Horace White, of Alexandria Appianus

The Roman History

Translated from the Greek by Horace White

Horace White, of Alexandria Appianus

The Roman History
Translated from the Greek by Horace White

ISBN/EAN: 9783744773690

Printed in Europe, USA, Canada, Australia, Japan

Cover: Foto ©ninafisch / pixelio.de

More available books at **www.hansebooks.com**

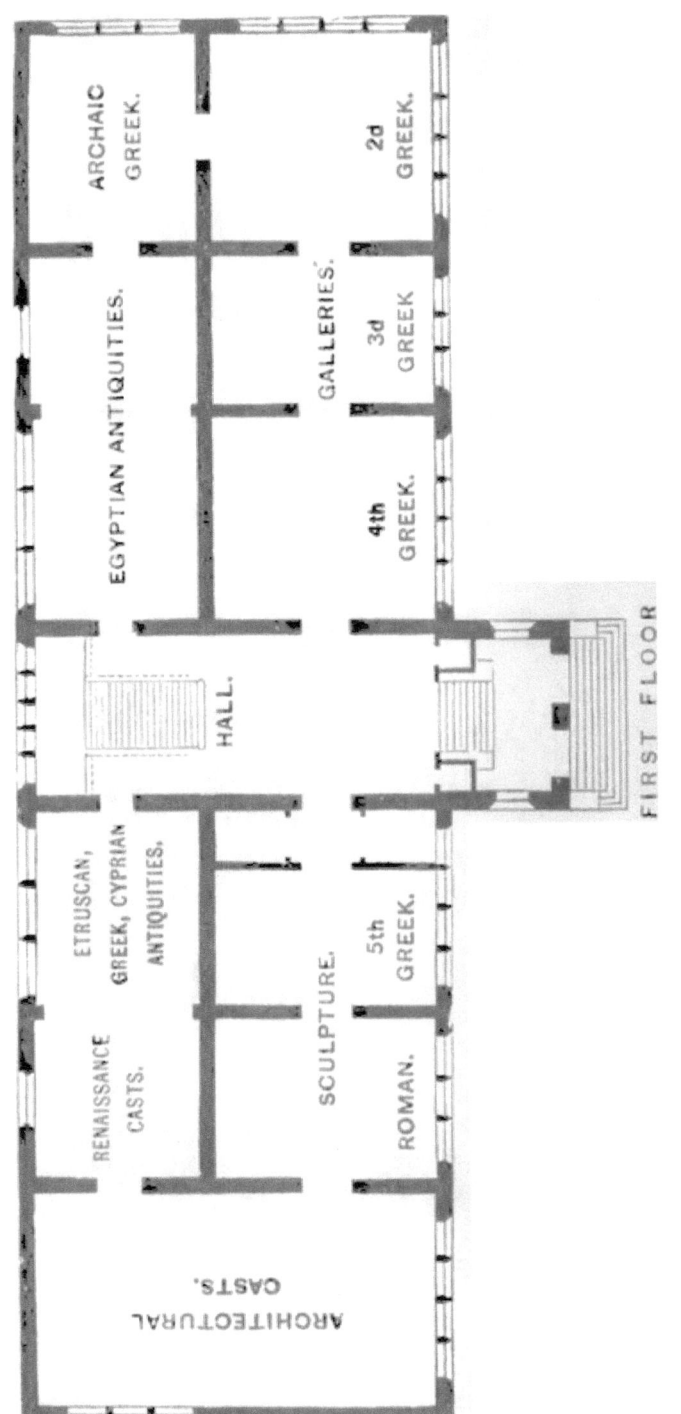

MUSEUM OF FINE ARTS.

DESCRIPTIVE CATALOGUE

OF THE CASTS FROM

GREEK AND ROMAN

SCULPTURE.

BY

EDWARD ROBINSON,

Curator of Classical Antiquities.

BOSTON:
PRINTED FOR THE MUSEUM BY ALFRED MUDGE & SON,
24 FRANKLIN STREET.
1887.

INTRODUCTION.

SINCE the publication of the former catalogue, the collection of casts has increased to such an extent that the Trustees of the Museum have found the continued issue of supplements impracticable, and have therefore ordered the preparation of a new catalogue. Advantage has been taken of this opportunity to offer what it is hoped may be both a guide for general visitors, and a useful handbook for students, for whom especially the notes following the title of each object are intended. The statements regarding restorations are based upon those of archæologists who have made especial studies of the respective objects, compared with photographs and with the author's notes. No attempt has been made to give the complete literature of each object, as this would have increased the size of the catalogue unnecessarily. The references are generally either to the best illustrations of the work described, or to one or two of the most important essays upon it, and are given partly as an assistance in identifying the casts with their originals, and partly for the benefit of those who may wish an exhaustive description of some particular work. In general histories and manuals of ancient sculpture students can easily find the allusions to the objects of which casts are here exhibited. A list of the more important of these histories is given below.

With few exceptions, the Greek names of deities and heroes are given, in preference to their Roman synonymes. For the convenience of those familiar only with the latter, the following table is appended:—

Greek.		Roman.	Greek.		Roman.
Zeus	is	Jupiter.	Hestia	is	Vesta.
Hera	"	Juno.	Dionysos	"	Bacchus.
Poseidon	"	Neptune.	Eros	"	Amor (*Cupid*).
Demeter	"	Ceres.	Asklepios	"	Æsculapius.
Persephone } Kora }	is	Proserpine.	Hades Eos	" "	Pluto. Aurora.
Artemis	is	Diana.	Nike	"	Victory.
Hephaistos	"	Vulcan.	Herakles	"	Hercules.
Athena	"	Minerva.	Polydeukes	"	Pollux.
Ares	"	Mars.	Aias	"	Ajax.
Aphrodite	"	Venus.	Odysseus	"	Ulysses.
Hermes	"	Mercury.			

The following-named works on Greek and Roman sculpture are recommended to those who wish to gain a general knowledge of the subject. The list is arranged alphabetically:—

Beulé, M. L'Art grec avant Périclès.
Brunn, H. Geschichte der griechischen Künstler, 2 vols. Braunschweig and Stuttgart, 1853–1859.
Collignon, Max. Manuel d'archéologie grecque. Paris, 1882.
——— The same, translated by Prof. John H. Wright. New York, 1886.
Friederichs, K. Bausteine zur Geschichte der griechisch-römischen Plastik. New edition by Paul Wolters, printed as the official catalogue of the collection of casts of the Berlin Museum. Berlin, 1885.
Lübke, W. History of Art, vol. I. Translated from the German by Clarence Cook. New York, 1878.

MITCHELL, Lucy M. A History of Ancient Sculpture. New York, 1883. This book is especially recommended for the amount of information it contains.

MÜLLER, K. O. Handbuch der Archäologie, 3d edition, by Welcker. Stuttgart, 1878.

—— Ancient Art and its Remains. A translation of the above, by John Leitch. London, 1852.

MURRAY, A. S. A History of Greek Sculpture, 2 vols. London, 1880-1883.

OVERBECK, J. von. Geschichte der griechischen Plastik; 3d edition, 2 vols. Leipzig, 1881-82.

PERRY, W. C. Greek and Roman Sculpture. London, 1882.

REBER, Franz. History of Ancient Art. Translated and augmented by J. T. Clarke. New York, 1882.

The Museum subscribes to the art and archæological periodicals named below, which are kept in the Library for the use of those who may wish to consult them:—

BALTIMORE. American Journal of Archæology.
LONDON. The Portfolio.
PARIS. Gazette des Beaux Arts.
    L'Art.
    Gazette Archéologique.
BERLIN. Jahrbuch des deutschen archäologischen Instituts.
    Jahrbuch der preussischen Kunstsammlungen.
    Antike Denkmäler.
    Repertorium für Kunstwissenschaft.
LEIPZIG. Zeitschrift für bildende Kunst.
ROME. Bulletino della Commissione Archeologica Municipale.
    Mittheilungen des deutschen archäologischen Instituts, römische Abtheilung.
ATHENS. Mittheilungen des deutschen archäologischen Instituts, athenische Abtheilung.
    Bulletin de Correspondance Hellénique.
    Ἐφημερὶς Ἀρχαιολογική.

FIRST GREEK ROOM.

ASSYRIAN RELIEFS.

A few Assyrian Reliefs are of necessity placed in this room for the present. A is an original slab added to the collection since the publication of the former catalogue. The description of the others is reprinted from that catalogue.

THE differences noticeable in the treatment of Assyrian reliefs mark three distinct periods, the first of which extends from the latter part of the tenth century (B. C.) to the beginning of the eighth; the second from the beginning of the eighth to the middle of the seventh (B. C. 721–667); and the third from the middle of the same to about forty years before its close (B. C. 667–640). The first, to which the casts in the Museum belong, are simply treated with plain backgrounds. In the second, landscape accessories, such as rivers, lakes, date-palms, etc., are freely introduced; swimming fish abound in the water-courses, and rustic scenes of all kinds are represented. These were executed during the reigns of Sargon, Sennacherib, and Esarhaddon.

The third class of reliefs, sculptured while Sardanapalus II. (Asshur-ben-i-pal) sat on the throne of Assyria, is easily distinguishable from the other two by its extreme minuteness of detail, more sober treatment of landscape in backgrounds, and less conventionality of vegetable forms. An examination of the first and second series of the plates in Sir Henry Layard's *Monuments of Nineveh* (atlas folio, 1853) will enable the student to appreciate the treatment of relief peculiar to each of the three periods referred to.

A. An original Assyrian Relief. From Nineveh.

Of alabaster. Ht., M. 2.30; width, 1.307; thickness, 0.11. Purchased by Mr. W. T. Shaw, of San Francisco, at Kouyunjik (Nineveh), about 1874. Sold at auction in New York, 1880, to G. L. Feuardent, of whom it was purchased by the Museum in February, 1881.

This relief, which is a part of a series, contains but one figure — a deified king, winged, standing in profile to the left, his right hand raised before him, the left grasping a sceptre or rod at his side. He is draped in a long, heavily fringed robe, and adorned with ear-rings, a necklace, arm-bands and bracelets, the last decorated each with a large rosette. The treatment of hair, beard, muscles, and drapery is an excellent example of the conventional style of Assyrian sculpture.

Crossing the slab horizontally is a cuneiform inscription of twenty-one lines, which is also carried across the right edge of the block, showing that the original composition ended at this point, as otherwise this part of the inscription would be covered by the adjoining slab. The inscription recounts the deeds of the king who is represented, and shows that he is Assur-nazir-pal, king of Assyria, B. C. 885–860.

B. Bas-relief (Plate 7 [A], first series, Layard), WINGED FIGURES KNEELING BEFORE THE SACRED TREE, the special emblem attached to the worship of Asshur, the Assyrian Jupiter. As an emblem it recalls the Tree of Life in Genesis, the Sacred Tree of the Hindoos, and the Zoroastrian Homa. This tree was the cedar, called the Tree of Paradise, whose pyramidal top represented a flame. In the Assyrian sculptures the arrangement of the flower petals resembles the Greek honeysuckle ornament.

C. Bas-relief from Nimroud, representing the INTERIOR OF A CASTLE, ground plan, and a pavilion or tent, under which some horses are drinking; and a groom is represented as in the act of currying a horse, whose natural action under the operation is faithfully rendered. "This bas-relief," says Mr. Layard (see Plate 30 and page 3, first series, of Description of the Plates in the Monuments of Nineveh), "probably represents the return home after battle." The general plan of the castle is divided into four compartments, in each of which is a group of figures, either engaged in domestic occupations or in making preparations for a religious ceremony or sacrifice. At the door of the tent stands a eunuch receiving four prisoners led by an Assyrian warrior. No explanation is given in the text of the lion-headed figures and their keeper in the upper right-hand corner of the relief.

D. RETURN OF A KING FROM A LION HUNT, not engraved in Layard's Monuments. The king, with attendants and horses, stands offering a libation over four dead lions lying at his feet. Another victim of the chase is brought in by some of the royal followers.

E. FIVE HORSES AND THREE RIDERS, one leading. From a slab in the British Museum, which represents a hunt of wild asses. Found by Mr. Layard at Kouyunjik.

F. WOUNDED LIONESS, bas-relief in the British Museum of a lion hunt, from Kouyunjik, Nineveh; date, about 700 B. C., reign of Sardanapalus III. This is a typical example of the Assyrian sculptor's wonderful ability to represent wild animals. Struck by an arrow in the spinal column, the dying lioness howls with rage and pain as she drags her paralyzed hind legs along the ground.

G. Bas-relief (Plate 56, second series, Layard), SCULPTURED PAVEMENT FROM KOUYUNJIK, in alabaster, between the winged bulls at entrance *c* of Chamber XXIV. Many of the entrances at Kouyunjik had similar slabs.

H. STONE, WITH THE FIGURE OF A KING IN RELIEF, and record of the sale of a field in the reign of Merodach Adan Akhi, king of Babylon, about 1150 B. C.

I. FOUR ASSYRIAN LION WEIGHTS, from the British Museum. At p. 601, Vol. III of Layard's Nineveh, the author says, "It is also highly probable that the curious series of bronze lions discovered at Nimroud during my first researches were used for a like purpose, as weights. The heads show that wonderful power of representing animal rage and suffering in which the Assyrians were unsurpassed. Their human figures are conventional, stiff, and unnatural, but their animals are living."

CASTS FROM GREEK SCULPTURE.

1. The Leukothea Relief, so called, in the Villa Albani, Rome.

Of Parian marble. RESTORATIONS: On the sitting figure the nose, lips, and part of right hand. On the small figure held by her, the right hand, left lower arm, and hand. On the large standing figure opposite, the face, both hands, and part of the object held. PUBLISHED: Zoega, *Bassirilievi*, vol. I, pl XLI; Winckelmann, *Monumenti Inediti*, No. 56; etc.

On a large chair at the left sits a goddess or woman with long flowing hair, clothed in the long-sleeved Ionic chiton, over which is an himation or shawl. With both hands she holds on her knee a small, full-draped figure, the right hand of which is stretched affectionately towards her. Facing these two at the left stands another large female, in a similar garment, holding a round object which is possibly a fillet. At her right stand two smaller figures, also full-draped.

From the time of Winckelmann, who first published this monument, explaining it as Leukothea nursing the infant Dionysos, the subject has been a matter of dispute. His interpretation is obviously wrong, the small figure in the lap of the seated one being evidently female, as indicated by the head-dress and the bands crossing the breast.

Comparison with archaic grave monuments discovered since Winckelmann's time shows that the relief belongs to that class of works, but whether the representation has a mythological or an every-day significance is not easily determined. It is often explained as a family picture, in which the deceased mother is represented playing with her child, her family about her. An objection to this theory is that the husband and father is not present. The small figure, too, appears to be not only female but an adult. It seems more probable, therefore, that the two large figures are goddesses, distinguished from mortals by their size, as is usual in early Greek art, and that the relief represents the reception of a woman into the lower world by the Great Goddesses, Demeter and Persephone. At Athens and elsewhere in Greece, Demeter was worshipped with Persephone as a power of the lower world, and **sacri**fices were made to her at funerals.

If this explanation is correct, Demeter **is the** seated figure, wearing the *sphendone*, a **form** of coronet, and Persephone stands opposite her. **The** smaller figures are mortal**s**, members of the family who bring offerings. (Cf. the Spartan reliefs on the adjoining wall, Nos. 7–12.)

The date of the relief is probably about 500 B. C., and its style is that of the early Ionic schools, which flourished along the coast of Asia Minor and among the islands of the Ægean Sea, whence they extended to Athens, their influence being predominant in the development of Athenian sculpture up to the **early** part **of the** fifth century, B. C.

2. **Figure Mounting a Chariot,** in the Akropolis Museum, Athens.

Of Parian (?) marble. The principal portion, with the figure, **found** near the Klepsydra, at the N. W. corner of the Akropolis, **in** 1822. The smaller block, with horses' tails, noted by Newton on the Akropolis in 1852. There are no restorations. PUBLISHED: Müller-Schöll, *Archäologische Mittheilungen aus Griechenland*, **pl.** II, fig. **4;** Overbeck, *Geschichte der griech. Plastik*, I, p. **153;** etc.

The theory has often been advanced, but without sufficient proof, that this relief was part **of the** frieze of the older Parthenon. We have no indication that the older building had a frieze, beyond the existence of this slab and one or two small fragments (cf. the head of Hermes, No. 31), and it is therefore more reasonable to suppose that this was an independent work, possibly the votive offering of **a** victor in the chariot races. The long flowing robe gives the figure a feminine appearance, but this costume is equally characteristic of male charioteers, as the paintings on vases testify, and the line of the breast, which is visible just below the arm, shows none of the marked fulness by which early artists distinguished female from male figures, as illustrated in the relief from the **Villa Albani**, No. 1, or the Harpy Monument. Probably, therefore, the figure is that of a youth mounting his chariot, and the fragment (No. 31) alluded to above, which unquestionably belonged to this group, shows that Hermes accompanied him, as he is often represented on early vases accompanying chariots.

This is a work of the Attic school, which, as mentioned above (No. 1), was largely under the influence of the Ionic, but differed from it in this, that while the Ionic sought to avoid the necessity of modelling the human figure by clothing it heavily with drapery, the Attic artists at an early date strove to emancipate themselves from this weakness, and to show the form through the drapery. Comparison of this relief with the one described above, or with those from the Harpy Tomb, will illustrate this point.

3. Herakles and the Stag, bas-relief in the British Museum.

> Of marble. Bought for the Towneley collection between 1770–1780. Passed with that collection to the British Museum. RESTORATIONS: part of each thigh. PUBLISHED: *Ancient Marbles in the British Museum*, II, pl. 7; Müller-Wieseler, *Denkmäler der alten Kunst*, I, pl. 14, No. 49. See also Keil in the *Annali dell' Instituto*, 1844, p. 175 ff.; etc.

This is a representation of one of the labors of Herakles, that of capturing the stag or horned hind which roamed about Mt. Keryneia, between Achaia and Arkadia, or according to other accounts, on Mt. Mainalos in Arkadia. The animal was sacred to Artemis, to whom it had been dedicated by the nymph Taygete, and Herakles secured it only after long wandering and toil.

Although treated in the archaic manner, especially the head of Herakles, the freedom in the action and the skill of the modelling indicate that this is not a genuine archaic work, but an imitation, probably of the Roman epoch. The size of the block, and the presence of the moulding about the edge, suggest that it may have been inserted as a panel in an altar or pedestal.

4. Pedestal of a Tripod, in the Museum of Antiquities at Dresden.

Of Pentelic marble. Formerly in the Chigi collection, in the Palazzo Odescalchi, Rome. Since 1728 in Dresden. There are no restorations. PUBLISHED: Becker, *Augusteum*, pl. 5-7; Hettner, *Bildwerke der Antikensammlung zu Dresden*, 1881, p. 76, No. 80; etc.

Each of the three sides of this pedestal is decorated with a relief of a religious significance, two referring to the sacred character of the tripod, and the third a subject difficult to explain. The first panel represents Apollo recovering the Pythian tripod from Herakles, who stole it from its place at Delphi. The scene of action is indicated by the *omphalos*, the cone-shaped object between them, which is symbolic of Delphi, the omphalos or navel of the earth, as it was regarded by the Greeks. A stone of similar shape stood there.

The second scene is the consecration of an object usually explained as a torch, which is placed upon a tall pillar by a priest and priestess. The significance of this ceremony is by no means clear. It is still open to question whether the consecrated object be really a torch, though this explanation of it is pretty generally accepted, and the bowl below it is said to be for the reception of embers that fall when the torch is lighted. The ritualistic character of the ceremony is shown by both priest and priestess standing on their toes, and by the manner of holding their hands (*priore digito in erectum pollicem residente*).

On the third side is the consecration of a tripod, which, placed upon a pillar, is decorated with a fillet by a priestess, while a priest stands by holding the besom, or broom, used to purify the temple.

Although the figures are modelled with the stiffness of primitive art, this is not a genuine archaic work, as some of the details, and especially the elaborate decorations at the top and base, show more freedom and command over the material than was possible in real archaic sculpture. The imitation of archaic art was cultivated at Rome during the early part of the empire by the priestly orders, who thus preserved the old types of divinities, and by many fashionable amateurs, who affected the simplicity of early Greek art. To this period the pedestal probably belongs. The subjects represented point to a hieratic purpose, and the presence of Sileni, grapes, etc., in the decoration suggest that the tripod which it supported may have been erected in honor of a Bacchic triumph.

5. **Archaic** Head, in the British **Museum.**

Of marble. There are no restorations. PUBLISHED: *Ancient Marbles in the British Museum*, pt. 9, pl. ii, fig. 4.

An example of the early Doric style, similar to the Apollo statues from Thera (No. 20), and Orchomenos (No. 21). Like them it is beardless, and the face has the archaic smile. The hair, which is bound by a fillet, falls in symmetrical curls behind the ears.

6. **Reliefs from the Harpy Monument.** In the British Museum.

Of white marble. Ht., M. 0.90; br. on east and west sides each 2.37, north and south each 2.15. Discovered by Sir Charles Fellows at Xanthos in Lykia, 1838. Carried to England 1842, and placed in the British Museum. There are no restorations. PUBLISHED: Fellows' *Journal of an Excursion in Asia Minor*, London, 1839, p. 231, his *Lycia*, 1841, p. 170; Rayet, *Monuments de l'Art Antique* I, pls. 13–16; etc. COLORS: At time of discovery colors on the reliefs were noted as follows: on the background traces of blue; on the crest of the warrior, and the sandals of some of the figures, red; and on the chair of the figure on the north side, traces of a pattern of rosettes, etc., in color.

The monument from which these reliefs were taken is a solid rectangular block of limestone, measuring about 8 ft. 4 in. on its longest side, and, with the base upon which it stands, about 20 ft. in height, surmounted by a low, broad cornice and a flat, square top. Just below the cornice was placed this marble frieze, encompassing the four sides of the monument, with a small opening on the west side (see below), through which the remains of the dead were passed into a chamber cut in the rock. The tomb itself, deprived of its frieze, is still standing in its original position.

Beginning the description on the left, we have first the three blocks of the SOUTH side. At the two corners of this are flying figures, each with the head, breast, and arms of a woman, the claws, wings, and tail of a bird, and an oval body. Each bears in its arms a small human figure, full-draped. Between these a seated figure, probably male, though the face is much destroyed, holds in each hand a pomegranate, perhaps just taken from the figure opposite, who holds a bird as though in the act of offering it. Following this is the WEST side, in which is the small opening alluded to above, and over it a cow suckling a calf. To the left of this block sits a female holding out a patera in the attitude of a goddess accepting a libation; to the right three female figures approach a seated female, who holds in her right hand a flower, in the other a pomegranate. Next comes the EAST side. The central figure here is a male, bearded, seated on a large throne, holding a flower in his right hand, the left leaning against a long sceptre. Two large male figures approach the throne from behind, while in front a smaller one holds out a cock and an egg (?) as an offering to the seated figure. In the right corner stands a large figure facing the others, holding a staff in one hand, and an unrecognizable object in the other, accompanied by a dog. Finally the NORTH end, similar to the south, except that the central group is that of a young warrior delivering up his helmet to a seated male divinity, under whose throne is a bear. In the lower right-hand corner is a figure in an attitude of grief gazing at the group above it.

Without doubt the subjects of these reliefs relate in some manner to death and the divinities connected with it, but a satisfactory interpretation of the figures and scenes has not yet been reached. It can only be presumed that the larger figures are divinities of the lower world, and the smaller figures mortals in the act of sacrificing, but with our present limited knowledge of the Lykian religion or its adaptation of Greek forms, a closer identification is not possible. Although this monument derives its name from the figures on the two narrower sides, it may be questioned whether these are really Harpies. In spite of the fact that they have generally been accepted as such, it is much more probable that they are Sirens. In Greek literature Harpies do not appear as creatures of the underworld. They are beings of the storms and rushing winds, and therefore were sometimes supposed to have carried off people who disappeared suddenly or mysteriously; but this cannot be regarded as a necessary association with death. Sirens, on the other hand, are intimately connected with Persephone and Demeter, and appear as beings of the lower world in the service of the former. The tradition was that they received the very form in which they are represented on this monument, either to enable them to fly over the sea in search of Persephone, or as a punishment for not preventing her capture. Moreover, we know both from existing monuments and from ancient writers, that they were often represented on grave monuments, as for example, on those of Sophokles, Isokrates, and Hephaistion, and many now preserved in the museums of Athens and other cities. The small figures they carry are not to be regarded as infants, the difference in size being a common way of distinguishing mortals from divinities in archaic art (cf. the "Leukothea" relief, No. 1 and the Spartan reliefs Nos. 7-12), and it is probable that these groups represent the transport of souls to the lower world.

In style, these reliefs correspond so well with early Ionic works that we may suppose them to have been the work of Greek sculptors of that school, which, as mentioned above (p. 11), spread its influence along the Asiatic shores as well as into Greece itself. This explains the resemblance between this work and the archaic reliefs found in Athens. At this early period, neither Attic nor Lykian art was dependent upon the other, but both were under the influence of a third school, the Ionic, whose principal seats lay between the two. Comparison with other Ionic works indicates the end of the sixth century B. C. as the probable date of the Harpy Monument.

7–12. Spartan Grave Reliefs.

Found at various times in and about Sparta. No. **8 was** purchased by Count Saburoff, formerly Russian minister to Greece, and bought of him in 1884 by the Berlin Museum, in which it now is. The others are in Sparta. Material, a coarse bluish gray marble found in **the** locality. 7, ht., 0.29, br., 0.37. **8,** ht., 0.87, br., 0.65. **9,** ht., 0.28–30, br., 0.22. **10,** ht., 0.25, br., o 24. **11,** ht., 0.60, br., 0.64. **12,** ht., 0.36, br., 0.35. There **are no** attempts at restoration. PUBLISHED: *Mittheilungen des deutschen Instituts in Athen,* II (1877), pp. 303 ff. and **pl. xx–xxv**; Furtwängler, *Die Sammlung Saburoff,* pl. I; etc.

As Nos. **7, 8, 11, 12** are variations of the same type, a description of **No. 8,** the best preserved, will answer for all. On a throne wrought with considerable **elaboration** sit two persons, who from their size, as compared with that of the other two figures in the **relief,** are doubtless divinities. The outer of these, a male with a slight beard, regards the spectator with a look intended to be expressive of good-will. In his right hand, extended, he holds a kantharos, or drinking cup. His left, also extended, is open, perhaps to receive the offerings brought to him by the smaller figures. At his left sits a female in profile, holding in her right hand a pomegranate, and with the left drawing aside her veil to disclose her face. Of the smaller figures, evidently mortals, the foremost brings a cock and an **egg,** the other a pomegranate and a flower. Behind the **throne** stands erect a serpent, his tail curled under the seat, **and** his head coming over the back. Nos. **9** and **10** are fragments of grave **monuments:** No. **9,** a woman with a flower; No. **10,** a figure turned towards the left with the right hand raised. The remains of another hand adjoining it indicate that a corresponding figure stood on the other half of **the relief.**

These slabs were originally erected over graves, and on some of them we can still see remains of the rough-hewn bases by which they were set up. The **subject** represented is an offering either to the deceased, or to the deities of the lower world, to whom the pomegranate was especially dear; the cock and egg also occur frequently in representations of offerings to them, as, for example, on **the** Harpy Monument. It is a suggestive fact that among the Greeks these also symbolized the reproductive powers of nature. The serpent was believed to possess mysterious connection with both the upper and the lower world.

In these reliefs we have some of the earliest existing monuments of Lakedaimonian art. They are not all of the same epoch, as will be seen by a comparison of Nos. 8 and 12, the latter of which, though not so well preserved, is much more developed in style. This may date as late as the fifth century B. C., though the others belong in the sixth. A striking peculiarity in the earlier examples is the manner of their execution. It will be noticed that the upper surface is quite flat, and the edges instead of rounding off as in most stone reliefs even of the archaic period (cf. Harpy Mon., relief in Villa Albani, No 1, etc.), is cut away sharply, in a manner more characteristic of primitive wood-carving, where the nature of the material would render it to a certain extent necessary. This is a very interesting circumstance, because we know that the early Spartan sculptors, the pupils of Dipoinos and Skyllis, worked only in wood, gold, and ivory. These slabs therefore probably reproduce in stone, the earlier with mechanical exactness, a type that was traditional in wood.

13. **The Stele of** Aristokles, in the Theseion, Athens.

>Bas-relief of Parian marble. Found 1838 near a tumulus in the village of Velanideza, on the coast of Attika, east of Hymettos. There are no restorations. PUBLISHED: Laborde, *Athènes*, atlas, pl. 7; *Mus. of Class. Antiq.*, I, p. 252; etc. COLORS upon it, still brilliant in parts, are as follows: on background traces of red, hair and beard brown, helmet and cuirass a very dark color (black ?) on which are patterns in brighter colors, a star on the shoulder-plate, meander under the shoulder, zigzag girdle about the waist, etc. On the flesh slight traces of a rather dark color particularly in the ears and about the finger-nails. On the chiton red.

The stele of Aristokles, as it is called from the name of the artist inscribed below the figure, is one of the oldest Greek grave monuments yet discovered. The form of the letters in the inscription shows it to be an Attic work of the time of the Peisistratids, *i. e.*, the latter half of the sixth century B. C. The figure is intended as a portrait of the man to whose memory the stone was erected, represented as a warrior in full armor. The name Aristion inscribed on the base of the stele — not shown in the cast — is probably that of the deceased.

An idea formerly prevalent, that this monument commemorated one of the Athenians who fell in the battle of Marathon, has been dispelled by the fact that the inscription places the monument much earlier than the battle, as well as by the site of the discovery, which was in quite another part of Attika.

This is an interesting example of the constant upward tendency of early Greek art. Obliged to crowd his figure into the limits of a form of monument that was probably traditional, the sculptor had little opportunity to display freedom of action, and in pose the figure is quite as stiff as those of a still earlier epoch. Yet with this stiffness is combined an earnest effort to arrive at the truth of nature in the shape of the figure. In the arms and legs we can see how the artist has endeavored to represent muscular development. He has spared himself no pains to represent faithfully every small detail; and though in this instance success was not achieved, it was this unflagging care and thought, of which every early Greek monument is a witness, that finally resulted in the perfection of the Parthenon frieze.

14. Grave Stele from Bœotia, in the National Museum, Athens.

Of gray Bœotian marble. Date of discovery unknown. Seen by Dodwell at the beginning of this century in the village of Petro-Magula, close to the site of Orchomenos. Afterwards carried to Rhomaïko, about an hour distant, and in 1880 placed in the National Museum, Athens. There are no restorations. PUBLISHED: Conze, *Beiträge*, p. 31 ff., pl. xi, fig. 1; Körte, in *Mittheilungen des Instituts in Athen*, III (1878), p. 315; etc.

The deceased, clothed in a long mantle (*himation*), and leaning upon a staff, is represented in an every-day act, playing with his dog, who springs to catch a grasshopper from his hand.

On the base of this stele — not shown in the cast — is a metrical inscription, which, translated, reads, "Alxenor the Naxian made this; only look at it!" Although this invitation may not excite in us the admiration which is evidently expected, the inscription is valuable because it shows that the sculptor belonged to the Ionic school, Naxos being an Ionic state. The relief therefore bears important testimony to the extent of the influence of that school in early Greek art, being an instance of the employment of an Ionic sculptor in the heart of Greece, and in an un-Ionic locality. As mentioned above, p. 11, the chief seats of the school were on the coast of Asia Minor and the adjacent islands.

Of Alxenor nothing is known, but we see that in his treatment of the human figure he followed the characteristics of his school, as described on p. 12. In contrast to the stele of Aristokles, this relief exhibits little effort to display the form itself; beneath the folds of the himation there is no suggestion of modelling, and only in the stiff line of the left leg is there a hint of the figure. Compare this with an example of the early Attic style, the chariot relief, No. 2, where the lines of the whole body are easily traceable through the drapery.

The date of this monument is not later than the first part of the fifth century B. C.

15. Grave Stele, in the Museum at Naples.

Of Greek marble. Formerly in the Borgia collection, beyond which nothing is known of its history. RESTORATIONS: End of the nose, the right hand, a piece on the right arm, greater part of the left hand and nearly all the ring on the left wrist, and a piece of the stick above left hand. PUBLISHED: Rayet, *Monuments de l'Art Antique*, I, pl. 19 (Martha); *Museo Borbonico*, XIV, pl. x; Conze, *Beiträge*, p. 34, pl. xi, fig. 2; etc.

Subject similar to the preceding, but the style more advanced, and the relief bolder. The man is clothed in an *exomis*, a short tunic which leaves much of the body nude, and holds nothing in his hand. His dog, seated at his feet, looks up at him affectionately.

Although the composition is awkward, especially in the clumsy manner in which the man's left shoulder is brought forward, and in the anatomically impossible setting of the dog's head upon his shoulders, the nude parts are modelled with much more knowledge and feeling than in the work of Alxenor (No. 14). In this respect the relief has some affinity to the Stele of Aristokles (No. 13), but the high relief and the muscular proportions of the figure are more characteristic of early Doric than of early Attic or Ionic sculpture. Notwithstanding the impossibility of tracing the history of this stele beyond its presence in an Italian collection, its technical characteristics prove that it is a genuine archaic Greek work, dating not later than the first half of the fifth century B. C.

16 A-O. Sculptures from the Temple of Athena in Ægina, in the Glyptothek, Munich.

Found in a very fragmentary condition by a company of English and German explorers, in the vicinity of a temple on the east side of the island of Ægina, in 1811. Bought for Ludwig I., of Bavaria, then Crown Prince, in the following year. Of Parian marble. The fragments were put together by Thorwaldsen, who also made the following extensive RESTORATIONS: A, end of nose, right forearm, most of the left hand, right leg from knee to ankle, and toes of both feet. B, crest of helmet, end of nose, right hand, left forearm and most of hand, left foot, and fore-half of right. C, head, left forearm, right arm, from middle of upper arm, and hand, most of the pendants on front of armor, and left leg from knee down. D, head, right shoulder with adjoining parts of breast and ribs, fingers of right hand, and ends of the fingers of left, greater part of shield, piece on right leg from ankle half way up to knee, front part of right foot, toes of left foot. E, neck, right shoulder and piece of breast, lower part of right hand, fingers of left, the toes except the great ones, pieces in the crest. F, nose, thumbs, right hand, ends of two fingers of left, small pieces in drapery, also in ægis, crest, and shield. G, end of nose, crest, half of right forearm, end of left thumb, one third of shield, and both legs. H, point of cap, nose, end of chin, parts of fingers of both hands, front half of left foot. I, head, right shoulder, fingers of right hand, left arm from just above elbow, right leg from knee down, left knee with part of thigh, and front part of foot. J, head, left arm, parts of right arm and hand, both legs from knee down. K, head, right arm, greater part of left arm, including elbow and shield, the entire right leg, left leg from knee down, and piece of greave which projects above knee. L, head, both hands, including wrists, entire left leg, right thigh, shield, except where it touches shoulder and lower arm. M, nose, both arms, greater part of right foot, left foot with ankle. N, end of nose, piece on the back under left shoulder, several pendants of the armor, left hand, right forearm, half of right foot, left leg from lower half of knee down. O, crest, part of nose, several fingers and toes, right leg from middle of thigh down. PUBLISHED: Cockerell, *Temples of Ægina and Bassae;* Blouet, *Expédition Scientifique de Morée*, III, pl. 58, ff.; etc. Described in detail in Brunn's *Beschreibung der Glyptothek*, München, 1879, from which are taken the facts stated above.

These statues formerly adorned the pediments of the temple near which they were found. A–J are from the western pediment, K–O from the eastern. Although the former group is the more complete of the two, smaller fragments discovered in the immediate vicinity show that originally it contained still more figures, especially one corresponding to M in the eastern pediment, the lower parts of whose legs have been found.

The scene represented in the western pediment is a battle, which takes place in the presence of Athena. The pointed Asiatic cap suggests a scene from the Trojan war, and the interpretation of the group as the contest over the body of Achilles is generally accepted. If this is the subject, the figure (E) lying at the foot of Athena is Achilles, while over him Aias Telamonios (D) and Æneas (G) engage in a combat which is shared by all the others. Names have been assigned to all, but as these are simply conjectural they are not repeated here. The archer (H) is possibly Paris. The attitudes of the five figures, K–O, and the character of the smaller fragments discovered, among them a head of Athena, indicate that a similar scene was represented in the eastern pediment. As the figure N is evidently Herakles, distinguished by his heavier proportions and by the lion-skin cap, this battle is supposed to be that fought over the body of Oïkles, in which tradition assigned parts to Herakles and Telamon, an Æginetan hero.

These figures exhibit the climax of Æginetan art. In the early development of Greek sculpture, particularly in bronze, Ægina occupied a foremost position among the Doric schools, Kallon and Onatas, both Æginetans, being regarded among the greatest masters of those schools. Soon after the Persian wars, in the early part of the fifth century B. C., the island lost its independence, and its school gave way to the two more powerful growing up on either side of it, — those of Athens and Argos.

It was principally in the Doric schools that skill in representing the nude body was developed. While the Ionic artists sought to avoid the necessity of modelling the form by covering their figures with drapery, the earliest Doric works extant (cf. the metopes from Selinus, Nos. 26

and 27, and **the "Apollo"** statues Nos. 20 and 21) show that from the very beginning these artists struggled for the truth of nature; and the sculptures from Ægina show how far they had advanced by the beginning **of the** fifth century, the probable **date** of the temple being about 479 B. C. Freedom of **action, a** great stumbling-block to the early sculptors, **is here** attained with considerable success, **even** without the tree-stumps **and** other artificial supports **to which** even later sculptors resorted. Each figure **rests** easily and firmly upon **no** other support than **the feet,** even when the weight **of** a shield is added on one side. Archaism is most apparent in the treatment of the heads. The hair is stiff and wiry, the eyes are expressionless, and the **faces wear** the proverbial "Æginetan smile." In the history **of the** development **of** Greek sculpture, **the** head **was** the **last member that** received perfect treatment, a **circumstance due to the** fact that Greek artists regarded the body, not the **face, as** the chief vehicle **of expression,** and until the beginning of the **fourth** century B. C. were more or less indifferent to the latter.

The proportions, also, are characteristic **of the** archaic style, the shoulders being broad and the hips narrow; and the modelling still lacks the free handling of a confident **master.** The manner in which the figures **are treated** is strongly suggestive of early bronze work, **in which the** Æginetan sculptors excelled.

17-19. Three **Terra-cotta Reliefs,** in the British Museum.

> Nos. 17 and 18 from the island of Melos, No. 19 of uncertain provenance. PUBLISHED: Nos. 17 and 18, Millingen, *Ancient Unedited Monuments,* II, pls. 3, 2; No. 19, Welcker, *Alte Denkmäler,* II, pl. xii, 20; Overbeck, *Geschichte der griech. Plastik,* I, fig. 32; etc.

These are specimens of what are commonly known as "Melan" reliefs, because many examples of this class have been found in **the** island of Melos. It does not follow that they were **made there, as** similar reliefs are found in other places, but **the name serves** as a convenient designation for **a** very **distinct style of** technique, the chief characteristic of which is that the relief is made à jour, that is, without background, the outlines of the figures being cut through the material. The relief itself is flat and the plates are thin, probably affixed originally to some other material such as wood, and used decoratively. The round disks which serve as a background for the casts are not part of the originals. No. 27 represents Bellerophon and the Chimæra; No. 18, Perseus beheading Medusa, from whose neck springs not Pegasos, as according to the common legends, but Chrysaor; and No. 19 is usually explained as Alkaios and Sappho, though this interpretation is not certain. These reliefs are of an advanced stage of archaic art, and probably date from the first half of the fifth century B. C.

20, 21. Statues of Apollo. (?)

No. 20, of marble, found about 1830 in the vicinity of some rock-graves on Mt. Exomytis in the island of Thera. Carried to Athens, 1835. Formerly in the Theseion, now in the National Museum, Athens. The neck is repaired with plaster. PUBLISHED: Newton, *Antiquities at Athens*, 18; Overbeck, *Plastik*, I, p. 89, fig. 9; etc.

No. 21, of grayish Bœotian marble. Formerly in Skripù (Orchomenos). Discovered there about 1850; brought to Athens, 1880, and since then in the National Museum. There are no restorations. PUBLISHED: Collignon, in the *Bulletin de la Corr. Hell.*, V (1881), p. 319, and pl. iv; Körte, *Mittheilungen des Inst. in Athen*, III (1878), p. 305; etc.

These are two of the earliest Greek works existing, and undoubtedly date not much later than the beginning of sculpture in stone. We see in them the struggle of the primitive artist to represent the human form, hindered both by his lack of training and his ignorance of the possibilities of the material in which he worked. The arms cling firmly to the sides, and lest even in this way they should not be strong enough, only a small portion, at the elbows, has been freed from the body. To give some life to the figure, one foot is advanced a little. The muscular surfaces are indicated with more feeling than knowledge, especially in the Theran statue, in which the body has a certain softness in spite of its extreme archaism. It was evidently in the face of this figure that the sculptor had the most difficulty. The eyes are scarcely sunk at all, the hair on the brow is indicated by a series of spirals traced with a pointed instrument in the stone, and the attempt to give individuality to the features has resulted in the bland smile which characterizes nearly all archaic Greek works.

It is, however, in the effort to express individuality that works of this class differ radically from similar Egyptian statues. The Theran and Orchomenos figures are two of a considerable number of statues reproducing the same type, which have been found in various parts of Greece and the islands; they are Doric works, and not improbably products of the school of the Dædalids, which travelled all through Hellas. This school originated in Crete, and therefore came under the influence of Egyptian art, whence it is easy to account for the canonical form of these statues; yet, while Egyptian heads through all epochs preserve the same passionless features, we see in the two figures before us how early the Greek sculptors broke away from this canonicism, and strove to attain individuality.

The Dædalid school, to which we have referred the type of these two statues, was chiefly noted for its works in wood, and these figures may well represent a wooden type transferred to stone. Of the two, the Theran is undoubtedly the older, as the other, although more roughly executed, displays a greater advance in knowledge, especially in the muscles of the torso. Both date probably from the first half of the sixth century B. C.

Whether the statues of this class, which is quite numerous, really represent Apollo is difficult to determine, because it is evident that the early Doric type of Apollo was very similar to that of athlete statues, both being characterized by nudity and by the long, flowing locks. Pausanias (VIII, 40, 1) describes an archaic statue of a boxer which he saw in Phigaleia as having the feet slightly parted and the arms close to the sides; from which it has been argued that this was the common athlete type in early Doric art, and that these "Apollos" are merely statues of athletes erected over the graves of victors in the Olympic and other games, a number of them having been found in or near ancient cemeteries. But on the other hand it must be remembered that several have also been found in sanctuaries of Apollo, and that the archaic statues of him which stood in the temples of Delos and Miletos are shown by extant reproductions to have been of precisely the same type as these, though differing slightly in action. It may be concluded, therefore, that as Apollo represented the ideal of manly youth to all the Greeks, and especially to the Dorians, their early artists, who were unequal to subtle distinctions, used the type of one to represent the other as it suited their purpose.

22. Male Figure carrying a Bull. Statue in the Akropolis Museum, Athens.

> Of bluish marble, supposed to be from the quarries of Nausa, on the island of Paros. Found on the southeast part of the Akropolis, the upper part 1864, lower part the following year. There are no restorations. PUBLISHED: Overbeck, *Plastik*, I, p. 148, fig. 25; Veyries, *Les figures Criophores*, Paris, 1884, pp. 4, 16 f.; etc.

This figure has been variously interpreted as Apollo Nomios (*i. e.*, guardian of the flocks) and Hermes Moscophoros (the bull-bearer). The beard and the shape of the cap are more in conformity with the type of Hermes, though there are a few examples in archaic art of Apollo with a slight beard. In spite of the fact that it was found on the Akropolis, the statue is evidently not a work of Attic art, being decidedly Doric in style; and, as has been suggested, is probably the dedication of a colony or another state. Its style is considerably more developed than that of the two statues Nos. 20, 21, and shows considerable knowledge in the treatment of the muscles. The artist has been so careful to represent the form faithfully that the drapery which covers it is perceptible only on close inspection, though undoubtedly it was originally made plainer by color. The middle of the eyes was of another material set into the marble.

The existence of this statue, the date of which is probably the second half of the sixth century B. C., and of others similar to it, equally ancient, shows how much older than Christian art is the type of the "Good Shepherd."

23. Fragment of a Male Statue, in the Museum at Sparta.

<small>Marble of a rather fine grain. There are no restorations. PUBLISHED: *Mittheilungen des Inst. in Athen*, II (1877), p. 298, No. 2.</small>

This small figure, so much worn as to be of little value for purposes of study, belongs, like the statues Nos. 20, 21, to the Doric school, and is probably a product of Spartan art of the early part of the sixth century B. C.

24. The Lions from the Gate of Mykenæ.

<small>Of a fine, smooth, greenish gray limestone, probably from quarries in the neighborhood. The heads were affixed, perhaps of metal. PUBLISHED: *Archäolog. Zeitung* 1865, pl. 193; Schliemann's *Mycenæ*, p. 32 ff., and pl. III; etc.</small>

This, the oldest sculptured work in Greece, dates from the pre-Homeric epoch, and represents a civilization earlier than the Hellenic. The slab decorated by these lions was inserted in a triangular opening over the principal city gate, the uneven line of the bottom showing where it fitted the top of the lintel, a huge block of breccia. That the slab and its relief are coeval with the walls about them, which rank among the oldest in Greece, there can be little doubt; and it was probably placed there with some armorial significance, like the escutcheons on mediæval buildings. Although all traces of the walls of many cities built in later epochs have disappeared, this gate and the wall about it still stand firmly, and the lions above still guard the entrance. The under part of the gate, with its threshold, was cleared and brought to light by Dr. Schliemann in 1876, but the upper part, including the lions, has probably been always above ground.

In 1874, Prof. Ernst Curtius, writing of this monument, spoke of its strongly marked Asiatic character, which had been noticed by other archæologists, and prophesied that investigations in Asia Minor would bring to light other similar monuments. The prophecy was fulfilled in 1881 by the discovery, by Prof. W. M. Ramsay, of a large grave monument in the heart of Phrygia bearing a relief of precisely similar design (see Journal Hellenic Studies, III, pl. xvii, p. 19 and 256 ff.). This discovery was of great importance regarding the lions of Mykenæ, because it proves that the old tradition, that Mykenæ was founded by a race coming from Asia Minor, had some foundation in fact, and explains the presence in Mykenæ of a type that is foreign to Greece. This and other recent discoveries have proved that civilization came from the East to Greece not only by sea along the southern shores of Asia Minor, but also overland, throught the great Phrygian country.

25. Head of Medusa. Relief in the Museum at Argos.

PUBLISHED: Milchhöfer in *Mittheilungen des Inst. in Athen*, IV (1879), p. 156 d.

This is a piece of very late and coarse decorative work, probably architectural.

26, 27. Two Metopes from Selinus, in the Museum at Palermo.

Of brown tufa, found in the locality. Discovered by the English architects, Harris and Angell, in the winter of 1822-23, and carried to Palermo. RESTORATIONS: *Perseus Metope*, on the female, almost the whole neck, larger part of breast and of the knees; Perseus, middle part of sword, and parts of hands and arms. *Herakles Metope*, small bits in hair, and in thighs of Herakles. COLORS: When discovered slight traces of color were noted as follows: *Perseus Metope*, background red; female, brownish black on brows, lids and pupils, red on borders of garment, yellow on garment. Perseus, green in garment, red on belt and cap, blue on belt. Medusa, yellow in face, red in eyes. Eyes of Perseus and wings of Pegasos had also indications of color. *Herakles Metope*, red on background; Herakles, red on right thigh, on arm directly under shoulder, on sword, belt and scabbard; also red on the bands, shoulders, and upper arms of the Kerkopes. PUBLISHED: Benndorf, *Die Metopen von Selinunt*, Berlin, 1873, and authorities there quoted.

These two metopes are from the oldest of seven temples the ruins of which still exist at Selinunte, on the south coast of Sicily. This town, the ancient Selinus, was founded by a Greek colony from the eastern part of the island, probably in the year 628 B. C. The temple to which these metopes belonged was built soon after, so that the year 600 may be considered an approximate date for the sculptures, which are therefore among the oldest surviving works of Greek art. The first represents Perseus slaying Medusa, while a female, possibly his protecting goddess, Athena, stands by. Both conception and composition display the childishness of primitive sculpture. Without regard to the action, all three faces are turned toward the spectator, and the lower parts of the figures are in profile. Perseus seizes the monster's hair with one hand, and with his sword severs her head from her body. Medusa is conceived with all the hideousness that characterizes representations of her throughout archaic art. According to the legends, Pegasos sprang from the throat of the Gorgon when her head was cut off, and the artist, desiring to remind the spectator of this fact, has placed the horse in her arms. Attempts of this kind to combine two successive stages of an event in one scene are very common in early Greek art.

The subject of the second metope is Herakles bearing the Kerkopes, a pair of rascally gnomes who disturbed and robbed him when asleep, in return for which he caught and bound them, and carried them off. The Kerkopes are here represented bound, hand and foot, and suspended, heads downward, from a pole borne by Herakles on his shoulders.

Selinus was a Dorian colony, and both the architecture and sculptures of this temple are Doric in style. The characteristics of early Doric sculpture have been described above, p. 22; and these reliefs testify to the very early date at which the effort to represent the nude body in action was begun in that school. The figures all show a strong appreciation of muscular play, rudely as it is expressed, and are executed with such careful endeavor to indicate the modelling of the body that one hardly realizes that every figure is clothed. In this characteristic, and in the boldness of the relief, the figures being almost entirely free from the background, these metopes present a very strong contrast to the early works of the Ionic school. (Cf. Nos. 1 and 6.)

28 A-E. Reliefs from the Temple of Assos. A in the Louvre, B in our Museum, C–E in the Museum of the Tchinly-Kiosk, Constantinople.

<small>Of the dark gray trachyte of which the temple was built. A, carried from Assos to Paris, 1838, by Raoul Rochette; the others discovered during the excavations in **1881**. PUBLISHED: A, *Monumenti dell' Inst.*, III, pl. xxxiv; **Clarac,** *Musée de Sculpture*, pl. 116 **A,** Texte, vol. II 2, **p. 1149;** etc. B–E, Joseph Thacher Clarke, *Report of Investigations at Assos*, 1881, Boston, 1882; B, pl. 16, C, pl. 19, D, pl. 17, E, pl. 21; Wolters' Friederichs, Nos. 8–12; etc.</small>

The temple of Assos possesses an especial interest for Americans as the scene of the first organized work of our country in the field of classical archæology. The site of the town is on the southern coast of Mysia, in Asia Minor, opposite the island of Lesbos. It was a Greek town, undoubtedly of great antiquity, as its remains testify, but although several eminent travellers have described the place during the present century, and a party sent out by France in 1838 carried away a number of monuments lying about the surface, no systematic excavations were undertaken there until 1881, when the Archæological Institute of America despatched an expedition for the purpose, under the leadership of Mr. J. T. Clarke. During the first season the site of the temple and many of its members, including the reliefs in the Entrance Hall of the Museum, and those of which B–E are casts, were discovered. With the exception of E, which is a metope, all these reliefs decorated the architrave of the peripteros; that is, they were sculptured on the beam directly over the outer columns, as is proved by the presence of *regulæ* and other distinctive peculiarities on the blocks. This is the only instance of sculpture applied to this member in all known examples of Doric architecture, and apparently bespeaks an epoch before the principles of that style became established, as the extremely archaic character of the sculpture also indicates. The temple is, therefore, a most important monument in the history of the early development of Greek architecture, combining as it does the elements of both Eastern and Western art. The building was Doric, a style whose chief seats were in the western parts of Hellas, but the sculptures show unmistakably the influence of Asiatic art. Semper (Stil, I, p. 404 ff.) thinks the idea of decorating the architrave thus was borrowed from the Oriental practice of covering exposed wooden parts of buildings with metal, decorated with *repoussé* work.

A represents a banquet at which four bearded men are reclining in the Asiatic fashion, which was introduced into Greece after the Homeric age. A youth pours wine into the cup held by one, and in the foreground are a number of vases of an archaic type. B, two sphinxes, couchant, face to face, one paw of each upon an indeterminable object between them. This group probably had an armorial significance, and is believed by Mr. Clarke to have formed the centre of the composition on the front of the temple. C is a fragment of a design similar to the above, the second figure of which is among the sculptures in the Louvre. D represents a lion attacking a boar, biting him in one of his hind quarters. This group and the sphinxes show that, like the Assyrians, the early Greek sculptors had much better appreciation of animal than of human life. Both of these figures are well drawn, although in their action there is less vigor than in most archaic representations of wild beasts. E, as stated above, is a metope. Two figures are represented; one is pursuing the other, whom he catches by the elbow. As the pursuer is bearded, there can be no doubt of his sex, but that the other is a female, as described by Mr. Clarke (Report, p. 117), does not appear certain in the cast. It was apparently beardless, and wore a garment which appears to have reached to the knees.

Mr. Clarke (*ubi supra*, p. 104) places the temple and its sculptures in the epoch following the Persian wars, *i. e.*, later than 479 B. C., and attributes the numerous archaic characteristics of both to provincialism. This opinion, which is contrary to that generally accepted, is based upon the resemblance of certain features of the architecture to that of the Theseion at Athens, and the temple of Sunion, both buildings of about the middle of the fifth century. That an architect familiar with a style so developed as theirs, should have retained, in many important particulars, the defects of a much earlier period, seems improbable; as does also the assumption that a city situated on the highway between the great Ionian cities and their northern colonies should be so provincial as to remain nearly a hundred years behind the rest of Greece in the development of its sculpture. Until, therefore, more convincing evidence of the late origin of the reliefs is offered, they may be judged according to the rule usually followed in estimating the date of such works. Their technique and composition are extremely primitive, the type of the figures resembles that on the earliest Greek sculptures extant, and in one of the reliefs in the entrance hall Herakles appears without the lion-skin, which became a characteristic attribute of him as early as the end of the seventh century B. C. These characteristics render the sixth century B. C. the latest date that can safely be assigned to the reliefs, and it is not improbable that they may have originated in the early part of that century.

29. **Fragment** of a bas-relief, in the Museum at Sparta.

Of the local bluish stone resembling marble. PUBLISHED: *Mittheilungen des Inst. in Athen*, II (1877), p. 313, No. 4.

A nude youth stands by his horse, in profile towards the left. Touching the horse's head is that of another horse, apparently standing opposite. The relief when entire, therefore, probably represented the Dioskouroi, Kastor and Polydeukes, who are often thus represented, and were worshipped at Sparta, where this fragment was found.

30. Bas-relief in the Museum at Sparta.

Not archaic. Of coarse white marble. PUBLISHED: G. Hirschfeld in *Bulletino dell' Inst.*, 1873, p. 182 ff.; Dressel and Milchhöfer, in *Mittheilungen des Inst. in Athen*, II (1877), p. 418, No. 259.

At the left a youth (Orpheus?) sits in a cave, holding a lyre. About him are four animals, a horse, bull, sheep, and stag. Opposite, a man, bearded, appears to be reading from a scroll. Behind is perched on the rocks a large bird, and in a small niche at the right is a figure, clothed in a mantle, carrying a shield on the breast and two lances in his hand. The cave and the group of animals suggest that the chief figure is Orpheus, represented in his Thracian grotto, and that the relief is the dedication of a poet to him. The presence of such a votive offering at Sparta, however, is somewhat surprising, as no sanctuary of Orpheus is known to have existed there.

31. **Head of Hermes.** Fragment of a bas-relief in the Akropolis Museum, Athens.

Of Parian (?) marble. Found 1859, near the wall on the south side of the Akropolis. PUBLISHED: Conze, in the Nuove Memorie dell' Instituto, pl. XIII; etc.

This fragment has already been spoken of in connection with No. 2, to which it originally belonged. Although it bears the stamp of archaism, it is modelled delicately and with a sure hand. Hermes is represented bearded and wearing the petasos, a kind of hat worn by shepherds and travellers, which is one of his distinctive attributes. It will be noticed that his hair is arranged in the same manner as that of the figure mounting the chariot in No. 2, an argument for the sex of the latter.

32. **Relief from Samothrake,** in the Louvre.

Of white marble. Found 1790 on the island of Samothrake. Formerly in the possession of Count Choiseul-Gouffier, and since 1817 in the Louvre. There are no restorations. PUBLISHED: Millingen, Ancient Unedited Monuments, ser. II, pl. 1; Clarac, Musée de Sculpture, pl. 116, No. 238; Wolters' Friederichs, No. 34; etc.

Although the edges of this relief show that it is but a fragment, the purpose it served and the object of which it formed a part are difficult to conjecture. It is apparently not an architectural decoration, and the scroll on the right side is suggestive of the arm of a seat, but there is nothing to prove just what it was. The subject, however, is more easily determined, as the name of each figure is inscribed at its side. The seated figure is Agamemnon. Behind him stands his herald Talthybios, bearing the herald's staff; and the third figure is Epeios, who built the wooden horse.

The scene was continued to the left, and probably represented a council of the Greek chiefs before Troy.

This relief is an interesting example of early art in the northern part of the Ægean Sea. Its date is probably not later than the second half of the sixth century B. **C**.

33. Bas-relief in the Museum at Sparta.

> Of the local bluish stone resembling marble. Found in Sparta. Below it, on the same stone, is part of an inscription. PUBLISHED: Conze and Michaelis, in the *Annali dell' Inst.*, 1861, p. 39, B, and pl. D, 2; Dressel and Milchhöfer, in the *Mittheilungen des Instituts in Athen*, II (1877), p. 385, No. 203; etc.

In the middle of the relief is a female image of extremely archaic style, holding in each hand a fillet, such as were used on festal occasions for the decoration of the images of divinities.

At either side stands a youth, nude, wearing a cap, and holding a sword and spear. Both are in profile, facing the middle. As noted above, this relief served as the heading of an inscription of a public character, and the figures represented are probably the Dioskouroi, Kastor and Polydeukes, standing before an image of Helen, their sister. All three were worshipped as divinities at Sparta, their reputed birthplace.

34. Seated Athena. Statue of Parian marble, in the Akropolis Museum, Athens.

> The date of discovery not known, but the statue was formerly among the débris of the Akropolis below the north wall, where it was seen and sketched by Gell. Carried up to the Akropolis about 1840. There are no restorations. PUBLISHED: Collignon, *Archéologie Grecque*, p. 129, fig. 38; Overbeck, *Plastik*, I, p. 145, fig. 24; etc.

One of the earliest Athenian sculptors of whom we have any account, Endoios, was remembered in later times as having made a number of seated figures of Athena. One of these Pausanias saw in the Erechtheion, identified by an inscription. It has often been argued that this is the very figure described by Pausanias, but the fact that another statue, very similar in style, has also been found on the Akropolis, weakens the claim to that distinction on the part of either. At all events, this statue accords very well in style with the epoch in which Endoios is supposed to have lived — the latter part of the sixth century B. C. — and is undoubtedly an Attic work. The goddess is represented in the type common in early art, a distinguishing feature of which, aside from the stiffness, is the large size of the ægis, which covers the whole bosom, and hangs very low behind (cf. also the Dresden Pallas, No. 35). The holes along the edge of the ægis indicate that the serpents which fringed it were affixed, and probably of metal.

35. The Dresden Pallas, in the Museum at Dresden.

Statue of marble. Formerly in the Chigi Collection, in the Palazzo Odescalchi, Rome. Sold with that collection to the king of Saxony (August II.), and carried to Dresden, 1728. RESTORATIONS: Both feet, where they project from the drapery. PUBLISHED: Becker, *Augusteum*, pl. 9; Overbeck, *Plastik*, I, p. 195. fig. 46; Hettner, *Bildwerke der Antikensammlung*, Dresden, 1881, p. 67, No. 61 ; etc.

This is a pseudo-archaic statue, as is shown by the studied stiffness of the folds of the drapery, too elegantly executed for genuine archaic work, and still more by the free style of the reliefs on the stripe running down the front of the garment.

It represents Athena Promachos (*i. e.*, as champion), and reproduces a type which vases and small figures prove to have been common during the early part of the fifth century B. C., and which doubtless originated in some famous statue now lost. The goddess is armed with the ægis, and in the uplifted right hand probably held a spear. The reliefs on the peplos represent the battle of the gods and giants, in eleven scenes.

That this statue is a reproduction of that which from the earliest times stood in the temple of Athena Polias at Athens, as has sometimes been argued, is highly improbable. What is known of that image indicates that it was of the rudest and most primitive kind of art. The original of the Dresden Pallas **could** hardly have been earlier than the **year 500** B. C., and may well have originated in the period immediately following the Persian wars, its warlike character corresponding **to** the spirit of that age.

36. Penelope, **so** called. Statue in the Vatican.

<small>Of white marble. RESTORATIONS: The drapery on the head, the nose, right hand, right foot and leg from knee down, left foot, and the rocks on which the figure is seated. PUBLISHED: Müller-Wieseler, *Denkmäler der alten Kunst*, I, ix, **35;** Wolters' Friederichs, No. 211; etc.</small>

This statue received the **name** by **which it is** popularly **known** because of its attitude of weariness **and** despondency, suggestive of Penelope mourning for Odysseus, and **also** because Penelope is thus represented on several ancient terra-cotta reliefs. As a matter of fact, however, the attitude is by no means distinctive of her, since there are numerous representations of other women in the same posture (compare, for example, Elektra in a relief illustrated **in** Overbeck's *Plastik*, I, **p. 164), **which was evi**dently one commonly** used by sculptors to express grief, **and not** as a **mark of** any individual. This being **the** case, it is doubtful whether the statue was anything more than a grave monument, representing the person whose grave it surmounted. It **was** evidently intended **to be seen** only from one side, being long and flat, and in its arrangement **more** like a high relief than a statue. Its date is uncertain. Many eminent authorities regard it as **a** genuine archaic work, yet there is in the treatment a suggestion rather of poor workmanship in a period of developed art than of real archaism; and the existence of another figure like it (**in** the Museo Chiaramonti of the Vatican) gives reason to believe that it is not an original work, but that both are reproductions **of** an older type.

Of the casts in this room Nos. 1–6, **13, 14,** 16 A–O, 24 and **35** were purchased from the bequest of Charles Sumner.

SECOND GREEK ROOM.

50-81.

SCULPTURES FROM OLYMPIA.

AMONG the many sites which legend and history made sacred to the Greeks, Olympia held the foremost place. It was here they recognized and expressed their unity as a people. Greece, it must be remembered, was not a nation, it was not governed by one body, nor in one city, but was broken up into almost an infinity of little states, extending over not only the main-land, the islands, and the coasts of Asia Minor, but also along the coasts of Italy and Sicily; states often at war with one another, allying themselves now with one power, now with another, as it suited their interests. In spite of these internal dissensions, however, they never forgot the great difference between themselves as a whole, however widely separated they might be, and the nations surrounding them; and in certain great national institutions, like the early Amphictyonic Councils, and the Oracle of Delphi, they manifested this sense of unity. Nowhere was it more religiously observed and more carefully fostered than at this little spot in the valley of the Alpheios, in Elis. About twenty miles above its mouth, in a long narrow valley, surrounded by well-wooded hills, this river is joined by the smaller stream of the Kladeos, coming from the north. In the angle formed by the two, tradition said, the Olympic games had been founded by the Idaian Herakles, a hero of earlier date than the famous one of the same name. It was here that the mythical chariot-race between Pelops and Oinomaos for the possession of the latter's daughter, Hippodameia, took place;

and **Pelops** having won and carried off his bride, **was** looked upon, and later worshipped, as the original Olympic victor. In an enclosure sacred to him, the remains of which **may** still be recognized, were afterwards raised the **trees** from which the olive-wreaths given **as** prizes were **cut.** Later, **the** famous Herakles instituted games and other religious ceremonies here, after slaying Augeas for his perfidy in not delivering the cattle which he promised as the reward **for** the cleansing of his stables. According to some legends this was the original foundation **of** the games.

The institution **was** for **a** considerable **period almost** local, until, probably in the eighth century **B. C.,** Iphitos, king **of** Elis, and the Spartan Lykourgos opened the historical epoch of the Olympic games, making them a **national** Hellenic festival, and establishing the principles **on** which, with the modifications caused by the development of Greek civilization, they were conducted for nearly twelve hundred years, until the decay of Greek religion brought them to an end, **A.** D. 394. The festival took place every four years, during the first full moon after the summer solstice, and lasted five days. During its continuance peace was proclaimed throughout Hellas, and any state violating this peace was suspended from the rights and privileges of participation in the exercises. From the year 776 B. C. the names of victors were preserved, **and** subsequently the occurrence of this festival became the basis of Greek chronology, which was reckoned by Olympiads, each Olympiad being a term of four years. Every free Greek, from whatever town or colony, could take part in the various contests, and the victor's name was proclaimed through the whole land. On the other hand **foreigners were** rigidly excluded. Even Alexander the Great **had to** prove his Argolic extraction before he was admitted, and though victorious was allowed only a second prize. Statues were erected to those who had conquered more than once, and these, with the votive statues erected **by states and** individuals in honor of various divinities, **made Olympia a** museum of art rivalling Athens and Delphi.

Olympia was not a city. **It was** a collection of temples, altars, and treasuries, in a sacred enclosure about which grew up, in course of time, other buildings connected with the festival, such as gymnasia, council halls, buildings for the entertainment of honored guests, etc. Everything was done under the immediate patronage of Zeus, the father of gods and of men. His was the chief shrine, under his image the prizes were awarded, and before him all oaths were sworn. In early times he was worshipped jointly with Hera in the very ancient temple known as the Heraion. There is no indication of a temple dedicated exclusively to him before the fifth century B. C., when was built the GREAT TEMPLE, from which the pediment groups (Nos. 50-65) are taken. This was begun probably about the year 470, with booty taken by the Eleans in a campaign against their neighbors, the architect being LIBON, a native of Elis. Just when it was finished is not known. Herodotos speaks of it as complete in 445, but it must have been finished some time before then, as we read of the Spartans placing a golden shield on the apex of the eastern pediment after a battle at Tanagra, in 457. The great STATUE OF ZEUS, of gold and ivory, which stood in the interior, was made by Pheidias after he had completed the statue of Athena for the Parthenon, which was dedicated in the year 438.

Through the whole course of Greek civilization Olympia retained its influential position, and even after Greece had lost her independence, her foreign rulers held the Olympic festival in the greatest respect, placing themselves in the position of servants rather than masters of its priests and judges. The Macedonian rulers not only entered the contests, as we have seen, but dedicated magnificent offerings in the sanctuary; and even Nero sought to win himself glory by appearing as a competitor in the games. With the decay of the old civilization and the rise of Christianity, the work of Olympia was done. Theodosius suppressed the games at the end of the fourth century after Christ, earthquakes completed the ruin that had been begun by robbers and barbarians, and Time began its slow work of burial. The two rivers, which at certain seasons bring down large quantities of soil, became choked at their outlet, and overflowed the plain for many years, until the cluster of once famous buildings was buried in soft alluvium, in some places to a depth of nearly twenty feet.

The idea of excavating there has been shared by many people during the last hundred years. In 1829 slight excavations were undertaken by the French on the site of the Zeus Temple, but it remained for Germany to do the work thoroughly. For this we are indebted to Prof. ERNST CURTIUS, author of the History of Greece, who secured the interest of the German Emperor and Crown Prince in the project; and after many vexatious delays and disappointments, a convention was signed by the German and Greek governments, in 1874, by which the former was allowed to excavate for five years on the site of Olympia, *on the condition that nothing be taken away*, Germany retaining as her only right the privilege of being the first to publish the discoveries and the exclusive power to make and sell casts and other reproductions of the objects found. In this disinterested spirit, acting solely for the benefit of science, the Germans conducted their excavations during the years 1875–81 (the term being extended one year), at an expense of $200,000, placing the work in charge of three directors in Berlin, and a corps of thirteen archæologists and architects at Olympia, among whom the superintendence of the work was divided. In that time was laid bare a space which might be roughly described as a square, measuring about one thousand feet on each side, comprising the Zeus Temple and all the other buildings within the sacred enclosure, and many important buildings about it. These and the sculptural discoveries, which were very extensive, illustrate every epoch of Greek art from the time when it was under the influence of the older arts of the East to the Byzantine period. With the exception of a small collection of duplicates presented to Germany and now in Berlin, all the objects found are in a museum recently erected at Olympia. The specimens in our Museum include but a few of the more important sculptures discovered.

For a history and description of Olympia and the excavations, see Adolf Bötticher, *Olympia*, 2d ed., Berlin, 1885, and an essay by C. T. Newton in his *Essays on Art and Archæology*, p. 321 ff. The discoveries are fully illustrated in the *Ausgrabungen zu Olympia*, 5 vols. Berlin, 1876–81.

50-65. Figures from the Pediments of the Temple of Zeus.

Of Parian marble; now in the Museum at Olympia. There are no restorations. Nos. 50-58 from the EASTERN pediment are results of the first year's excavations (1875-76), and are published in Vol. I of the *Ausgrabungen zu Olympia* as follows: **50** pl. viii; **51** pl. vii; **52** pl. ix; **53** pl. xii; **54** pl. x, xi; **55** pl. xiii; **56** pl. xiv; **57** pl. xv; **58** pl. xvi A.

Nos. 59-65 from the WESTERN pediment. Published in the *Ausgrabungen* as follows: **59** II, pl. xxi, xxii, and III, pl. x; **60** II, pl. xxiii, xxiv; **61** II, pl. xxv, and III, pl. xi; **62** II, pl. ix B; **64** II, pl. xv; **65** I, pl. xviii B. These were found during the season of 1876-77. COLOR was noted on the upper lip of No. 54, and on the chlamys of No. 59. Red in both cases.

The subject of the eastern or principal front was the opening of the chariot race between Pelops and Oinomaos for the possession of Hippodameia, over which contest Zeus presided, as he did over the Olympic games. The manner of representation may be seen more easily in the small model of the pediment above the figures, the latter being too fragmentary to show the composition. The central figure (50) is Zeus, on either side of whom stand the competitors. That to the right of Zeus (52) is Oinomaos, by whose side is his wife, Sterope. To balance this figure on the left of Zeus, Hippodameia (51) stands by Pelops. These five form the principal group; beyond them on either side are the four-horse chariots, with their charioteers and attendants, every figure on the right side being balanced by a corresponding one on the left; and the ends of the pediment are occupied by personifications of the rivers Kladeos (56) and Alpheios (57), who appear as spectators, to indicate the locality of the action.

The WESTERN FRONT represented the battle between the Lapithæ and Kentaurs at the wedding of Peirithoös and Deidameia when Eurytion attempted to carry off the bride. This is a favorite subject in Greek, and especially Attic, sculpture, and is usually considered as symbolic of the struggle between civilization and barbarism. At Olympia it was probably intended to enforce the principle of order at a gathering of kinsmen such as the festival brought together; for the Lapithæ and Kentaurs, though of widely different natures, were of the same race, both being descendants of Apollo. In the midst of the confusion caused by the attempted rape, appears **Apollo** himself (59), the stern punisher of lawlessness **and** disorder, who with the calmness of divinity repels the drunken Kentaur simply **by the** force of his outstretched arm. The small model **shows the** correct grouping of these figures, **by** which it **will** be seen that the hand of the god came in contact with **the** Kentaur's head. Here, as in the eastern pediment, there was the rhythmical balancing of figures on the two sides. The woman rescued by Apollo is evidently Deidameia (61); the fragments, Nos. 62, 63, **have been** recognized as those of Peirithoös, but the others have not been identified.

Pausanias, who described Olympia very minutely **in** the second **century** after Christ, says that the eastern pediment group was the work of Paionios of Mende in Thrace, **the** western that of Alkamenes of Athens. Paionios we **know** only through one other work, the Nike (No. 73), which is ascribed to him by both Pausanias and the inscription on its pedestal. Of Alkamenes no identified work remains, but through literary sources we know him as one of the great masters of the Athenian school at its greatest epoch, a younger contemporary and pupil of Pheidias. We may judge of his style, therefore, by the existing sculptures of that school and period. Both these and the Nike show such a great advance beyond the art of the Olympian groups as to render the assertion of Pausanias regarding either of these sculptors almost incredible. Yet the rejection of an ancient authority is unwarrantable with**out** positive proof of error, such as in the present case **does** not exist. Our knowledge of the history **of** Paionios **and** Alkamenes is very slight, and though it is evident that **they** could **not** have executed these groups when under the **influence of** Pheidias, it is still possible that they may **have done** so at an earlier period. Unfortunately we have **not the** material necessary to either confirm or disprove the statement of Pausanias, and must judge the sculptures simply by their style. This shows **that** in **the history** of Greek art **they** occupy **a place** midway **between** the Æginetan groups and those of the Parthenon, in which respect they correspond with the date of the completion of the Zeus Temple, about **460** B. C., when they were probably made. They are of great importance in illustrating the condition of sculpture just before it felt the influence of Pheidias. In execution there is little advance beyond the Æginetan figures. The muscular surfaces are hard and flat, the action is not yet freed from archaic stiffness, the hair is either treated in a wiry, mechanical manner as in the Apollo (59) and the Lapith head (64), or left to be expressed entirely in color, as in the Peirithoös (62). In the drapery there is some improvement. The folds are less stiff and symmetrical than in works of the beginning of the century, yet they are neither vigorous nor graceful. The sculptor has no idea of the value of drapery as a means for expressing the character of the figures; his effort was apparently that of mere imitation, and in this he has not wholly succeeded. On the other hand, the faces display character. The "Æginetan smile" has disappeared, and although there are no lines expressive of mental emotion, individuality has been attained.

It is, however, chiefly in conception that these sculptures are superior to earlier works. The Æginetan figures do not indicate that their sculptor had any higher aim than the representation of the body in action. The absence of any attempt to express an intellectual idea deprives them of impressiveness. The Olympian figures, on the contrary, are full of dignity; they possess the ethical quality which distinguishes a great from a clever work. In spite of technical shortcomings, the Apollo is a superb conception of divinity, and in all the figures there is a suggestion of self-restraint which harmonizes well with the Doric architecture of the temple. They show the spirit of the greatest epoch, without its power of expression.

66. Metope from the Zeus Temple, Herakles and Atlas.

Of Parian marble; in the Museum at Olympia. Found in the Pronaos of the Temple, April 19, 1876. PUBLISHED in the *Ausgrabungen* I, pl. xvii.

The metopes over the outer columns, unlike those of the Parthenon, were without any plastic decoration, but over the inner columns, at the front and rear of the building, ran a smaller frieze of triglyphs and metopes, the latter carved in high relief. Of these there were six at each end, representing the twelve labors of Herakles. That here exhibited is one of the best preserved, and is from the eastern end. In the middle stands Herakles bearing the burden of Atlas, who, having secured the apples of the Hesperides, now offers them to the hero. The globe of heaven is not represented here, its weight being suggested by the cushion held by Herakles, on which it is supposed to rest. At the left stands a young woman with hand uplifted as though to assist him. This is possibly a daughter of Hesperos.

The style of this metope presents the same characteristics as the pediment sculptures, a fact which furnishes another argument for the dating of the latter; as the metopes, from their position on the temple, were most probably executed before the completion of the building.

67. Fragment of another Metope.

From the east end. Found Jan. 25, 1876. In the Museum at Olympia. PUBLISHED: *Ausgrabungen*, I, pl. xviii A.

This almost unrecognizable fragment represents the jar in which Eurystheus tried to hide himself when frightened by the Erymanthian boar, brought to him by Herakles. Early vases, on which the subject frequently occurs, show that Herakles, of whom only one foot remains in this fragment, carried the boar on his shoulders, threatening to drop him on the terrified king whose head and arms protrude from the jar.

68-71. Four of the Lion's Heads, placed at intervals along the cyma, or moulding at the edge of the roof, of the Zeus Temple, to drain off the rainwater. These heads show considerable individuality and variety in their treatment, and are evidently the work of different hands.

72. LION'S HEAD of terra-cotta, used like the preceding, on another building.

73. The Nike of Paionios. In the Museum at Olympia.

Of Parian marble. Found Dec. 21, 1875, on its original site, east of the Zeus Temple; the fragment of the head found Nov. 3, 1879, at a considerable distance from the statue. PUBLISHED: in the Ausgrabungen, *I, pl. iii-vi; Overbeck,* Plastik, *I, figs. 88, 89; etc.*

Nike, the goddess of victory, is represented as descending through the air with outspread wings, traces of which remain on the shoulders. The right arm was raised, the left bent backward and downward, but in what manner the hands were occupied there is, unfortunately, nothing to indicate. From under the drapery at the left flies out an eagle, to signify that the figure is in mid-air. At the back are remains of a large mantle, which was filled out by the wind so as to be almost entirely clear of the figure.

The effect originally produced by the statue is almost unappreciable in its present position. It stood facing the Temple of Zeus, on a slender, three-cornered pillar, about nineteen feet (6 M.) high, and was therefore seen only from below. From this point of view the figure appeared entirely free, as the support under the left foot was not visible, and the light, airy folds of the drapery gave no suggestion of the burden they bore.

An inscription (No. 74) on the pedestal stated that the "Messenians and Naupaktians dedicated this statue to Zeus with a tithe of the spoils taken from their enemies." The campaign referred to is not mentioned, but was probably that of Sphakteria, B. C. 424, in which both fought with the Athenians against the Spartans.

A smaller inscription below this records the name of PAIONIOS of Mende as the sculptor, "who was also victorious making the *akroteria* on the Temple." Whether the word *akroteria* here means the pediment groups, or the objects which stood at the three angles of the roof, on each front, is a disputed point which has not yet been determined. Pausanias describes a Nike of gilded bronze above the middle of the pediment, and it has been suggested that the statue dedicated by the Messenians and Naupaktians was a copy in marble of that figure, the object of the inscription being to show that it was by the same sculptor. The technical characteristics of the Nike certainly lend force to this argument, the character of the support and the broad, flat mantle behind being more adapted to bronze than to marble.

However this may have been, the Nike is a striking example of the extraordinary development of sculpture during the years that followed the completion of the Zeus Temple. It was during this time that the art attained perfect mastery over its material. The stiff pose and ungraceful drapery of earlier sculpture have here given place to perfect freedom of movement, and beauty in every line. The figure is conceived in the attitude most difficult of all to study, yet executed with such consummate skill as to give no hint of the difficulty. The action of the wind on the drapery brings the exquisite proportions of the body into full relief, and this manner of treatment, as well as the type of the goddess, bears such a strong resemblance to the balustrade of the Temple of Nike Apteros at Athens (see Nos. 165–171, especially 167) as to lead one to believe that Paionios had his training in the Attic school.

74. Inscription from the pedestal of the Statue of Nike.

"The Messenians and Naupaktians dedicated this to the Olympian Zeus, a tithe of spoils taken from their enemies. Paionios of Mende made it, who was also victorious in making the akroteria upon the Temple."

75. The Hermes of Praxiteles.

Statue of Parian marble; in the Museum at Olympia. Found May 8, 1877, lying near its pedestal in the ruins of the Heraion. COLOR: Traces of red were found on the mouth and the sandal, reddish brown in the hair. PUBLISHED in the *Ausgrabungen*, III, pl. vi–ix, and V, pl. vii–x; Treu, *Hermes mit dem Dionysosknaben*, Berlin, 1878; etc.

Pausanias (V, 17, 3), describing the works of art in the Temple of Hera at Olympia, speaks of a number of archaic statues, and continues: "In later times other works also were dedicated in the Heraion, a Hermes of marble, bearing the infant Dionysos, the work of Praxiteles." This, the only work of that master mentioned at Olympia, was discovered lying face downward close by its original position, buried in a mass of clay and tiles, the débris of the temple. Hermes is represented as the youthful messenger of Zeus, by whom he has been intrusted to carry the newborn Dionysos to be nursed by the Nymphs. With one hand placed upon his shoulder the child looks up affectionately at the face of his protector, who regards him with womanly tenderness. The right arm of the Hermes was raised, and probably held some object. With the left, on which the infant rests, he leans upon the trunk of a tree, over which he has thrown his cloak, in an attitude which gives beautiful variety to the modelling of the figure, one side being at rest, the other in action.

Although we must regret the lost parts of this statue, the beauty of what remains is so impressive as to render comment upon it impertinent. The exceptionally fine preservation of the head and torso enables us to appreciate for the first time the quality for which Praxiteles was most famous in antiquity, his marvellous technique in marble, in which he was said to "surpass even himself." This, of course, copies cannot reproduce. They indicate the type and attitude, and sometimes suggest the spirit of the original; but the soft, elastic texture of the skin, the infinite modulations of the surface, the exquisite outline of the figure from every point of view, and the extreme sensitiveness of the face, these only the subtle hand of the master could impart to the marble.

In conception as well as in execution, refinement is the most prominent characteristic of the Hermes. It is the embodiment of the spirit of the fourth century, the age of Praxiteles, in which the sublime ideals of the Pheidian epoch had given place to the desire for the expression of pure beauty. More delicately modelled than the statues of the Parthenon, it is also less majestic. They command the admiration of the spectator, while the Hermes appeals to it. To use the distinction of Aristotle, the influence of the one is purely ethic, that of the other pathetic.

76. Fragment of a Roman Statue.

Of white marble. In the Museum at Olympia. Found March 30, 1876, and published in the *Ausgrabungen*, I, pl. xviii C.

This statue was one of the many hundred dedicated at Olympia by individuals. It was found near a pedestal bearing the name of Caracalla, and may have been a portrait of him, in which case its date would be about 212 A. D. The head was of a separate block.

77–81. **Five** inscriptions, found during the first year's excavations at Olympia, and published as follows: 77, *Archäologische Zeitung* 1875, p. 183; 78, *Arch. Zeit.* 1876, p. 47; 79, *Arch. Zeit.* 1876, p. 47; 80, *Arch. Zeit.* 1876, p. 48; 81, Röhl, *Inscriptiones Graecae Antiquissimae*, 46.

82. Satyr in the Capitoline Museum.

Statue of Pentelic marble. Found 1701, near Civita Lavinia, where there was formerly a Villa of Antoninus Pius. Placed in the Museum of the Capitol by Benedict XIV., in 1753. RESTORATIONS: the nose, right forearm with hand and pipe, three fourths of left arm with all except two fingers of the hand, also part of the base. PUBLISHED: Müller-Wieseler, *Denkmäler der alten Kunst*, I, pl. xxxv, 143; Overbeck, *Plastik*, II, p. 41, fig. 103; etc.

This, the "Marble Faun" of Hawthorne, is a copy of a lost work which must have been very famous in antiquity, as more replicas exist of it than of any other ancient statue. Almost every museum in Europe contains one or more, among which the Capitoline figure ranks as the best because of its fine preservation. In technique it is surpassed by a fragment in the Louvre, which is, however, too mutilated to give a complete idea of the original.

Praxiteles has long been considered as the sculptor with whose style, as described by ancient writers, this Satyr best corresponds, and the discovery of the Hermes (No. 75), which enables us to study the master through an original work, has confirmed this judgment. The conception of the two figures is very similar. Both Hermes and the Satyrs are beings with whom the reflective faculty is least associated; the essence of their natures is a restless activity. One appears as the swift-footed messenger of Zeus, or the patron of athletics and the traffic of the market-place, or the guardian of shepherds and their flocks; the others as wild roamers among the hills, or the noisy companions of Dionysos, their animal nature being emphasized in most representations by the attributes of tails, goat-feet, or coarse, sensual faces. Yet in this Satyr as in the Hermes it is to the psychical rather than the physical qualities that the artist has given most attention. Each is represented in an attitude of meditation, with a face indicative of a sensitive character, which in the original of the Satyr must have been quite as marked as in the Hermes. The tendency to refinement which was noticeable in the latter, is carried still further in the Satyr, in whom there is no suggestion of the animal except the pointed ears. He is simply a beautiful boy, "easy, mirthful, apt for jollity, yet not incapable of being touched by pathos,"— a purely poetic, almost sentimental, ideal of these creatures of the woods and streams.

Praxiteles is known to have made at least three Satyrs, one of which stood on the famous street of Tripods in Athens, the second in a temple of Dionysos at Megara, and the third was in Rome in the time of Pliny, who speaks of it as "the one which the Greeks called 'Periboëtos' (famous)." As there remains no description of any of these, it is impossible to say which, if either, is reproduced in this figure.

Hawthorne's description of the statue shows such keen appreciation of its qualities as a work of art that the visitor will be glad to read it with the figure before him:—

"The Faun is the marble image of a young man leaning his right arm on the trunk or stump of a tree; one hand hangs carelessly by his side; in the other he holds the fragment of a pipe, or some such sylvan instrument of music. His only garment, a lion's skin, with the claws upon his shoulder, falls half-way down his back, leaving the limbs and entire front of the figure nude. The form thus displayed is marvellously graceful, but has a fuller and more rounded outline, more flesh and less of heroic muscle, **than** the old sculptors were wont to assign to **their** types of masculine beauty. The character **of** the face corresponds with **the** figure. It is most agreeable **in outline and** feature, but rounded and somewhat voluptuously **developed,** especially **about** the throat and chin. The nose **is almost** straight, but very slightly curves inward, thereby acquiring an indescribable charm of geniality and humor. The mouth, with its full yet delicate lips, seems so nearly to smile outright that it calls forth a responsive smile. The whole statue, unlike anything else that **ever was** wrought in that severe material of marble, conveys the idea of an amiable and sensual creature,— easy, mirthful, apt for jollity, yet not incapa**ble of being** touched by pathos. It is impossible to gaze **long at this** stone image without conceiving a kindly senti**ment** toward it, as if its substance were warm to the touch, and imbued with actual life. . . .

"The animal nature, indeed, is a most essential part of the Faun's composition; for the characteristics of the brute creation meet and combine with those of humanity in this strange yet true and natural conception of antique poetry and art. Praxiteles has subtly diffused throughout his work that mute mystery which so hopelessly perplexes us whenever we attempt to gain an intellectual or sympathetic knowledge of the lower orders of creation. The riddle is indicated, however, only by two definite signs; these are the two ears of the Faun, which are leaf-shaped, terminating in little peaks, like those of some species of animals. . . . In the coarser representations of this class of mythological creatures, there is **another** token of brute kindred, — a certain caudal append**age, which,** if the Faun of Praxiteles must be supposed to **possess it at** all, is hidden by the lion's skin that forms his garment. The pointed and furry ears, therefore, are the sole indications of his wild, forest nature.

"Only **a** sculptor **of the finest imagination, the most** delicate taste, the sweetest feeling, and **the rares**t artistic skill — in a word, a sculptor and a poet, **too — could** have first **dreamed** of a Faun in this guise, **and** then **have** succeeded in imprisoning the sportive and frisky thing in marble. Neither man nor animal, and yet no monster; but a being in whom both races meet on friendly ground."

83. Apollo Sauroktonos, in the Vatican.

Statue of Carrara marble. Found among the ruins of the House of Augustus on the Palatine, during the excavations of the Abbé Rancoureil, 1777. The figure was seriously mutilated, and has undergone the following extensive RESTORATIONS: The head was much damaged and broken from the statue, the face especially being freely restored; also a piece in the front of the neck, the right forearm and hand (?), a large piece in the upper side of the left upper arm, the wrist and upper portion of the left forearm and fingers of the left hand, the right leg from middle of the thigh down, left foot and leg from the knee. Of the tree, a piece at the top, and the lower half, including the greater part of the lizard's tail, are modern. PUBLISHED: Clarac, *Musée de Sculpture*, pl. 475, No. 905 A; Welcker, *Alte Denkmäler*, I, p. 406 ff.; Rayet, *Monuments de l'Art Antique*, II, pl. 46; etc.

Apollo is represented as a boy amusing himself by striking at a lizard on the tree beside him. In the right hand should be an arrow, to correspond with Pliny's description of a statue by Praxiteles (N. H. XXXIV, 70): "He made also a young Apollo lying in wait with an arrow for a lizard creeping towards him, which they call the 'Sauroktonos' (lizard-killer)." The type and attitude of the figure before us correspond so well with this description that it may safely be regarded as a copy of the one referred to. As we have seen in the Hermes (75) and the Satyr (82), this leaning posture was characteristic of Praxiteles, who probably originated it. The older statues, when not representing figures in action, stood either firmly upon both legs, or with one slightly drawn back (see the Eirene, No. 85). By making the figure lean upon some artificial support, great variety is given the modelling of the different parts of the body, even in repose. The lines of the figure become more undulating, and the effect, though less vigorous, is more graceful.

As the lizard is known to have had some connection with the oracular mysteries of Apollo, the attempt has been made to give this statue a religious interpretation, as of the divinity engaged in some rite. The purely decorative style of the work, however, makes this supposition extremely improbable. The act of killing the lizard was probably invented merely to give a motive to the figure.

This statue is reproduced in a number of marble copies, and one of bronze in the Villa Albani. According to Pliny's description the original was of the latter material.

84. Silenos and the Infant Dionysos, in the Louvre.

Group of grechetto marble. Found at Rome during the sixteenth century, near the gardens of Sallust, and formerly in the Villa Borghese. RESTORATIONS: Of Silenos, the end of the nose, parts of the hair, both hands, and three toes of the right foot. Of the infant, the nose, chin, arms, and legs. Also pieces of the nebris, the greater part of the tree-trunk, and the back of the base, with the plant. PUBLISHED: Clarac, Musée de Sculpture, pl. 333, No. 1556; Müller-Wieseler, Denkmäler der alten Kunst, II, pl. 35, No. 406; etc.

Silenos, the old satyr to whom some of the Bacchic legends attributed the guardianship and education of Dionysos, leans against a tree, holding in both arms his young charge. His satyric character is indicated first of all in the face, which is of a coarse, sensual type, but not lacking in good-nature; and also in the distinctive attributes of satyrs,—the long, pointed ears, the tail, and the nebris or fawn's-skin which hangs on the tree. From the birth of Dionysos, Silenos was his constant companion, and the affection of the two for each other is expressed in the grim smile in the older face, and the merry laugh in the younger.

Like the two preceding numbers, this statue is reproduced in a number of extant copies (there is one in the Glyptothek, Munich, another in the Vatican), from which circumstance it may be inferred that the original was a well-known work in antiquity. What, or by whom, that original was, we have no means of knowing. The attitude is somewhat suggestive of Praxiteles, but certain peculiarities, such as the lengthened proportions of the legs, and the realistic treatment of the face of the Silenos, are more characteristic of the epoch following that of Praxiteles. It is not probable that the original dated earlier than the end of the fourth century B. C. The manner in which the hair and wreaths are treated, and the sharpness in the modelling of the muscles, indicate that this original was of bronze.

85. Eirene and Ploutos, in the Glyptothek, Munich.

Group of Attic marble. Formerly in the Villa Albani, whence it was carried to Paris by Napoleon I., after whose fall it was purchased by Ludwig I., of Bavaria, then Crown Prince. RESTORATIONS: Of the Eirene, the lower half of nose, the right arm, the fingers of the left hand, with the vase, and pieces in the folds of the drapery. Of the child, both arms, the left foot, the fore part of the right foot, and the neck. The head, with restored end of nose, is antique, but of Parian marble, and probably belonged to an Eros (Brunn). PUBLISHED: Winckelmann, *Monumenti Inediti*, 54; Brunn, *Die sogenannte Leukothea*, Munich, 1867; etc.

This group, which was formerly thought to represent Ino-Leukothea with the infant Dionysos, has been shown by Brunn to be a replica of a work by Kephisodotos the elder, probably father of Praxiteles, representing Eirene, the goddess of peace, as nurse or protectress of Ploutos, the personification of wealth. The original was erected at Athens in commemoration of the victory of Timotheos over the Spartans at Leukas, B. C. 375, by which the naval power which Athens lost in the Peloponnesian war was for a time restored. In representations of that group on certain Athenian coins Brunn detected the strong resemblance to the Munich group, and thereby established the identity of the latter. The coins show that the uplifted right hand held a long sceptre which rested on the ground, and that the restoration of the left hand with the vase is wrong, the original having held a small cornucopia, the attribute of Ploutos. A small fragment of another copy of the group, consisting of only the infant with the left forearm of the goddess, discovered a few years since in the Piræus, shows the cornucopia as represented on the coins. (See *Mittheilungen d. Instituts in Athen*, 1881, pl. xiii.)

This is a most interesting monument of the transition from the older to the younger Attic schools, of the epoch between Pheidias and Praxiteles. The goddess of peace is represented with the full matronly figure indicative of fertility. As in works of the older school, the figure rests firmly upon one leg, allowing the garment to fall in straight vigorous folds, in the style of the maidens of the porch of the Erechtheion (see the cast in the Architectural Room), and those on the Parthenon frieze. The treatment of the

drapery, though not stiff, is as simple as possible, and gives **great dignity to** the figure. In these and in the technical **characteristics** we are reminded of the age of Pheidias, but **in the** almost pathetic expression of the face, and the delicate turn of the head, there are suggestions of Praxiteles and the masters of the younger school.

86, 86 A. The so-called Apollo and the Omphalos, in the National Museum, Athens.

> Statue of Pentelic (?) **marble. Found** July, 1862, in **the** Dionysiac Theatre, Athens, the statue behind the stage of Phaidros, near the left Parodos, according to the official report, and the Omphalos near by, between the parallel walls of the same Parodos. Formerly in the Theseion. There are no restorations. PUBLISHED: Conze, *Beiträge*, pp. 13 f., and pl. iii-v; Waldstein, in *Journal Hellenic Studies*, I, pp. 168 f., and, II, pp. 332 f. (reprinted in his *Essays on the Art of Pheidias*, pp. 323 f.); Schreiber, in *Mitth. d. Inst. in Athen*, 1884, **pp.** 234 f. and pl. ix; etc.

The Omphalos (navel) **was a stone at** Delphi which marked that place as the navel **or centre of** the world, and is therefore intimately connected with Apollo, in representations of whom it often occurs (see, for example, the Rape of the Tripod in No. **4,** First Room). It is always represented as a cone-shaped object; and usually, as here, bound with fillets. When, therefore, this statue was found, and the omphalos with the marks of feet on its upper surface, near by, the two were thought to belong together, and to represent Apollo standing upon the omphalos. A slight examination will show that this is an impossible restoration. The feet of the figure could not be made to **fit the** marks on the omphalos, being both too large and placed at **a** different angle. Moreover, a long, narrow projection on the outside of the right leg indicates that the statue leaned against **an** artificial support, perhaps the trunk of a tree, of which there are **no traces** on the omphalos. The impossibility of the connection was at once recognized by the authorities of the Berlin Museum, who set **up** their casts of the figure and the omphalos separ**ately,** and was afterwards proved by Dr. Waldstein, in the **articles** mentioned above.

Whether the statue is that of Apollo or an athlete, is not easy to determine. Apollo is the divinity that typifies the perfection of youthful manhood, and therefore, without some special attribute, it is difficult to distinguish his statues from those of victorious athletes. Like them, he is represented as a well-built, muscular youth, and generally nude, except in his character of the god of music. The lost hands and support of this statue deprive it of the distinguishing attributes it may once have had. The arrangement of the hair is peculiar, especially the long front locks, and this same arrangement is seen in an Apollo on a relief of the Twelve Gods in the Capitol. Another copy of the same figure, the "Choiseul-Gouffier Apollo" in the British Museum, is in a better state of preservation, possessing both feet and the tree-trunk against the right leg. On the tree are the remains of a long, narrow object not unlike a slightly curved stick. Waldstein regards this as the strap used by pugilists for binding the hand, and argues therefrom that the figure is a pugilist. Against this theory is the shape of the ears, which in pugilists are represented as hard and solid, a feature on which they prided themselves (see the Head of an Olympic Victor among the small casts in the Room of Greek Vases). The object is much more probably a bow, and adds at least some weight to the generally accepted theory that the statue is an Apollo.

In style, this statue corresponds to works of the middle of the fifth century B. C., the period immediately preceding that of Pheidias. Both feet were placed firmly upon the ground in an attitude not quite free from archaism; the square shape of the body, the broad shoulders, narrow hips and long legs, and the flat, mechanical treatment of the abdominal muscles, resemble the Apollo of the Zeus Temple (No. 59) sufficiently to suggest that both originated in the same stage of the development of sculpture, though the types of the two figures indicate that they are the creations of different schools. The original of the "Omphalos" Apollo, Conze attributes to Kalamis, Schreiber to Kallimachos, and Waldstein to Pythagoras of Rhegion. Our knowledge of all these artists is too limited to warrant our ascribing it positively to either of them, but it is safe to assume that it was a work of the Attic school, a famous statue, as testified by the number of existing replicas, and that it dated about 460–450 B. C. The careful though mechanical treatment of the hair, and the sharpness of the brows and eyelids, as well as of the outlines of the muscles, suggest that the original was of bronze.

87. **Satyr,** in the Museum of Antiquities, Dresden.

> Statue of marble. Said to have been found at Antium. **Formerly** in the Chigi collection, in the Palazzo Odescalchi, Rome. **Sold** with that collection to August II., of Saxony, in 1728, and since then in the royal collection of antiquities. RESTORATIONS: The left hand. The face has been worked over, but is original. PUBLISHED: Clarac, *Musée de Sculpture*, pl. 712, No. 1695; Hettner, *Bildwerke der Antikensammlung zu Dresden*, 1881, p. 81, No. 87; etc.

This is evidently a Roman copy of a work of the Praxitelean type (see the Capitoline Satyr, No. 82), in which the animal side of the satyr nature is almost entirely suppressed. Unlike the satyrs of both earlier and later art, this figure has no tail, and his pointed ears are half disguised by the curls. The head is bound with a fillet, and adorned with a garland of grape-leaves. In the uplifted right hand was formerly an *oinochoë* or wine-jug, from which he was pouring into a cup in his left hand.

Intrinsically this statue does not rank high. It bears numerous evidences of being the work of an ordinary copyist, yet it is instructive because its type indicates that its original was of a fine period, and if not by Praxiteles himself, undoubtedly of his time and school.

88. **The** Eleusinian Slab, in the National Museum, Athens.

> **Bas-relief of** Parian marble. Found May, 1859, in Eleusis, close by the chapel of S. Zacharias, during excavations for the foundations of a school-house. Carried at once to Athens and placed in the Theseion, whence it was subsequently moved to its present place. The cracks between the several fragments composing the slab have been partially filled up with plaster, otherwise there are no restorations. PUBLISHED: *Mon. dell' Instituto*, VI, pl. xlv, and Welcker in the *Annali*, 1860, pp. 454 f.; Fr. Lenormant, *Gazette des Beaux Arts*, 1860, p. 65; Overbeck, *Kunstmythologie*, Demeter, pp. 426 ff., 564 ff., and Atlas, pl. xiv, No. 8; etc.

88. THE ELEUSINIAN SLAB.

In the centre of the relief is a boy from whose shoulders has fallen his chlamys, leaving the figure nude. He stands in profile towards the left, his right hand uplifted to receive some object from the large female whom he faces. She wears rather short, wavy hair, and is clothed in a Doric sleeveless chiton. In her left hand she holds a long sceptre. The right evidently held some small object, and small holes drilled in the marble, not visible in the cast, show that this was of metal, affixed. Behind the boy stands another female, clothed in an Ionic chiton, over which is a shawl or himation, who with the right hand was placing an object, probably a wreath or crown, on his head. This object was also of metal. In her left hand she holds a large torch.

There can be no doubt that these two females are the Great Goddesses of Eleusis,—Demeter, and Kora or Persephone. Which of them is Demeter, however, is not easy to determine. In the forms of the two there is no distinction between mother and daughter. Both the sceptre and the torch are attributes of each. If we assume the boy to be Triptolemos, then we have a probable interpretation of the relief in the story of his being sent forth by Demeter to carry the blessings of agriculture to mankind. This is a favorite subject of vase paintings, many of which represent Demeter in the act of handing Triptolemos the ears of wheat as a symbol of his mission, and is most probably the subject of the relief. If so, the figure to the left is Demeter, and in her hands were the ears of wheat, of metal, which Triptolemos is about to receive, while on the other side Kora crowns him with the laurel-wreath which he is usually represented as wearing when starting out. Although Iakchos and Ploutos have also been suggested as the youth in the centre, and the subject some rite connected with their worship, the explanation given has the most ground for acceptance, both for other reasons and because the relief was found on the site of a small temple, the situation of which corresponds with Pausanias' mention of the temple of Triptolemos, near the great temple of Demeter.

This is an original work of the fifth century B. C., and dates from about the time of the Parthenon. It has the severe character of a purely religious work, but unlike the later so-called Hieratic sculptures, of which there are several specimens in the First Greek Room, there is no affectation in the conception of the divinities. Demeter and Kora are represented as the Greeks of Perikles' time really imagined them. The tranquil spirit of the group, and the absence of all sensationalism or sentiment, are characteristic of all similar compositions of the great age of sculpture.

This cast was presented to the museum by Mr. C. C. Perkins.

89. **Torso of Eros, in the** Museum at Sparta.

> Statue of marble of medium grain, white. Probably found in the locality, and formerly in private possession at Sparta. PUBLISHED: Dressel and Milchhöfer in *Mitth. d. Instituts in Athen*, II (1877), p. 325, No. 38; Martinelli's Catalogue, No. 316.

The figure of a nude boy, identifiable as Eros (Cupid) by the holes in the shoulder-blades for the insertion of wings. The shape and size of these holes indicate that the wings were of metal. A long square hole in each arm, just at the point where it was broken off, is indicative of other objects in metal affixed. The figure is **too** fragmentary to give any suggestion of its motive. **It** is well proportioned, and is one of the best pieces in the collection at Sparta.

90. **Statue of an Amazon,** in the Capitoline Museum, Rome.

> Of Greek marble. Formerly in **the** Villa d'Este at Tivoli. Placed in the Capitoline Museum by Benedict XIV., in 1753. RESTORATIONS: The head is ancient, but does not belong to the statue; half of the nose, the neck and part of breast, the entire right arm with a portion of the shoulder, the upper half of left arm **and** some of the fingers of the hand, almost the entire bow, the right foot, end of the left foot, parts of the rim of the shield, **the** helmet and the entire plinth. PUBLISHED: Nibby, *Sculture del Campidoglio*, II, 22; Michaelis, in the *Jahrbuch des archäolog. Instituts* 1886, p. 14 ff. (p. 18, m., and p. 19, β); *Nuova Descrizione del Museo Capitolino*, 1882, p. 326, No. 4; etc.

This statue, which is a replica of the type better known through the Mattei Amazon in the Vatican, represents an Amazon drawing a bow from her shoulder. She is clothed in a short chiton which has fallen from one shoulder, and carries her quiver at her left side. On **the** tree at her right are her shield and battle-axe, and on her left foot is the strap of her spur. Amazons are always represented as wearing the spur upon that foot only. The figure is largely restored, and the restoration of the arms has been made the subject of much discussion, as it is claimed by many authorities that the original Amazon of which this and other similar statues are reproductions, was represented as leaning upon a spear, not holding a bow, this opinion being based upon the analogy of an ancient gem on which is engraved an Amazon of this same type, in the position described. But the restoration with the bow is justified, at least in our example, by the fact that the piece of the bow which passes through the left hand is original, and is too slender to have been part of a spear. Although this statue was probably executed in the Roman period, its original was undoubtedly a work of the fifth century B. C., with which epoch the type and proportions of the figure correspond. The character of the technique, especially the manner in which the chiton is wrought, indicates that bronze was the material of the original. The head, too, although not that which belongs to the statue, reproduces a type of the same period and material, as shown by the wiry treatment of the hair.

Pheidias, Polykleitos, and other great sculptors are said to have made statues of Amazons for the Temple of Artemis at Ephesos, a shrine with which these female warriors had an especial connection because of the tradition that they took refuge there when vanquished by Dionysos and his followers. Attempts are commonly made to identify this and other extant Amazon types with the works of those sculptors, but our knowledge of their statues is too slight to make such identification possible.

91. Hermes, Statue from Andros, in the National Museum, Athens.

Of Parian (?) marble. Found, 1833, in the western part of the island of Andros, near the site of the ancient city, in the vicinity of a grave. With it was found the statue of a draped female of the same style and epoch. RESTORATIONS: The lower half of left leg to the ankle. PUBLISHED: von Sybel, *Katalog der Sculpturen zu Athen*, No. 264, and authorities there quoted.

The many-sided Hermes is here represented in his character of a deity of the lower world. He was regarded as the one who conducted the souls of the dead to Hades; and was therefore honored with sacrifices at funerals, and with festivals at certain seasons of the year. Statues were sometimes erected to him over graves, and this figure from Andros illustrates the type of those statues in the fourth century B. C. It belongs to a rather numerous class, all of which reproduce the same characteristics, with slight modifications. That the type originated in a famous statue is very probable, but it is doubtful whether all the existing members of the class are to be considered as replicas in the usual sense. It is more likely that the type itself became a general one, as it served a general purpose.

Around the tree-trunk is coiled a serpent, symbolic of the connection between the upper and lower world. Other copies of the figure show that the cloak was wound about the left arm, and that the left hand held the caduceus, or herald's staff, while the right rested against the hip. The proportions of the figure remind us that Hermes was also the god of the palæstra, the patron of gymnastic exercises. The form is that of a perfectly developed athlete, powerful yet not suggestive of brute force. The type, as we have said, is that of the fourth century B. C., but whether this statue dates from that time it is not possible to say. Comparison between this and the adjoining Hermes of the Belvedere will bring out the characteristics of each to better advantage than is possible in studying them separately.

92. Hermes of the Belvedere, in the Vatican.

Statue of Greek marble. Found in the early part of the sixteenth century, near the Church of S. Martino at Monti, on the Esquiline, Rome (or according to other accounts, near the tomb of Hadrian). Placed by Paul III. in the Belvedere of the Vatican. There are no restorations. The right leg was broken between ankle and hip, and is not well joined to the foot. PUBLISHED: Visconti, *Museo Pio Clem.*, I, pp. 40 f., pl. 7; Treu, *Hermes mit dem Dionysosknaben*, Berlin, 1878, pp. 8 f.; etc.

Like the preceding, this represents Hermes in his relation to death. The attitude, the arrangement of the cloak, and the general composition of the figure resemble the statue from Andros, yet there are certain points of difference that seem to indicate that the two are reproductions of a general type rather than copies from the same original. Such is, for example, the character of the two heads. That of the Belvedere Hermes is smaller in proportion to the body. The face of the Andros statue is broad, the forehead flat, and the contour round, while that of the other is long, the shape more oval, the eyes nearer together. The shoulders of the Belvedere figure are broad as compared with the hips, those of the Andros figure more nearly equal. Had these been copies of some one original, measurements would probably have prevented these discrepancies.

Both are finely modelled statues, though the surface of that of the Belvedere has suffered from polishing and retouching, which is especially noticeable about the eyes and face. The proportions of the two figures resemble those of the Hermes of Praxiteles, and the slight bend of the head is suggestive of the style of that artist, yet the resemblance as a whole is indicative rather of the same stage in the development of art than of the work of the same sculptor. The elaboration with which the muscles are treated, causing a delicate play of light and shade over the figure, is a characteristic of the refining tendencies of the younger Attic school, in which it is probable that this type originated.

These two statues illustrate one distinguishing quality of Greek sculpture of the best period. Their conception is so simple as to lead one to think there is none whatever, that they are merely figures of fine men standing in an easy posture. Yet this simplicity is a mark of the highest art, which does not strive for effect, but instead of trying to catch the eye by dramatic action, aims to delight it by the beauty of pure form. To accomplish such ideals demands refinement in the spectator as well as in the artist; and the designs of their vases and other ordinary utensils show how keenly sensitive the Greeks were to this charm. To them this beauty of form in statues was more than a pleasure to the mind and eye. It was the type of ideal manhood; it represented health, education, and religion; it meant refinement of mind as well as body, and it suggested many other qualities the appreciation of which is difficult, if **not** impossible, to us, because of the great difference in the standards of modern life.

93. The so-called **Ilioneus,** in the Glyptothek, Munich.

<small>Statue of Parian marble. Discovered probably between 1556-62 in Rome, then became the property of Cardinal da Carpi. At the beginning of the seventeenth century was in the palace of the Emperor Rudolph II., in Prague; towards the end of the last century fell into the possession of a stone-cutter, from whom it was acquired by a Dr. Barth of Vienna, who sold it in 1814 to Ludwig I. of Bavaria, then Crown Prince. Now in the Glyptothek, Munich. There are no restorations, but the surface has been worn somewhat by polishing and cleaning. PUBLISHED: Müller-Wieseler, *Denkmäler d. alten Kunst*, I, pl. xxxiv E; Stark, *Niobe*, pp. 255 ff.; Brunn, *Glyptothek zu München*, p. 172, No. 142; etc.</small>

This is the figure **of a boy** who, fallen upon his knees, **is trying to** avert some danger **from above.** Although the **head and arms** are gone, their attitude **is** clearly indicated, and shows **that** the action of **the** figure is that of fear. The right arm was stretched at full length in the direction towards which the head was turned, and the left was extended more in front of the figure, and perhaps bent at **the** elbow. From **a** general resemblance to the **figures** in the famous Niobe group (see under No. 154), **this was** formerly thought to have belonged either to the **original** or to an early copy, **and to** have represented Ilioneus, who, according to Ovid, was the last of the children to die, **and whose** fate excited the compassion of Apollo. At present this interpretation is not generally accepted, **the** principal argument against it being **the** fact that in all **other** existing representations of the **death of the** Niobids, whether reliefs **or** statues, **the** youths without exception wear some drapery about them, **while** this **figure is** perfectly nude. Whether this circumstance **is sufficient to prevent** its having belonged **to** the group **may be questioned.** In motive it corresponds better with that **than** with any **other** known work, and its interpretation as a Niobid suits the figure better than any other that has been suggested.

The exquisite grace of the statue, and the beautiful modelling, are indications of original Greek work of the second half of the fourth century B. C. In its softness and refinement it suggests Praxiteles, to whom it has often been attributed, but its technical qualities are more characteristic of the epoch following him, and it may therefore be a work of his school. Scrubbing and polishing have worn away the freshness of the surface, and impaired the delicacy of the modelling; yet this is still one of the most beautiful fragments of ancient sculpture that have survived.

Of the casts in this room, Nos. 50-58, 66-71, 73, 74, and 77-81 are the property of the Boston Athenæum.

Nos. 87, 92, 93 were purchased from the bequest of Charles Sumner.

No. 88 was presented by Mr. C. C. Perkins.

(For the Parthenon Frieze, of which there are specimens on two walls of this room, see the following pages.)

THIRD GREEK ROOM.

100–113.

SCULPTURES FROM THE PARTHENON.

THE Parthenon is the grandest of all monuments of Greek art. It embodies the perfect union of the arts of sculpture and architecture, each in the highest state of development, since it was built in that short epoch when sculpture, having overcome every obstacle of execution, used its technical perfection for the expression of only the loftiest ideas, and when the architect made it his ambition to "surpass the magnificence of his design with the elegance of the execution," as Plutarch says. Such was the spirit of the age of Perikles, the first to reap the benefits of the victorious struggle against barbarism, by which the independence of Greece was maintained, and the country aroused to the full consciousness of her intellectual superiority over her older neighbors. In the Persian wars intelligence had triumphed over numbers. The gods of Greece had shown their love for the land by imparting counsels to its people which enabled them to overcome by craft the brute force of the barbarian, and thus vindicate civilization. In Athens especially the stimulus of this victory was of the most intense nature. Religion and patriotism, the two greatest powers that move the soul of man, were there strained to their highest pitch. It was she who had taken the foremost part in the banishment of the Persian; and although her citizens had seen the city laid waste, its temples razed, and the Akropolis, with the shrine of their goddess Athena, made desolate, they returned full of gratitude to their patron divinity, and determined to make her city the centre of the civilization they had saved. In the years that followed, every form of literature and art was developed with a rapidity which will always excite the wonder of the world. Sculpture broke through the bonds of archaism, and not merely reproduced, but idealized, the human form. PHEIDIAS carried the art to perfection; in his works were established for all time the laws of beauty and sublimity in art. The ideals of his school and age have never been surpassed. He was the confidential friend and adviser of Perikles, and with him perhaps originatd the idea of dedicating to Athena a new and splendid temple upon the Akropolis, to be a fitting emblem of the city's recognition of her, and an immortal monument of Athenian art. To Pheidias was given the charge of the work, and under him was gathered such an assemblage of architects, sculptors, and artisans of all schools and trades as only Greece in her most glorious epoch could bring together.

In what year the Parthenon was begun is not known. In 438 B. C. it was opened, and the great statue of Athena that stood in its principal hall was dedicated (see below, under Nos. 112, 113). The architects were IKTINOS and KALLIKRATES. The style of the architecture was Doric, but with modifications peculiarly Attic, which relieved the severity of the pure Doric style as it is exemplified in the temple of Zeus at Olympia. The length of the building is 228.15 ft., width 101.25 ft. (equivalent to 225 × 100 Attic feet); the proportions being 9 to 4, instead of 7 to 3 as in the Zeus Temple. The height to the top of the pediment was originally about 59 ft., not including the krepidoma, or platform of three steps from which the building rose. The Doric temple usually has six columns on the front and thirteen on the sides, but the Parthenon had eight on the front and seventeen on the sides. At either end, within the outer row of columns, was a second row of six, of smaller dimensions. Except the roof, which was tiled with Parian marble, the whole building and its sculptural decorations were of the purest white Pentelic marble.

This not only gave material splendor to the building, but by the firmness of its texture afforded opportunity for the display of skill in the **execution of** details, such as is unequalled in any other structure.

PUBLICATIONS: The Parthenon and its sculptures are treated more or less fully in all histories and handbooks of Greek sculpture, and the student is referred to the list at the beginning of the catalogue. Of special works on the subject the number is very large. The most important of these is Michaelis, *Der Parthenon*, Leipzig, 1870, where a summary of all the previous literature may be found. Besides this may be especially recommended: Stuart and Revett, *Antiquities of Athens*; Laborde, *Athènes aux XIVme XVme et XVIme Siècles*; Penrose, *Principles of Athenian Architecture*; Petersen, *Die Kunst des Pheidias*, Berlin, 1873; Brunn, *Die Skulpturen am Parthenon*, in the Abhandlungen d. bayerisch. Akademie, 1874; Dörpfeld, *Untersuchungen am Parthenon*, in the Mittheilungen des deutschen Instituts in Athen, 1881, p. 383 f.; Waldstein, *Essays on the Art of Pheidias*, 1885; *Guide to the Parthenon Sculptures in the British Museum*, 3d ed., 1886; Collignon, *Phidias*, Paris, 1886; etc.

100. The Frieze encircled the walls of the temple on the outside, at a height of about 39 feet above the floor, crossing the two ends above the inner row of columns. Its total length was about 523 **feet, and its** height about 3 feet 3 inches. The subject, although disputed, most probably relates to the greater Panathenaia, or festival of Athena. This, the chief of **Attic** festivals, was held every four years, lasting five days, and consisted of games, athletic contests and other amusements, as well as sacrifices and ceremonies in honor **of the** goddess. Its culmination was the traditional birthday of Athena, on which a procession passed through the city and up to the Akropolis, carrying to the ancient image of Athena in the Erechtheion (see below, p.178) the saffron-colored peplos woven for it by daughters of the great Athenian families. The dedication **of this** robe, which was renewed every four years, was the principal object of the festival, and this we believe to be the theme of the frieze. The subject is not treated in a literal or illustrative way, nor does it represent any one moment of time, but is an artistic combination of the principal features of the day and its ceremony, carrying the spectator forward from one event to another, all of which it suggests rather than describes. The design began at the southwest corner of the building, and was divided into two parts, one running along the southern wall, the other along the western and northern, so that they met at the eastern front, over the main entrance to the building.

On the western frieze, of which there are specimens in the Second Greek Room, are the preparations for the procession. One youth is fastening his sandal, others are harnessing or holding their horses, some are mounting, and some are already on their way. Along the north and south walls the movement grows more rapid, the procession is in motion. The horsemen here are massed thickly together, their horses prance impatiently, and everything is full of action. Before them go the chariots with horses equally spirited. Then, as the eastern end is approached, the movement becomes more solemn. The dignitaries of the city, or its elder citizens, and musicians, take the place of the cavaliers. Next, the sacrificial animals, sheep and bullocks, sent by the colonies to the mother city, are led by priests and their attendants, before whom go youths and maidens bearing utensils for the sacrifice. At this point the processional element ceases, and we come upon the central group—the seated figures representing the divinities assembled to take part in the festival. Unfortunately our selection of the frieze is especially defective in this, the principal portion of the frieze, which in the original consists of two groups, each of six seated figures and one standing, separated from each other by a third group, the subject of which is not so obvious as to be beyond dispute, though it probably represents the priest and priestess of Athena receiving the peplos from a boy, and attended by two maidens, each of whom bears a chair on her head. The last two figures are to be seen directly over the statue of Demosthenes; at their right are Athena and Hephaistos, beyond which should be five other divinities to correspond with the group on the left. The chief figure of this group is Zeus, at whose side is Hera, drawing the veil from her face, attended by Hebe. The remaining figures cannot be named with certainty, although many attempts at their identification have been made.

The enumeration of all the peculiarities and beauties of this composition would occupy much more space than the limits of a catalogue afford. **It must be borne in** mind that the projection of the roof beyond the wall of the temple prevented all direct light from reaching the frieze, which therefore received only reflected light from below. This circumstance, and the sharp **angle at** which it was seen, the gallery between the columns and wall of the temple being only about nine feet wide, explain the sharp cutting of the under surfaces in contrast to the gradual rise of the upper from the background. By this device the details are more clearly defined, though just how minutely **those** were brought out we cannot tell without the **aid of the colors** which were originally applied to the marble. Another artistic convention which the character of the composition necessitated was the Greek principle of *Isokephalism*, that is, the placing of all the heads, whether of riders, footmen, or **seated** figures, at the same level; and this is perhaps the best illustration of the marvellous skill **of** the execution; for **even** when the fact becomes apparent, it is not in the least disturbing, and one can hardly realize that it is not **true** to nature. The most wonderful quality of the work, however, is the ease and naturalness of the composition. **In** relief which is never more than **2 1-4** inches high, this band, more than 520 feet in length, contained over 350 human figures, as well as the animals, and in no part is there the slightest suggestion of repetition or of the introduction of a figure to fill up space. Every man and every horse is an individual. In the grouping there is neither constraint nor effort; the figures are brought together as easily as they would be in life; and every figure, whether young or old, male or female, is beautiful. No two riders sit their horses in just the same position, yet each **one** is graceful. In the drapery there is not an inexpressive or a superfluous line. From whatever point of view we study it, there is no work of sculpture which requires such long and careful observation **for** the proper appreciation of its many beauties.

101-106. **Statues from the Pediments.** The subject **of** the eastern pediment **was the** birth of Athena, an **event** having direct connection with the Panathenaic festival, as we have seen. In what manner it was represented we have no means **of** knowing, as quite half the group, including the principal figures, disappeared at an unknown age, and no description of them remains. Yet in the fragments that survive there is abundant testimony of the grandeur of the conception and the power with which it was expressed. These fragments show that at the left end of the pediment Helios, the sun, in his four-horse chariot, rose from the sea; while at the right Selene, the moon, in hers, sank into the darkness. Immediately adjoining Helios and facing him was a youth, No. 101, of strong, muscular build, reclining upon a rock over which lies a lion's skin. The athletic character of the figure suggested a hero, and it was long thought to represent Theseus, the mythical founder of the Attic state. Unfortunately in this, as in nearly all the pediment statues, there is no distinguishing attribute by which it may be positively identified. Herakles, Kekrops, Dionysos, and other names have been advanced, but none of them with sufficient ground for acceptance. The most poetical suggestion is that of Brunn, who sees in this figure the personification of Mt. Olympos, where the birth of Athena took place. This would explain the rugged character of the modelling, the rocky seat, and the indifference to the important event towards which his back is turned. Grouped thus with Helios, Olympos would be the first to catch the light of the glorious day which dawned when Athena was added to the gods of Greece.

At the other end of the pediment, adjoining Selene, were grouped three females, two of which are No. 102. The number three gave rise to the idea that they represented the Fates, but again the lack of distinguishing attributes prevents our affirming or denying the correctness of this and the other appellations they have received. Brunn sees in them the clouds that still hung over the West when Helios rose, symbolic of the gradual disappearance of darkness in the wake of Selene. Whoever they may have represented, they are splendid examples of the sublimity of Pheidian art, displaying the highest type of female beauty, in which there is no hint of sensuousness, although the forms are clothed in drapery so light as to act only as a thin veil. The execution of the drapery and its graceful disposition show how completely the sculptor mastered his material. Although the figures could be seen only from the front, every fold in the drapery behind is wrought with the same care and precision as though it were visible, — a mark of the sculptor's enthusiasm for his work.

The mutilated torso, No. 103, was also from this pediment. Large square holes **on** the back show that wings **were** formerly inserted; and the figure being that of a youthful female, has been called NIKE (Victory), the constant companion **of** Athena.

No. 104 is the head of one of the horses of Selene; a beautiful specimen of the spirited representations of this animal which characterized the art of Pheidias. **Selene was represented as sinking below the level of the pediment, and this head is all there was of the animal to which it belonged.** A notch cut in the lower jaw shows where it projected beyond the ledge on which it rested. Both the "Theseus" and the "Fates" also projected beyond the **line** of their base, the intention being evidently to break **the rigidity of** the architectural lines of the pediment.

The **WESTERN PEDIMENT** represented the contest between Athena and Poseidon for the dominion over Attika. This contest was believed to have taken place on the Akropolis before a council of the gods, who were to determine which of the two was most deserving of the honor. To show his power, Poseidon struck his trident into the rock, and immediately a salt spring started out. Then Athena with her lance raised up an olive-tree, — the emblem of Attika's commercial prosperity, — and the prize was at once awarded to her. At present the Museum possesses but one of the figures of this group, No. 105, which belonged at **the** left or north end of the pediment. From **its** reclining position, and the soft, flowing lines of the modelling (note the contrast to No. 101), this has been supposed to be a personification of the river KEPHISOS, the bed of which lies to the north of the Akropolis. The attitude shows that he had been roused from his repose, and without altering his position had turned his head to watch the result of the competition. The treatment of the skin of this figure, which is **soft** and elastic, **without** being in the slightest degree effeminate, the fine anatomy, and most of all, **the** majestic spirit in which it is conceived, show that the sculptures of this pediment were not inferior to those of the eastern.

The FEMALE HEAD, No. 106, is believed to have belonged to this pediment. In breadth and simplicity of treatment it resembles the other sculptures of the two groups, and although its dignity has suffered somewhat by the restorations, which give a mechanical rigidity to the nose, and a trivial expression to the mouth, it still possesses the character of the Pheidian style, and corresponds in size to the pediment figures. It is usually supposed to be the head of the NIKE of the western pediment, but there are several other statues in the group to which it may equally well have belonged.

> This, sometimes referred to as the "Weber" Head, was formerly built into the wall of a staircase in the house of the San Gallo family in Venice, to which city it is supposed to have been brought by a member of the family who was secretary to the Venetian general Morosini at the time of the siege of Athens in 1687. From this family it passed through several hands until in 1823 it came into the possession of an amateur, David Weber, whose family sold it later to the Comte Laborde. It was then carried to Paris where it is at present, in the Laborde Collection. RESTORATIONS: The nose, small piece in upper lip, the middle of lower lip, the chin, and part of the back of the head. Michaelis, pl. 8, fig. 6, p. 195; Collignon, *Phidias*, 1886, p. 54.

No. 107, on the pedestal of No. 102, is a restoration, on a very small scale, of the group above it, by Clevenger.

108–111. Four Metopes from the Parthenon. Michaelis, pl. 4, Nos. XXXI, XXX, XXIX, and pl. 3, IV.

The metopes, ninety-two in number, placed between the triglyphs, directly under the cornice of the temple and above the columns that surrounded the building, were brought into direct juxtaposition with the members that supported the roof, and, in conformity with the character of these, were sculptured in bold, high relief with designs representing vigorous action, the sharply defined lines of which gave vitality to the architecture. So far as can be learned from the remaining metopes, the subjects had direct reference to Athena or the Athenians. On the eastern end was a series of scenes from the battle of the gods and giants. On the south was represented the fight between the Kentaurs and Lapithæ, in which Theseus and other Attic heroes took part. Of the west and north the series are too fragmentary to admit of a definite interpretation, though they show that fighting was the principal theme.

Because of the position they occupied on the temple, the metopes were most probably the first of the sculptures to be finished; and the four specimens here exhibited testify that the marvellous development of sculpture under Pheidias took place even during the building of the Parthenon. These metopes are of a distinctly earlier style than the other sculptures of the building. Though they possess all the vigor of the pediment statues, they are less gracefully composed, and in this sometimes awkward expression of force, as well as in the characteristics of the modelling, they still retain some of the traits of archaic art. Between them and the western pediment of the Zeus Temple (Second Room, Nos. 59–65) there is a strong affinity, which suggests that both originated under a common influence. It is a curious fact that in both this pediment group and the Parthenon metopes the faces of the Kentaurs are strongly marked with rage, fear, exultation, and the other sensations of defeat or triumph, while those of their victims and adversaries are quite devoid of all expression.

STATUETTES OF ATHENA PARTHENOS.

112. The "Lenormant" Statuette.

Of **Pentelic marble.** Found, 1859, during the construction of a **road west of the Pnyx,** Athens. Now in the office of the Ephor of Antiquities, Athens. Unfinished behind, and on the right side, where the marble is left rough. PUBLISHED: Fr. Lenormant in the *Gazette des Beaux Arts*, 1860, VIII, pp. 129 ff., 203 ff., 278 ff.; Conze, in the *Annali dell' Instituto*, 1861, p. 334, pl. OP; etc.

113. The "Varvakeion" Statuette.

Of Pentelic marble. Found Dec. 30, 1880, just north of the Varvakeion, Athens (*i. e.*, close by the northern limit of the ancient city), among the ruins of a house of the Roman epoch. Now in the National Museum, Athens. Many traces of COLOR were found on the figure, which are described in the following

PUBLICATIONS: Lange, in the *Mittheilungen d. Inst. in Athen*, V, 1880, p. 370 ff.; VI, 1881, p. 56 ff. and pls. i, ii; Hauvette-Besnault, in *Bulletin de Corresp. Hellénique*, V, 1881, p. 54 ff.; etc.

Although intrinsically of little artistic value, these statuettes are of extreme importance as being the best existing reproductions of the colossal figure Athena Parthenos (the Virgin), which Pheidias made for the Parthenon. Together with the Zeus which he made for **Olympia**, that statue was considered the greatest work of the **master**; and until the discovery of these figures, it was **known** only through various fragmentary allusions in **ancient authors**, from whom it has been gathered that the statue was, **with its** base, about thirty-eight **feet** high, made of a kernel of cedar, **over which was laid** gold **and** ivory, the latter in the nude parts **of** the **figure.** The goddess stood upright, clothed in a long **chiton,** and wearing the ægis. On her head was a helmet adorned with a sphinx, and on either side of this a griffon. The right hand, extended, held an image of Nike (Victory). The left rested on her shield, which was **of** gilded silver decorated with reliefs **on** both sides. In this hand, or leaning against **the** arm, **was a** long spear, near which on the ground **was** the serpent Erichthonios, the autochthonous hero of Attica, and foster-son of Athena.

These **statuettes, although** evidently **the work of** unskilled artisans, reproduce to a certain extent the type of the goddess, and show the disposition of the accessories mentioned in the various descriptions. **The V**arvakeion figure follows the details of these most minutely, although the decorations of the shield were probably represented in color **instead of** relief, as on the Lenormant figure. Comparison of the **two** shows that the face **of** the Pheidian goddess was broader and rounder **than the** later type of Athena, which is more familiar **to us (see** Nos. 125 and 126); and **that she** wore the close-fitting **Attic** helmet instead of the Corinthian, which has openings for the eyes and nose. In the ancient descriptions of the statue there is no mention of a crest, but the Varvakeion statuette shows the helmet to have been surmounted by a high crest and **long** plume. Whether the column under the right hand was originally a part of the great statue is at least questionable. Not only is it a weak and clumsy device, but in the original would have been so large as to dwarf all the columns of the hall in which the statue stood; and it is moreover of a type which conforms much better to the age of the statuette than of its original. There can be little doubt that Pheidias contrived some more artistic means for the support of the Nike, such as could easily have been introduced into the framework of the statue.

Both statuettes show that the Parthenos was composed with the extreme simplicity becoming a colossal figure. The drapery hangs in big, straight folds, which add to the dignity expressed in the attitude. Undoubtedly color contributed largely to the impressive effect of the statue; for it is not to be supposed that the natural colors of the gold and ivory were the only ones employed, but that, as in other works of the toreutic art, these materials were colored, the gold with enamel, so that the brilliancy of the surface was toned, and a more natural appearance produced than is possible with the simple combination of gold and ivory. As mentioned above, the Varvakeion statuette retains many traces of color, which are unfortunately not sufficiently well preserved to permit of a restoration.

114. Relief in the Museum at Argos.

Of white marble, of rather fine grain. Said to have been found south of the ancient theatre of Argos. PUBLISHED: Furtwängler in *Mittheilungen des Inst. in Athen*, III, 1878, p. 287 ff., and pl. xiii; Milchhöfer, ibid., IV, p. 153, No. 502.

This relief, which is probably of a votive character, represents a nude youth, standing in profile towards the right, and holding in the left hand a long spear, which rests upon his shoulder. Behind him is a horse facing in the same direction. The design is of especial importance, because in the youth we have a reproduction of the most famous work of Polykleitos, the great Argive sculptor, who was the master of the school of Argos at the time of Pheidias' activity in Athens. The work referred to was the bronze statue of a Doryphoros, or spear-bearer, which was celebrated throughout antiquity for its magnificent proportions. It has long been thought that copies of this were to be recognized in several marble statues of similar type, the best examples being in the museums of Naples (a photograph of which hangs under the relief) and Florence; and with these the youth on this relief, found in the town where Polykleitos lived, corresponds in all essentials. The original dated from about the middle of the fifth century B. C., but this relief is a much later, possibly Roman, production.

115. **Jason, so called,** in the Louvre.

> Statue of Pentelic marble. **Formerly** in Rome, in the Palazzo Savelli, later in the Villa **Montalto** (?). Purchased of Cardinal Savelli for Louis XIV., in 1685, and by him placed at Versailles, whence it was subsequently removed to the Louvre. RESTORATIONS: The head, which is antique but does not belong to the statue, the end of the nose, the lower lip, chin and occiput; also the left shoulder and arm, half the right forearm and the hand, the right leg down to ankle, and parts of the left leg. On various parts of figure and drapery small pieces are inserted to fill up fractures. PUBLISHED: Clarac, *Musée de Sculpture*, pl. 309, No. 2046; Froehner, *Sculpture Antique du Louvre*, No. 183, p. 210; etc.

This statue, of which there are several extant replicas, is probably a copy of a work of the latter part of the fourth century B. C. Its motive, that of a figure with one foot raised upon a rock, was a favorite one among the sculptors of that epoch, and probably originated with Lysippos.

Winckelmann was the first to give the statue the name by which it is popularly known, but which rests upon insufficient evidence. More probably the statue is simply that of an athlete tying his sandal, the attitude being chosen because of the opportunity it afforded for giving variety to the play of the muscles in different parts of the figure.

116. **Inscription,** in the British Museum, from Orchomenos.

It records the payment, by the town of Orchomenos, of two sums of money to one Euboulos of Elateia, on account of a loan made by him to the city, and gives him the right to pasture 220 oxen and horses and 1000 sheep upon its land for a term of four years.

PUBLISHED: *Greek Inscriptions in the Brit. Mus.*, pt. II, No. CLVIII; *Elgin Inscriptions*, No. 377.

117. **Inscription**, in the British Museum.

A fragment, the beginning of which is lost. It apparently contains the names and tribes of Athenians who fell in some battle of the Peloponnesian war. Its date is 425 or 424 B. C.

PUBLISHED: *Greek Inscriptions in the Brit. Mus.*, pt. I, No. XXXVIII; *Elgin Inscriptions*, No. 173.

118. **Bronze Tablet**, in the British Museum.

Found at Olympia, whence it was carried to England by Sir Wm. Gell, 1813. PUBLISHED: *Greek Inscriptions in the British Museum*, pt. II, No. CLVII, and pl. 1, fig. 3.

This is the record of a treaty of alliance, for a period of one hundred years, between the Eleans and the people of Heræa, a town in Arkadia. The date of the treaty, as indicated by the character of the inscription, is probably the latter part of the sixth century B. C.

119. **The Pourtalès Apollo**, in the British Museum.

Head of Parian marble. Formerly in the Giustiniani collection, Rome, from which it passed into the possession of the Comte de Pourtalès, and was purchased for the British Museum at the sale of his collection in 1865. RESTORATIONS: The nose, part of the lips, the lobes of the ears, and a small piece in the neck. COLOR: In the hair are traces of red. PUBLISHED: *Galleria Giustiniana*, II, pl. 42; Müller-Wieseler, *Denkmäler d. alten Kunst*, II, pl. xi, No. 123; etc.

The resemblance between this head and that of the Apollo Belvedere shows it to be a work of the same period and school, and it dates therefore probably from the third or second century B. C. The manner in which the hair is treated, and the sharp lines of the brow and eyes, indicate that it is a copy from a bronze. That the head originally belonged to a statue is evident, and Newton thinks it likely to have been an Apollo Kitharoidos (playing on the lyre), which would account for the sentimental expression in the face.

120. **Head of Apollo**, in the British Museum.

> Of **Parian** marble. Formerly **in** the possession of Cardinal Albani, **from** whom it was acquired by Towneley in 1773, on its removal **from a** figure of Bacchus, to which it had been wrongly attached. RESTORATIONS: The nose, the knot of hair above forehead and that on the back **of** the head. PUBLISHED: *Ancient Marbles in the British Museum*, pt. XI, pl. iv.

From its resemblance to the head **of the** "Apollino" of Florence, and those of similar statues in **the** Louvre **and** Capitoline Museum, this may be supposed **to** have belonged to a **statue** like **them,** which represented the god **of** music leaning against **a tree in** the "Praxitelean" attitude, **with** the right arm resting **on his** head. If that be the proper restoration, the original would probably be a work **of** the latter part **of the** fourth **century** B. C., with which period the type of this head corresponds. In the face there is the softness characteristic of the younger **Attic school,** while the hair is treated in a less exaggerated manner **than** in works of the following epoch, like the Pourtalès Apollo (No. 119) and the Apollo Belvedere (No. 215).

121. **Statuette of Aphrodite,** in the Museum at Argos.

> Of white marble. Found near the **ancient** theatre of Argos. **There** are no restorations; PUBLISHED: Conze in the *Archäolog. Anzeiger*, XVI, 1858, p. **198;** Milchhöfer in the *Mittheilungen d. Inst. in* **Athen,** IV, **1879,** p. 150, No. 489.

In this little figure we have a variation of **the type** that is best **known** through **the** Venus of Melos, representing the goddess **with** one arm raised and the left foot resting upon **an object** which varies with the different examples. In this case it is **a** swan, **one** of **the** attributes of Aphrodite. The figure is of slender proportions, the **lower** half being particularly good, the upper part **less** so. **The** drapery is light and gracefully managed. **The** statuette is probably a copy of a larger work of the **fourth century** B. C.

122. **Grave Stele,** in the Berlin Museum.

> Of Parian marble. Found at Karystos in Euboea. Formerly in the possession of Count Saburoff, ex-minister of Russia to Greece, and by him sold to the Berlin Museum in 1884. There

are no restorations. PUBLISHED: Furtwängler, *Die Sammlung Saburoff*, pl. vi; Berlin Museum, Ancient Sculptures No. 736.

The figure of a bearded man, clothed in an himation, standing in profile to the left, his right hand raised to the chin. This is one of the most beautifully executed grave monuments that exist. The relief has the character of the best period, and reminds one of the figures on the Parthenon frieze. The hair is treated easily and naturally, the head is of a fine type, and the drapery is remarkable for grace and simplicity. This is probably a work of the Attic school of the second half of the fifth century B. C., and is an interesting monument of the period of transition between the earlier style of grave stelai, like those in the First Greek Room, Nos. 13-15, and that of the fourth century (Nos. 178-188, Fourth Room).

123. Inscription, in the British Museum.

On the original from which this cast is taken, the inscription is engraved on both sides of the stele. It is from Oropos in Bœotia, a public decree enacting the appointment of three special commissioners to examine the gold and silver articles in the temple of Amphiaraos, with a view to recasting those found unfit for service.

PUBLISHED: *Greek Inscriptions in the Brit. Mus.*, pt. II, No. CLX; *Elgin Inscriptions*, No. 378.

124. The Borghese Achilles, so called, in the Louvre.

Statue of Parian marble. Formerly in the Borghese collection, Rome, from which it passed to the Louvre in 1808. RESTORATIONS: Half of the right hand, left arm from deltoid, three toes of the right foot, big toe of the left foot. PUBLISHED: Clarac, *Musée de Sculpture*, No. 2073, pl. 263; Wolters' Friederichs, No. 1298; etc.

The name Achilles became attached to this statue because of the ring above the right ankle, which was thought to indicate the vulnerable part of Achilles, and to have been placed there as a sort of defence to the heel; but the right explanation of the ring is probably that given by Ravaisson, — that it is "nothing else than a kind

of pad worn by Greek warriors on the leg to receive the
weight of the greave, and to protect the ankle from contact
with it." Thus all attributive significance disappears, and
we have simply the figure of a warrior, wearing an Attic
helmet, and holding a spear in his left hand. The name
Ares (Mars) has also been applied to the statue; and with
the rough, sturdy character of the god of war, the heavy
proportions correspond better than with that of the active,
lithe Achilles. The square, thick frame, the short, powerful legs, and the general character of the muscular development, as well as the type of the face, are suggestive of
the style of Polykleitos, and it is possible that this statue,
of which several copies exist, — especially a fine head in
Munich, — may be a late replica of a work of his school.

125. **The Giustiniani Minerva, in the Braccio Nuovo
of the Vatican.**

Statue of Parian (?) marble. Found close by the church of Santa
Maria sopra Minerva, Rome (not, as according to popular
tradition, in the temple of Minerva Medica). Date of discovery unknown. In the beginning of the 17th century, it was
in the possession of the Giustiniani family, from whom it passed
to Lucien Bonaparte, and was bought of him by Pius VII. for
the Vatican. RESTORATIONS: The right forearm with the
hand holding the spear, and fingers of the left hand. PUB-
LISHED: Müller-Wieseler, *Denkmäler d. alten Kunst*, II, xix,
205; Gerhard, in the *Beschreibung der Stadt Rom*, II 2, p. 91,
No. 23; etc.

This was formerly thought to be a reproduction of the
type of Pheidias' Parthenos statue, but the statuettes Nos.
112 and 113 show that to have been of quite a different
style. Not only is the face of a different type, but the
helmet is of another variety. The drapery is much more
elaborated in the Giustiniani figure; and the ægis, which on
the Parthenos covered both shoulders and was made a
prominent feature, is here comparatively insignificant, being entirely hidden on the left shoulder beneath the folds
of the himation, — a garment which the Parthenos statue
did not wear. The type to which the Giustiniani Minerva
belongs is of a decidedly later origin, though just when
and in what school it originated is not known. The over-
elaboration of the drapery is characteristic of the virtuos-

ity of the sculptors of the Roman epoch, who attempted to make up what they lacked in originality by elegance of detail. The fact that the statue was found in the immediate vicinity of the church of Santa Maria sopra Minerva, which was built over the ruins of the temple of Minerva Campensis, has led to the opinion that this may have been the temple-image of the goddess. The attitude and the inclination of the head correspond with the character of such an image, and the execution is quite in keeping with the art of the first century B. C., in which the temple was built.

The presence of the serpent has been thought to indicate that this is a figure of Minerva Medica, as the serpent is closely associated with the divinities of health; but in the present instance it is evidently the symbol of Erichthonios, as he is thus represented in the Parthenos statuettes. This is a distinctively Attic attribute of Athena (Minerva), and indicates that although the statue itself may have been executed in Roman times, the type originated in Greece.

126. Colossal Bust of Athena, in the Glyptothek, Munich.

Of Pentelic marble. Found near Tivoli, and formerly in the Villa Albani. RESTORATIONS. The head of the serpent on the helmet, and the points on front of same; the nose, part of the under lip, and some of the serpents in the ægis. PUBLISHED: Bouillon, *Musée des Antiques*, I, 66; Müller-Wieseler, *Denkmäler d. alten Kunst*, II, xix, 198; Brunn, *Beschreibung der Glyptothek*, p. 115, No. 92; etc.

The head of this bust is of the same type as that of the Giustiniani Minerva (No. 125), characterized by the Corinthian helmet, the long, oval face and the arrangement of the hair. As in that, the ægis is small and partially concealed beneath the himation on the left shoulder. The treatment of the under surface shows that this was never part of a statue, but made as a bust. The execution indicates that it originated in the Roman epoch, but like the Giustiniani and other similar statues, it probably reproduces a Greek original, which was possibly as early as the fourth century B. C.

127. The Farnese Diadumenos, in the British Museum.

Statue of Pentelic marble. Date and site of discovery unknown. In the 16th century in the Villa Madama, Rome (pub. by Cavalieri, 1585); afterwards in the Farnese Gardens on the Palatine, and later in the Palazzo Farnese. Acquired by the British Museum, 1864. RESTORATIONS: The nose. PUBLISHED: Michaelis in the *Annali dell' Inst.*, 1878, pl. A and p. 20; etc.

Polykleitos, the Argive contemporary of Pheidias, made two statues which were famous throughout antiquity. One of these was called the Doryphoros (see No. 114), the other the Diadumenos. Of the latter, this figure is among the best of a number of replicas. It represents an athlete binding his hair with the broad band that indicated a victor in the games. Evidently this copy reproduces but little of the spirit of its original, as it has the technical characteristics of ordinary Roman workmanship; yet it is useful because it gives us an idea of the proportions and the general style of Polykleitos' statues. The original having been of bronze, the tree-stump against the right leg was probably absent, and the figure rested firmly and easily upon that leg without artificial support. The frame is powerful and of rather heavier proportions than the athlete statues of the Attic school. This appears especially in the development of the muscles of the chest and shoulders. There is no attempt to idealize the human figure, such as characterized the art of Pheidias, and in this respect the statue well illustrates what we know of the art of Polykleitos from the statements of ancient writers, — that it was scholarly rather than poetic; and that in statues of athletes his style was characterized by fidelity to nature at her best, but without the realism of later epochs.

Among the replicas of the Diadumenos there is considerable variation in the head. Which of them comes the nearest to the original it is impossible to determine, but the large eyes and the almost sentimental expression in the face of this figure are characteristic of a later epoch than that of Polykleitos, and indicate that the head is a free rendering of the original.

128. Inscription, in the British Museum.

A gravestone, recording the names of Aristophose, mother of Amphenor, and others. Believed to be a forgery. PUBLISHED: *Greek Inscriptions in the Brit. Mus.*, I, No. CXXXV*, *Elgin Inscriptions*, No. 266.

129. The so-called Germanicus, in the Louvre.

Statue of Parian marble. Date and place of discovery unknown, but in Italy, and probably during the last half of the 16th century. In 1685 it was sold by Cardinal Savelli to Louis XIV., together with the so-called Jason; and placed first at Versailles, afterwards in the Louvre. RESTORATIONS: The thumb and forefinger of left hand, and some pieces in the drapery. PUBLISHED: Rayet, *Monuments de l'Art Antique*, II, pl. 69, 70; etc.

This statue is an illustration of the custom, very general at Rome, of representing individuals in the form and with the attributes of divinities, the types of which were copied from well-known statues. Thus there are many existing examples of Roman ladies having their heads and features represented on figures of the type of the Venus de' Medici. The head of the "Germanicus" — a name which rests upon no foundation whatever — is probably that of some Roman orator, combined with a statue of Hermes Logios, the god of speech and patron divinity of orators, as statues of Hermes in precisely the same attitude exist in several museums, apparently reproductions of some famous original. (The best of these is in the Villa Ludovisi, published in Müller-Wieseler *Denkmäler d. alten Kunst*, II, 318, and represents the god as youthful, wearing the winged cap.)

In this statue the features are too individual for those of a divinity, and the manner in which the hair is worn indicates the Roman. The action of the fingers of the left hand shows that it held some long object, which may well have been the caduceus, or wand of Hermes. Identification with this god is emphasized by the presence of the turtle on which the drapery rests, — the distinctive attribute of Hermes and Aphrodite. On its shell is an inscription which translated reads, "Kleomenes, the son of Kleomenes, of **Athens, made this."** Of this artist we know nothing, but **the** character **of the** inscription and style of the sculpture warrant **our placing** him in the first century B. C., and he was probably **one** of the many Greek artists who found employment in **Rome** at that time.

The proportions of the figure **are** fine, **and its preservation** remarkable. Excepting the thumb **and forefinger of the** left hand, **which are** restored, it has **survived without a** blemish.

130. **The Ludovisi Juno,** in the Villa Ludovisi, Rome.

Head of coarse Greek marble. Date and place of discovery unknown. It was formerly in the Villa Cesi, and was acquired by Cardinal Ludovico Ludovisi in 1622. RESTORATIONS The end of the **nose** and **part** of right nostril, the curls on right side of the neck, and all **but** small fragments of those on the left. Also smaller pieces **in various** parts of the head. The surface has been worn by over-cleansing and rubbing of the marble. PUBLISHED: Kekulé, *Hebe*, Leipzig, 1867, pl. II; Overbeck, *Kunstmythologie*, III (Hera), p. 83 ff., and Atlas, pl. IX, 7, 8; Schreiber, *Antike Bildwerke der Villa Ludovisi*, No. 104; etc.

This **head** was formerly considered the grandest of **all** existing types of Hera (Juno), **and** thought to reproduce the head of the colossal statue made by Polykleitos for **the temple of Hera** at Argos, a work which ranked second **only to** the great creations of Pheidias in the estimation of **antiquity.** That idea has long since **been** abandoned, **because the** style of treatment could **not be** older than the **century following** that of Polykleitos; and the origin of **the head** is now a matter of dispute, some authorities dating it as **early as the fourth** century B. C., **others** at various subsequent **epochs, even as** late as the Roman. In technical characteristics it has a strong affinity with the sculpture of the early empire, and we are inclined to place it among **the** works done by **Greek** sculptors in Rome **about the** beginning of our **era.**

It may also be questioned **whether Hera** is the correct appellation. The authenticated **figures of the** bride of Zeus represent **her** according to the **Homeric** descriptions, rather matronly in both face and figure, with a sternness **about** the mouth **suggestive of** her disposition. To **these** descriptions the Ludovisi head does not correspond. It is dignified, but neither stern nor matronly, and appears to be that of a maiden-divinity. The stephané or crown is not a distinctive attribute of Hera, while the veil by which she is usually distinguished is wanting here.

The cutting of the under surface of **the neck shows that the** head once formed part of a **statue.**

131. Inopos, so called. Fragment of a statue, in the Louvre.

Of Parian marble. Found in the island of Delos, in the 18th century, and carried to Marseilles as ballast. There acquired by an artist named Gibelin (1739–1814), from whom it passed to the Louvre. RESTORATIONS: Part of the nose, and small pieces in the cheeks. PUBLISHED: Reinach, in the *Gazette Archéologique*, 1886, p. 186 ff., and pl. 22; etc.

What remains of the torso of this statue shows **it to have been in a** reclining posture, a fact which, in connection with **the** flowing hair and youthful face, gave rise to the idea **that** it was a personification **of** the river Inopos, which flows through Delos. It has also been considered a member of a pediment composition, like the so-called Kephisos of the Parthenon (No. 105), but **the** recent excavations in Delos have disclosed no temple large enough to include such a figure in its pediment groups.

The style of the sculpture **shows** it to be a work of **the** Hellenistic epoch (B. C. 332–150, see p. 131). This **is** indicated by the heavy masses in which the hair is treated, **and** by the detail **in** the modelling of the face, both distinctive characteristics of that epoch. The figure is executed **with** breadth and power, displaying the technical skill **which** distinguished the sculpture of the period to which it is assigned. (Compare with the relief from Pergamon, Fifth Room, No. 247.)

M. Reinach, in the article quoted above, attempts to establish this as a portrait of Alexander the Great, but its resemblance to authenticated portraits **of** him is not sufficiently close to make the identification unquestionable.

This cast was presented to the Museum by the late Mr. **Stephen H.** Perkins.

132. Sophokles, in the Lateran **Museum,** Rome.

> Statue of Greek marble. **Found at** Terracina, a town on the coast between Rome and Naples. The exact date of discovery is not known, but it was a few years before 1839, when the statue was presented by Count Antonelli of Terracina to Pope Gregory XVI., who at once placed it in the Lateran Museum. RESTORATIONS: the nose, small bits in the hair, beard, and face, the right hand, both feet with the base, the lower part of the garment behind, and the Scrinium, or box of rolls. These by Tenerani. PUBLISHED: Welcker in the *Annali*, 1846, p. **129** f., and *Monumenti dell' Inst.*, IV, pl. xxvii; Benndorf and Schöne's *Bildwerke des Lateran. Museums*, No. **237;** and pl. xxiv; etc.

The attempt has been made to see in this figure the copy of a bronze statue of Sophokles erected in the Dionysiac Theatre by **the Athenian** Lykourgos, which we know from allusions by **one or** two ancient writers, though no description or indentified copy of it exists. It is much more probable that this is itself an original **work of** the same period, — the latter half of the fourth century B. C., — as the movement has all the life, and the execution all the freshness, of an original work; the technique, **too,** has all the distinctive characteristics of pure marble treatment, in contrast to the reproduction **of** bronze work, as may be seen especially in the hair and beard. (On this **point** compare the Amazon, No. **90,** which, though of **marble, is** evidently a copy of a bronze original.)

The face has been identified as that of Sophokles by comparison with several antique busts on which **the name** was inscribed, — especially a small head in **the Vatican,** published by Visconti **in** the *Museo Pio Clem.*, VI, pl. **27,** and in the *Iconographie Grecque*, I, pl. iv.

A study of the Demosthenes (No. 138) in comparison **with this statue is** instructive, showing the fine appreciation by their sculptors of the distinction between the orator and the declaimer. The object of the one is to convince, of the other to move, his audience. In the attitude of the Demosthenes we see the careful balancing of thoughts before utterance, while that of **the** Sophokles is thoroughly dramatic; the **words** are committed, and the object of the speaker is **to deliver** them with proper effect.

133. The Praying **Boy, so called,** in the Berlin Museum.

> Statue of bronze. Probably identical with a statue that was in Venice in the 16th century. In the 17th century, the " Praying Boy " was in France, the property of the *Surintendant* Foucquet. By his son it was sold to Prince Eugene of Savoy at Vienna, 1717, after whose death it passed into the possession of Prince Wenzel Liechtenstein, by whom it was sold to Frederic the Great in 1747. It was then placed at Potsdam (Sans-Souci), and later in Berlin. Napoleon I. carried it to Paris, whence it was subsequently restored to Berlin. RESTORATIONS: Both arms to the shoulders, the second toe of the right foot, second and third of left foot, and the plinth. PUBLISHED: *Verzeichniss der Antiken Skulpturen im kgl. Museum*, Berlin, 1885, No. 2, and authorities there quoted; *Archäolog. Zeitung*, 1885, pp. 73 and 76; Conze, in the *Jahrbuch des deutschen archäolog. Instituts*, 1886, pp. 1 ff.; etc.

The investigations into the history of this statue which have been made recently by the authorities of the Berlin Museum have stripped it of its most distinctive feature, by showing that the uplifted arms, in which many generations have seen and admired the Greek attitude of prayer, do not belong to the original figure, but are a very skilful modern restoration, which is thought to have been made while the statue was in France, during the reign of Louis XIV., and to indicate merely what was the restorer's idea of the original motive of the statue. Of that motive there is little indication, except that the action of the shoulders shows that both arms were raised. It has been suggested that the work was of a *genre* or decorative character, and that the hands held some object, such as a large vase, but this is merely one of a number of possible restorations, including that which has actually been made.

Apart from the disposition of the arms, however, this is one of the most beautiful ancient bronzes that have come down to us. The attitude is graceful and easy, giving the figure a charming outline from every point of view; the proportions are ideal rather than realistic, in contrast to the " Spinario " (No. 136), and the modelling displays the delicacy and refinement of works of the second half of the fourth century B. C. In these qualities and in the type of the head there is a resemblance to the style of Lysippos, in whose school the statue may have originated.

134. The Otricoli Zeus, in the Vatican.

Bust of Carrara marble. Found at the end of the last century, during the excavations of Pius VI. at Otricoli, in Central Italy. RESTORATIONS: Only the mask is antique, and of this the following-named parts are restored: the end of the nose, nearly all the hair on the left side of the face below the level of the eyes. On the right side the hair next to face is original, the outer part modern, also bits set into the beard. PUBLISHED: Visconti, Museo Pio Clem., VI, 1; Müller-Wieseler, Denkmäler d. alten Kunst, II, 1; etc.

Although this may be considered one of the most majestic of extant heads of Zeus, the theory that it reproduced the Pheidian type has been generally abandoned. It is evidently the creation of a later epoch. If we can judge of the head of the Pheidian Zeus by reproductions of it on coins, its character was purely intellectual; the hair was treated simply, and the face was impressive by reason of its intrinsic dignity. In the Otricoli head, the animal predominates over the intellectual. It owes its impressive effect principally to exaggeration of physical qualities,— the extraordinary projection of the brow, the mane-like locks that frame the face, and the heavy, rugged masses of the beard. This attempt to produce effect by means of a sort of trickery, is a method of treatment characteristic of the art of the Hellenistic epoch (332–150 B. C.), in which the type of the Otricoli head probably originated. The head itself was executed not earlier than the time of Augustus, in whose reign the marble of Carrara (Luni), of which it is made, was first quarried.

135. Female Head, in the Berlin Museum.

Of Pentelic marble. Found at Eretria, in the island of Euboea, and formerly in the collection of Count Saburoff, ex-minister of Russia to Greece, by whom it was sold to the Berlin Museum in 1884. There are no restorations. PUBLISHED: Furtwängler, Sammlung Saburoff, pls. XII–XIV; Berlin Museum, Ancient Sculptures No. 743.

This beautiful head is from a grave relief, of the style of Nos. 178–188, in the Fourth Greek Room. It is a work of the Attic school of the fourth century B. C.

136. The "Spinario," in the Palazzo dei Conservatori, Rome.

<small>Statue of bronze. Date **and** place of discovery not known. As early as the end of the 15th century the statue was in a Roman collection. Carried to France after the treaty of Tolentino, and subsequently returned. There are no restorations. PUBLISHED: Rayet, *Monuments de l'Art Antique*, I, pl. 35; Brizio in the *Annali dell' Instituto*, 1874, p. 49, pl. M, and *Monumenti*, X, pl. ii; Robert, *Annali*, 1876, p. 124 f.; Furtwängler, *Der Dornauszieher*, Berlin, 1876; etc.</small>

This is one of the most interesting specimens of Greek *genre* sculpture that we possess. A purely decorative work, without either mythological or historical significance, it represents a boy wholly absorbed in drawing a thorn slowly and carefully from the sole of his foot. His spare form and slender arms and legs are rendered with more realism than the bronze boy in Berlin (No. 133), but the face is as devoid of expression as those of the statues of the early period. Several replicas of the figure exist, the best being the "Castellani" Spinario, of marble, in the British Museum (published by Rayet *ubi sup.*, pl. 36). In all of these the head is treated with as much realism as the figure; the hair is short and curly, and the face, with wrinkled brow and parted lips, expresses both the pain and the delicacy of the operation.

This difference from the more general type has made the Roman Spinario the subject of much discussion as to its date, the principal authorities who have made special studies of the figure differing from one another to the extent of 450 years. By some it is considered a work of the Attic school of the middle of the fifth century B. C.; by others it is placed as late as the beginning of the Christian era, when there was at Rome a school of sculptors who affected the simplicity of early Greek art, just as some artists of our time follow the methods of the pre-Raphaelite painters. While it is not possible to decide the question as to when the statue was actually made, its style is unquestionably that of the period preceding Pheidias. At that time there were at Athens sculptors who represented the human figure with all the realism of this statue; and the shape of the skull, high at the crown and

declining towards the forehead, the type of the face, and
the treatment of the hair, are in exact accord with many
existing sculptures of that epoch.

137. Bust of Zeus (?), in the British Museum.

> Of Pentelic marble. Formerly in the collection of Mr. Towneley,
> who bought it at the sale of the Duke of St. Albans' collection.
> Beyond this its history is unknown. RESTORATIONS: The
> nose, greater part of neck, and a piece in the left cheek. PUB-
> LISHED: *Ancient Marbles in the Brit. Mus.*, pt. X, pl. 1; Over-
> beck, *Kunstmythologie*, II (Zeus), p. 229, Atlas, pl. II, No. 17;
> etc.

Although this is quite generally regarded as a head of
Zeus, it has certain distinctive characteristics in which it
resembles the common type of Asklepios, the god of
health, more than that of Zeus. (Compare, for example,
the Otricoli Zeus, No. 134.) These are, first of all, the
youthfulness of the face and its mild, placid expression.
The formation of the head, also, varies somewhat from that
of Zeus in most representations of him, the forehead being
lower and broader, the brow less prominent, and the face
rounder and shorter. The hair and beard, though disposed
in the same manner as those of Zeus, are treated in lighter
masses, the general effect being decidedly less majestic.
In all these peculiarities the bust corresponds to the ideal
of Asklepios in the fourth and following centuries B. C.,
when sculptors distinguished him from Zeus by just such
minor details.

138. Demosthenes, statue in the Vatican.

> Of marble. Formerly in the Villa Aldobrandini, Frascati. RESTO-
> RATIONS: Both wrists and hands, with the scroll. PUBLISHED:
> Wagner, in the *Annali dell' Instituto*, 1836, p. 159 f.; Michaelis,
> in the *Archäolog. Zeitung*, 1862, p. 239, f.; etc. See also
> Michaelis, *Ancient Marbles in Great Britain*, p. 417 f.

It is easy to believe that this statue is an excellent portrait of the greatest of Greek orators. The combination
of resolution and weariness in the face, the peculiar con-
formation of the mouth, and the slight, weak body, correspond to Plutarch's description of Demosthenes, who is here
represented in the latter part of his life, yet with features

wrinkled more by toil and trouble than by age. The attitude is characteristically simple and dignified; the drapery is treated in the same spirit, and the face, especially the eyes, is thoroughly expressive of the tremendous earnestness of the man.

Polyeuktos, an Athenian sculptor, made a bronze statue of Demosthenes, which was erected at the public expense about the year 280 B. C. That is the only portrait of him mentioned, and as the Vatican statue and all other extant portraits are evidently replicas of one original, there is good reason for supposing this original to have been the statue of Polyeuktos, especially as the extremely realistic treatment of the face and nude portions of the figure, which is noticeable in our copy, is quite characteristic of the art of his time. His statue, however, had the hands clasped, as we know from an anecdote in Plutarch's life of Demosthenes (Chap. XXXI). The hands of the Vatican statue are modern, but that the restoration is correct is proved by a similar statue in the collection of Lord Sackville at Knole in Kent (described by Michaelis, *Anc. Marbles*, cited above), on which hands and scroll are original. In his description of that statue, Michaelis explains this divergence from the original type by supposing the extant figures to have been executed at a later epoch, when Demosthenes was admired more as an author than as a patriot, and therefore the scroll was substituted for the clasped hands.

139. Head of Demosthenes.

In the garden of the Royal Palace, Athens, where it was found. PUBLISHED: Mitchell, *History of Ancient Sculpture*, p. 547 f., fig. 223.

From a statue similar to the preceding.

140. The Venus of Melos. Statue in the Louvre.

Of Parian marble. Found 1820, probably in April, by a peasant, in a grotto about five hundred yards from the ancient theatre of the town of Melos, on the island of the same name. From its shape and character the grotto is supposed to have been a grave in which the statue was hidden. Bought for about 6,000 fr. by M. de Marcellus for the Marquis de Rivière, then French ambassador to the Porte. Carried to Paris, where it arrived in February, 1821, and was presented by de Rivière to Louis XVIII., who placed it in the Louvre. RESTORATIONS: The end of the nose, part of the lower lip, the left foot with the edge of the drapery covering the upper part, the big toe of the right foot, and various small pieces inserted to fill up small fractures in the body and drapery. On the original these restorations are in plaster. PUBLICATIONS: Of the inexhaustible literature on the subject of this statue, the essays by Göler von Ravensburg, *Die Venus von Milo*, Heidelberg, 1879, and Felix Ravaisson, *La Vénus de Milo*, Paris, 1871, may be especially recommended.

From almost the very year in which it was discovered, this, the most famous and most beautiful of all female statues, has been the object of incessant controversy among scholars and critics respecting its name, its date, and its original motive. Those who first saw the statue called it a Venus, and as such it was carried to Paris; but a few years after its arrival there the correctness of this appellation was disputed, and successive attempts have since been made to prove it the Protecting Nymph of Melos, a Muse, Elektra, Nemesis, Nike, Athena-Nike, Sappho, and even Phryne. In spite of these assaults, however, the original name remains both the most popular and that which is supported by the strongest evidence. The superb moulding and majestic proportions indicate that the figure is not only ideal, but of one of the greater divinities. Among these the disclosure of the form by the falling drapery is characteristic of the goddess of love, while the dignity of the bearing and the nobility of the countenance distinguished Aphrodite Urania, the heavenly Venus, from the vulgar goddess of the same name. The inspirer of the highest form of love, she is herself exquisitely lovely, yet with no suggestion of sensuality in her beauty. The splendor of her form is displayed with neither shame nor coquetry. Her face is as pure as it is beautiful, proud, yet sympathetic, combining in its expression the tenderness of the woman with the majesty of the goddess. These are the distinctive qualities of Aphrodite Urania, and their expression in sculpture is characteristic of the art of the fourth century B. C. in which this conception of the goddess undoubtedly originated.

Although its type may be confidently assigned to that

period, the date of the statue itself is a matter of uncertainty, being dependent upon its connection with an inscription found in the same place and carried to Paris at the same time, which read, "Agesandros [or Alexandros] son of Menides of Antioch on the Mæander made this." Many competent judges who saw the inscription believed the fragment containing it to be part of the base of the statue; others affirmed that there was no connection between the two. Before the matter was determined, the fragment disappeared from its place in the Louvre, and the diligent searches which have been made at different times since, have failed to recover any trace of it. If this inscription belonged to the statue, it would prove the latter to be the work of an otherwise unknown sculptor, who lived not earlier than the third century B. C., since Antioch on the Mæander was not founded before the year 281. As every thing possible was done by not over-scrupulous authorities to prove the Venus a work of Praxiteles or his time, the suppression of such weighty testimony to the contrary is not difficult to understand. The very fact of its disappearance at the time when it was so important is a strong argument for the connection between the inscription and the statue; and though absolute certainty is no longer attainable, it is extremely probable that the two did belong together.

 The argument that the execution of the Venus is too fine to have been the work of such a late period has been refuted by the recent developments in our knowledge of the art of the Hellenistic epoch (332-150 B. C.). The excellence of the sculptures discovered at Pergamon (see Nos. 217 and 247, Fifth Greek Room) and other Hellenistic sites, shows that the Venus might have been executed as late as the second century B. C. For, although the creative power of the preceding centuries was gone, the sculptors of that epoch still possessed marvellous technical skill, and their works display great power and refinement of execution. Among the extant works of the period are many fine reproductions of older types, especially of the higher divinities, which are marked by much greater sympathy with the spirit of the original, and more freedom in the treatment of details, than the mannered works of the Roman copyists. To this class of monuments the Venus of Melos probably belongs. It is probably a Hellenistic reproduction of an original that dated from the fourth century.

> The many attempts at restoration of the arms and determination of the original motive of this statue may be divided into three groups. The first represents the goddess as a Venus Victrix, holding the apple of Paris in the uplifted left hand; the second as grouped with Ares (Mars), her left hand on his shoulder; the third as supporting a shield on the left knee and holding it with the left hand. The first of these is based upon the fragments of a hand holding an apple, and of an arm, said to have been found in the same grotto two years after the discovery of the statue, but of doubtful connection with it. Each of the others is derived from the analogy of extant representations of Aphrodite, in which the attitude of the figure and the disposition of the drapery are precisely similar to those of the statue. Each of these three restorations has much evidence in its favor, but none is so absolutely satisfactory as to receive general acceptance to the exclusion of the others, and the motive of the statue is still a riddle which defies the ingenuity of those who try to solve it.

141. Model of the Akropolis of Athens, showing the relative position and size of its various monuments. The names of these, with their corresponding number, will be found on the key.

Of the casts in this room, Nos. 100-103, 105, 112, 116-120, 127, 132, 136, and 138 were purchased from the bequest of Charles Sumner.

Nos. 125, 126, 130, 134, 137, 140, are the property of the Boston Athenæum.

No. 107 is the property of the Institute of Technology.

No. 131 was presented to the Museum by Mr. Stephen H. Perkins.

FOURTH GREEK ROOM.

On the wall above the door leading to the entrance hall, —

150. The Wedding of Poseidon and Amphitrite, in the Glyptothek, Munich.

<small>Relief of Parian marble. Formerly in the Palazzo Santa Croce, Rome, later in possession of Cardinal Fesch. Bought in Paris, 1816, by von Klenze, and transferred to the Glyptothek. RESTORATIONS: "Many small pieces, including the ends of nearly all the noses, the left arm and hand of the woman on the bull, arms and head of the Eros behind her, the horns of the lyre, the shell and both forearms of the front Triton, part of the vase in the left hand of one of the Nereids, the left arm and wing of the Eros behind her, the whole of the floating Eros next to the pillar, except the lower half of the wing, the head and half of the neck of the sea-dragon, the three heads of the last group, with parts of the right arm of both females."— Brunn. The remains on the background of the relief were the basis of these restorations. PUBLISHED: Jahn, in *Berichte der Sächsischen Gesellschaft*, 1854, p. 160 ff., pls. III–VIII; Brunn, *Beschreibung der Glyptothek*, 1879, p. 146 ff.; Perry, *Greek and Roman Sculpture*, p. 395 ff., figs. 168 A–F; etc.</small>

The subject of this relief is the wedding of Poseidon and Amphitrite, or more exactly, the conduct of the bride to her new home by the bridegroom, one of the most important features in the Greek marriage ceremony. In a chariot, the back and arms of which are draped, sit Poseidon and Amphitrite, the latter wearing the bridal veil. The chariot is drawn by two Tritons, one blowing a sea-shell, the other playing upon a lyre. In front of and opposite the bridal couple, Doris, the mother of Amphitrite, rides upon a sea-horse, carrying the two nuptial torches, in accordance with a Greek custom dating from the earliest times, that the mother of the bride should accompany the pair as far as their new home, with torches lighted at the parental hearth. These figures form the principal group, at either side of which is another composed of three females riding upon fantastic beings of the sea, and carrying objects which are presumably the bridal gifts. The women may be Nereids, or possibly, since each group is composed of three, the Hours and Graces, who took part in the weddings of the gods.

Pliny (N. H., XXXVI. 26) describes a work by Skopas which in his time stood in the Temple of Domitius at Rome, representing Poseidon, Thetis, Achilles, Nereids, etc., and Brunn has attempted to establish the identity between that and this frieze. His opinion has been widely followed, but it rests upon evidence which is far too conjectural to prove that the two are identical. Of Skopas' work we do not even know whether it was a frieze or group, and of his style our knowledge is very imperfect. The character of this frieze is of a much later epoch than that of Skopas. Its style resembles that of the decorative work of the Hellenistic epoch, earlier than which it can hardly have originated.

On the adjoining and opposite walls, —

151. Selection from the Frieze of the Temple of Apollo at Phigaleia, in the British Museum.

Of Pentelic marble. Discovered among the ruins of the Temple in 1811, 1812, by Cockerell, Haller, Lynckh, Stackelberg, etc., and acquired by the British Museum in 1814. There are no restorations. PUBLISHED: Stackelberg, *Apollo-Tempel zu Bassae*, Rome, 1826; Blouet, *Expédition Scientifique de Morée*, vol. II, pls. 20-23; Combe, *Anc. Marbles in Brit. Mus.*, IV, pls. 25-28; Cockerell, *Temples of Aegina and Bassae*; etc.

The temple of Apollo Epikourios (the Succorer), from which this frieze was taken, was built by the people of Phigaleia, a town in the southwest corner of Arkadia, in recognition of their deliverance from a plague. It stood some distance from the town itself, on a spur of the neighboring Mt. Kotylios, at a place called Bassæ. The architect was Iktinos, the same who built the Parthenon.

The date of the construction of the temple is not known, but it was probably after the completion of the Parthenon (438 B. C.), and the plague referred to may have been that which visited Athens soon after the outbreak of the Peloponnesian war.

The temple was of the Doric style, but with Ionic half-columns in the interior; and it was over these, not on the outside of the building, that the frieze was placed, thus forming a decoration of the cella, the four walls of which it encircled. With unimportant exceptions the entire frieze has been found; it is about 101 ft. long, divided unequally into two subjects, the battle of the Greeks and Amazons, and that of the Kentaurs and Lapithæ, the former being the longer of the two. A selection from this is on the inner wall of the room, while the battle of the Kentaurs and Lapithæ is represented on the wall next the Third Greek Room.

Unlike that of the Parthenon frieze, these two subjects are represented without continuity. The battles are not followed from beginning to end, but each is depicted at its height, with no indication as to which is to be the victorious party. Among the Kentaurs, some are brought down by the powerful Lapiths; others have the advantage over their adversaries, and one is represented as killing his foe by biting his neck, kicking at the same time with both hind legs the shield of another Lapith who approaches from behind. The fate of the women is equally uncertain. From one the clothes are torn as she clings to the image of a divinity. Her companion, with outspread arms and upturned face, implores the aid of the gods, and another is seized by a Kentaur as she attempts to escape with her child. At the inner end of the wall is a chariot drawn by two stags, and bearing Apollo and Artemis, the former in the act of shooting.

The battle of the Amazons is represented with equal spirit, and the same uncertainty of result. Both of these subjects are treated not merely in the Attic style, but with actual imitations of works in Athens, and undoubtedly originated in the Attic school. There is the same ease and fertility in the composition that is noteworthy in all Greek works of this class and epoch, an infinite variety in the lines, all of which are vigorous, and fulfil the architectual object of the frieze by giving life and activity to the more serious members about it. The quality of the execution varies, often displaying a marked contrast to the excellence of the conception; yet it has the characteristics of the work of the fifth century, the faces lacking pathetic expression, and the proportions of the men less slender than in reliefs of the following century. (Compare the reliefs from the Mausoleum, Nos. 191–195.)

152. Helios and his Chariot. Metope from Ilion, in the Ethnographical Museum, Berlin.

Of white marble. Found by Dr. Schliemann during his excavations in 1872. There are no restorations. PUBLISHED: Schliemann, *Ilios*, fig. 1479, pp. 622–625; the same, *Troja*, fig. 109, p. 202; etc.

The original of this cast is an architectural fragment, combining a metope and two triglyphs, from a temple erected on the site of the ancient Troy. In the metope Helios, the Sun-God, is represented driving his four-horse chariot. Of the chariot itself nothing is to be seen, a fact which indicates that originally it was represented in color only. The design is spirited, the action of the horses showing unmistakably the Greek chisel, but the sculpture is not of the best period, and probably dates later than the year 300 B. C.

153. Fragment of a Relief, in the Vatican.

Of marble. Found near Præneste; date unknown. PUBLISHED: Visconti, *Museo Pio Clementino*, IV, pl. 9. p. 56 ff.

The relief of which this is a fragment contains in all six figures, arranged in pairs in the attitudes of these two, and, like them, wearing helmets and carrying shields. In their right hands were originally swords, probably of metal. The character and subject of this monument are explained by a similar one, more complete, in Athens (Beulé, *L'Acropole*, II, 314 and pl. IV), on which is an inscription showing it to be the pedestal of a statue dedicated by a victor in the Pyrrhic dance. In that relief the figures are arranged in two groups of four each; otherwise they are precisely like these, so that there can be little doubt that this was also portion of a pedestal, and that the dance represented is the Pyrrhic, not, as Visconti supposed, the wild, noisy dance of the Korybantes or priests of Kybele.

154. Niobe and her Youngest Daughter. In the Uffizi Gallery, Florence.

Group of Pentelic marble. Found 1583, near the Lateran, Rome. Purchased by Cardinal Ferdinand de' Medici, and placed in the Villa Medici. In 1775, removed to Florence. RESTORATIONS: On the Niobe, the nose, parts of lips, left lower arm with the piece of garment attached, and the right hand with half the lower arm. Daughter, the right arm, left hand, hair, nose, lower lip, left foot. PUBLISHED: Stark, *Niobe*, Leipzig, 1863, pp. 225 ff. and Plate X; Overbeck, *Plastik*, 3d ed., II, pp. 52 ff.; Clarac, No. 1260, pl. 583; etc.

These two figures were found with twelve others, at least seven of which evidently formed part of a group of which the Niobe was the centre. Since their discovery, statues in various museums have been identified as of the same group, so that there are now in all thirteen figures established as belonging to it, and several others about which there is still controversy. The subject represented is the climax of the well-known story of Niobe, and the moment chosen is that in which the slaughter is at its height. About Niobe are her sons and daughters, some already dead, some wounded, and some trying to escape. The haughty mother, punished for her arrogance, clasps her youngest daughter, still unharmed, to her knees, and with her mantle vainly tries to screen the child from the flying arrows, looking imploringly, yet despairingly, towards heaven.

The fact that the execution of these figures, which is hard and mechanical, is greatly inferior to the conception, warrants the belief that they are Roman copies of a Greek original; and that this was a famous work is indicated by the number of replicas of these same figures that have been discovered, both statues and reliefs. (See, for example, the sarcophagus, No. 173, in the same room.) Of the Niobe there is a head precisely similar to that of the statue, but of finer execution, in the collection of

Lord Yarborough, at Brocklesby Park. It is, therefore, probable that the original was the **group** of which Pliny (N. H., XXXVI. 28) speaks as **standing, in** his time, in the temple of Apollo Sosianus at Rome, and about which there was doubt as to whether it **was** the work of Skopas or Praxiteles. As no other ancient writer mentions the group, and we have not enough existing w**orks of the two** sculptors to **enable us to** make a decisive comparison **of** their styles, it is impossible to determine to which of **them** this is to be assigned. Moreover, the doubt existing in Pliny's time indicates that the work was not signed, **and** therefore there is no proof that it was by either of them. Whoever the artist may have been, the original was undoubtedly a work of **the first** half of the fourth century B. C., **as** all the existing copies bear resemblances **to** the general characteristics of that epoch.

155. **Niobid,** in the Vatican.

Statue of Greek marble. Discovered possibly in Hadrian's Villa in the 16th century. Formerly in the papal gardens of the Quirinal. There are no restorations. PUBLISHED: Stark, *Niobe*, p. 265 ff. and pl. XII; Murray, *History of Greek Sculpture*, II, p. 315 f. and pl. xxviii; etc.

This statue represents **one of** the elder daughters of Niobe fleeing from the arrows of Apollo and Artemis, **and is a** copy **of a** figure from the group mentioned above (No. 154), as famous in antiquity. The same figure is reproduced in one of the statues in Florence, though that is greatly inferior to this, which **is** by far the finest of all the extant Niobids, and doubtless reproduces much of the spirit of **its** lost original. In contrast to the stiff, mechanical action **of the** Florentine statue, which suggests **the** original in little **more than** attitude, **this** is **full** of life and excitement. The drapery is cut in deep, vigorous folds, that express all the rush of the movement, and is treated with a grace and power suggestive **of the** Parthenon sculp**tures,** although the original of **the group,** as stated above **(No.** 154), was probably **a work of the** century following **the** completion of **the** Parthenon.

156. Colossal Head of Kastor. From the statue on the Monte Cavallo, in front of the Quirinal Palace, Rome.

> **Of marble.** Formerly stood in front of the Baths of Constantine, from which it was removed to present position by Sixtus V., in 1589. There are no restorations on the head. PUBLISHED: Fogelberg in the *Annali dell' Instituto*, 1842, p. 194 ff.; Clarac, *Musée*, pl. 812 A, No. 2043; etc.

The statue from which this **head is** taken is one of two which formerly served as decorations to the entrance of the Baths of Constantine, representing the Dioskouroi holding in check their prancing horses. The figures are not mounted, **but** lead the horses by the bridles, and Kastor **looks back at his** horse, who rears behind and a little to **the left of him.** This explains the action of the head and **the excitement** in the countenance. On the chin there **still** remains **one** of the sculptor's measuring points, showing that the **statue was left** incomplete.

Upon **the** pedestal **of** this statue is the inscription, "Opus Phidiae"; on that of the companion, "Opus Praxitelis," which Pope Sixtus V. had copied from the earlier pedestals when the statues were removed. That the statues are the work of these masters, however, is impossible. They evidently date from the Roman Empire, but are possibly copies of works of the Hellenistic epoch.

157. Head of Demeter, in the British **Museum.**

> Of Parian marble. Discovered, with the statue to which it belongs, by Newton at Knidos in 1858. (The statue had been noted by Gell and his associates in 1812, headless and nearly covered with earth.) There are no restorations. PUBLISHED: Newton, *Halicarnassus*, p. 375 ff. and pls. LIII–LV; Brunn, in the *Transac. Royal Soc. of Literature*, new series, Vol. XI, pt. I, **p. 80 ff.;** Rayet, *Monuments de l'Art Antique*, II, pl. 49; etc.

This head is from a statue, probably of the fourth century B. C., representing Demeter seated upon a throne, her figure fully enveloped in drapery, and wearing the veil indicative of a matron. Between the head and that of the Venus of Melos, there is great resemblance in the treatment of the hair, the general character of the sculpture, **and** most of all in the manner in which **a** number of qualities are combined in the expression of the face. Demeter is here conceived in her relation to Persephone, the shrine in which the statue was found having been dedicated to both. A mother, she has not yet passed the bloom of womanhood, but is still beautiful in spite of the long mourning over her lost child. Grief has left its traces in the face, but only to soften the lines, and give expression to the submission with which her sorrow has been endured. There is also the kindliness which is born of resignation, making the countenance as tender as that of the Venus, in marked contrast to the stony face of mourning of the Niobe (No. 154). "It has been truly said that the countenance of this Knidian Demeter is, in expression, the most Christian work in ancient sculpture." — *Newton*.

158. Standing Diskobolos, in the Vatican.

Statue of Pentelic (?) marble. Found, 1792, by Gavin Hamilton, amid the ruins of an ancient villa on the Appian Way, and bought of him by Pius VI. for the Vatican. RESTORATIONS: The fingers of the right hand, and a few other unimportant pieces. PUBLISHED: Visconti, *Museo Pio Clem.*, III, pl. xxvi; Kekulé, in the *Archäologische Zeitung*, 1866, p. 169, ff. and pl. CCIX, 1, 2; etc.

This statue represents an athlete about to hurl the diskos, a favorite subject among the sculptors of the fifth century B. C., as the game of the diskobolia or diskos-throwing was one of the most popular among athletes, and formed part of the contests for which prizes were awarded at the great festivals. The diskos was a round object, sometimes lens-shaped, sometimes flat, and if we may judge by one found at Ægina, now in the British Museum, was of bronze, about eight inches in diameter, weighing a trifle less than four pounds. The object was to throw it the greatest possible distance, in a definite direction, but without regard to a goal.

The action of this figure is instantaneous. His feet firmly planted, and the right hand raised, the youth is estimating the ground preparatory to swinging himself into an attitude like that of the neighboring Diskobolos (No. 161). As is usual with works of the fifth century, the face expresses none of the excitement of the action.

Visconti, in describing this statue, considered it a copy of a Diskobolos by Naukydes, **a** pupil of Polykleitos, and therefore of the Argive school; but, although it is **still often** referred to as the "Diskobolos of Naukydes," there is no authority for the assumption that it is a work **of that** sculptor. In type and style it has more affinity with the Attic than the Argive works, and it may be a copy of some Athenian statue of the fifth century B. C., though to what sculptor it is to be assigned **we do** not know. Both Alkamenes and Myron have been suggested, but there is not sufficient evidence for ascribing it to either. The clumsy character of the support necessitated by the marble is disturbing to the effect of the action. The original was probably of bronze, in which material the statue would require no artificial support whatever.

159. Large Oval Sarcophagus, in the Vatican.

Of marble. Found 1777 in digging the foundations for the Sacristy of St. Peter's, Rome. (In it were two skeletons.) Placed by Pius VI. in the Vatican. RESTORATIONS: The head of the female in the middle group, lower part of faces of both lions, and the mask lying by the altar. PUBLISHED: Visconti, *Museo Pio Clem.*, IV, pl. xxix; Gerhard, in the *Beschreibung der Stadt Rom.*, II 2, p. 133, **No.** 37.

As is frequently **the** case with Roman sarcophagi, the subject represented **here** has the least possible connection with death or the purpose of the sarcophagus. The object of the relief is simply that **of** decoration, without especial significance, and the subject chosen is one of great popularity **in** decorative works of late Greek and Roman art, — a dance of Satyrs and Mænads or Bacchantes. Beginning **at** the extreme right, a Satyr, holding a thyrsus in his right **hand,** dances up to **a** Mænad, offering her a tambourine. **At his feet** leaps a panther in the same direction. Next **are another** Satyr and Mænad, dancing, she holding some **sacrificial** object in her left hand, while with her right she grasps her flying drapery. The **Satyr** holds a thyrsus in **one** hand, and stretches at full length his panther-skin garment with the other. His club has fallen at his feet. Under the two lion-heads on the front are Erotes (Cupids) riding on panthers, and holding wine-cups. In the centre is the most beautiful group, a graceful Mænad and Satyr swinging in a circle. Between them is a panther with one paw upon a goat's head, another Bacchic emblem. To the left another group of two dance about a small altar, on which is a Silenus mask. The manner in which the Mænad's drapery flies shows that she is whirling in the perfect abandonment of the Bacchic frenzy, while her companion dances around her. Finally, the last group represents a Satyr who for a moment stops piping to dance, and a Mænad playing the cymbals and apparently singing.

It is worthy of note that although this scene exhibits all the wildness of the Bacchic dance, of which the utmost liberty of gesture and movement was characteristic, it is yet absolutely free from coarseness or vulgarity. As becomes the devotees of the god of wine, the fun is boisterous, but it is always graceful and without an element of brutality.

160. Bacchanalian Vase, in the British Museum.

> Of marble. Found by Gavin Hamilton, on the site of the Villa of Antoninus Pius at Lanuvium. Formerly in the Towneley collection. RESTORATIONS: Of the Mænad adjoining Pan, everything except the feet; of the Satyr next to her, everything except the right leg, left foot, left arm, and part of the panther's skin; the face of the youth leaning upon a Mænad; the left arm and head of Pan, except his beard, and the greater part of the amphora which he carries. PUBLISHED: Ellis, *Towneley Gallery*, II, pp. 210-12; *Ancient Marbles in Brit. Mus.*, I, pl. 7.

The subject, like that of the preceding, is a Bacchanalian festival. Among the figures, the most easily recognizable is that of Pan, under the right handle, with long beard and goat-legs. Next him to the left, and leaning upon a bearded Satyr, is probably Dionysos, the short chiton and tall shoes with overlapping tops being characteristic of that divinity in later Greek art. The remaining figures are Satyrs, youthful and bearded, and Mænads whose flying drapery denotes the wildness of their movements.

Around the base is a decorative border of fantastic female figures, winged, joined to one another by the pateræ held in their hands.

The character of the rim, handles and base of the vase, indicates that it is a reproduction of metal work.

161. Diskobolos, after Myron, in the Vatican.

<blockquote>Marble statue. Found in Hadrian's Villa, 1791, and placed by Pius VI. in the Vatican. RESTORATIONS: The head, left arm, left leg from knee down, and the greater part of the diskos. PUBLISHED: Bouillon, *Musée des Antiques*, II, pl. 18; Welcker, *Alte Denkmäler*, I, p. 417 ff.; Collignon, *L'Archéologie Grecque*, fig. 45; etc.</blockquote>

Myron of Athens, pupil of Ageladas, and contemporary of Pheidias and Polykleitos, was one of the most famous sculptors of his age. Few of his works have survived even in copies, but the numerous allusions to him in ancient writers show his tendency as a sculptor to have been realistic, in contrast to both the ideality of Pheidias and the quiet scholarliness of Polykleitos. His favorite theme appears to have been the human figure in intense action, and one of his most celebrated works was a bronze statue of an athlete in the act of throwing a diskos, in the game described under No. 158. Lucian (*Philopseudes*, 18) describes the statue as "bent in the attitude of throwing, looking back at the hand which holds the diskos, and with one leg slightly contracted, as though to recover his balance after the throw."

The statue in the Vatican is in point of execution one of the best of the numerous extant copies of this figure. Lucian's description places the identity beyond doubt. The attitude of the head, which is modern, does not correspond with the original, but the muscles of the neck show that the restoration is incorrect, and that the head was originally turned in the direction described. Another marble copy, in the Lancellotti Palace, Rome, still retains its original head, which is so turned. A photograph of that statue hangs upon the pedestal.

These marble copies can hardly be regarded as anything more than suggestions of the original. They were executed during the Roman Empire, and while they show the type and attitude of the figure, they undoubtedly give but a poor idea of the modelling. The presence of the tree-stump, necessary for support in the marble, but not required in the bronze, seriously hinders an appreciation of what must have been the most striking feature of the original, — the wonderful balance in the pose. Fortunately, a small ancient copy of the statue in the material of the original has been preserved, and is now in Munich. A cast of it is in the case of small casts in the Greek Vase Room. That figure has no extraneous support whatever, yet contorted as the body is, the line of equilibrium falls perpendicularly through the centre from whatever point of view the statuette is seen, and gives a perfectly satisfactory sense of support in spite of the instantaneous character of the action.

162. Large Lekythos as Grave Monument, in the National Museum, Athens.

> Of Pentelic marble. Found 1849 in the eastern part of Athens, and formerly in the Theseion. There are no restorations, COLOR: Below the relief traces of red are still very distinct, and in the relief itself are numerous indications of the application of colors no longer distinguishable. PUBLISHED: E. Curtius, in *Archäolog. Zeitung*, 1864, p. 145 ff., pl. 183; Newton, *Travels and Discoveries*, I, p. 24; Mitchell, *History of Ancient Sculpture*, fig. 215, p. 505; etc.

This Lekythos, or oil-jug, belongs to a class of monuments described below (Grave Monuments, Nos. 178-188). It reproduces on a colossal scale the oil-jugs which were used at funeral sacrifices and placed on the graves by friends of the deceased. Grave monuments of this type were introduced in Athens as early as the middle of the fifth century B. C., but this example probably dates from the beginning of the fourth.

The relief represents a youth riding upon a spirited horse, the easy and graceful action of which is an indication of a fine period. Before him are two young warriors clasping hands. On the back, below the handle, another subject has been sketched, representing a woman seated in profile towards the left, behind and leaning upon whom is a girl. This sketch, although hasty, is extremely fine in spirit. Probably the monument was erected to the memory of a youth, and the subsequent burial of a female member of his family in the same place was thus commemorated, as the sketch was evidently inserted after the completion of the relief, with which it has no connection.

The color still existing on the vase, and the neglect to

represent in the sculpture accessories, such as the bridle, reins, and tail of the horse, the shoe and left foot of the rider and the spears of the warriors, indicate that the surface was extensively if not entirely painted.

163, 164. Two small Fragments from the Frieze of the Temple of Nike Apteros, at Athens.

These two fragments give but a meagre idea of the frieze to which they belong. The first represents two warriors in hand-to-hand combat, their shields pressed closely against one another. The second represents a female standing half in profile towards the right, her right hand resting on her hip, the left holding by the hand Eros who stands between her and another female. Of him scarcely anything is left except the large wings, the mutilated torso, and one leg. He bends towards the second female, who, turned from him, stands in a meditative attitude, her left foot upon a rock. The beautiful manner in which the drapery of these two females is treated is especially worthy of study.

165-171. Reliefs from the Balustrade of the Temple of Nike Apteros, Athens, in the Akropolis Museum, Athens.

> Of Pentelic marble. Found 1835-38 by Ludwig Ross and others, during excavations at the site of the Temple. There are no restorations. PUBLISHED: Ross, etc., *Der Tempel der Nike Apteros*, Berlin, 1839; and Kekulé, *Die Reliefs an der Balustrade der Athena Nike*, Stuttgart, 1881, where they are illustrated as follows: 165, pl. IV, fig. O; 166, pl. I, fig. A; 167, pl. IV, fig. M; 168, pl. IV, fig. N; 169, pl. III, fig. I; 170, pl. V, fig. R; 171, pl. II, fig. E.

The situation of the little temple which these reliefs adorned is shown by No. 8 on the model of the Akropolis in the Third Room. It was at the extreme western end of the Akropolis, on a bastion projecting from the south side of the Propylaia. Around the edges of this bastion, enclosing the temple on three sides and part of the fourth, ran a marble balustrade, decorated with reliefs on its outer side, so that these were seen as one passed up the approach to the Propylaia, while the inner side, facing the temple itself, was unsculptured.

As the temple was that of Athena Nike, — that is, of Athena in her quality of goddess of victory, — the reliefs bore reference to that fact, representing figures of Nike in various acts of sacrifice and triumph. As will be judged from the specimens here exhibited, the sculptures are in a very mutilated condition, but enough remains to show that no continuous subject or procession was represented, the figures being divided into groups like that of the two Nikes with the cow or bull, No. 166.

Greek art has left us no more delicate and graceful sculptures than these fragments, which combine many of the characteristics of the best work of both the fifth and fourth centuries B. C. In conception and composition they display the qualities of the period immediately following Pheidias, while in execution they show the refinement of the fourth century. No. 170 has the quiet spirit of the Parthenon figures; she stands firm and erect, her drapery falling in simple, straight folds, through which the form is not apparent. In strong contrast to this is the figure of the Nike untying her sandal. Through her soft, clinging drapery all the graceful lines of her form are displayed with the exquisiteness of technique which characterizes the art of Praxiteles, and renders the figure one of the most wonderful specimens of Greek art that survive.

The date of the temple and its decorations is still a matter of conjecture, as neither historians nor inscriptions have given any clue to it. Examination of the substructure shows that the building was begun later than the Propylaia (437 B. C.), and the style of the sculptures points to the end of that century or the beginning of the following as the date of their origin. Kekulé (cited above) thinks 407 the latest date that could be assigned them, in which year Alkibiades returned from his victories in Asia Minor; but their association with that event is purely conjectural, and it is very doubtful whether Athens was in a condition during the few years following to undertake a work of this kind. On both historical and artistic grounds the beginning of the fourth century is a more probable date for the origin of the balustrade.

172. **Fragment of a Sarcophagus**, in the Museum at Sparta (except the piece containing the head of the boy playing on the cymbals, which is in the National Museum, Athens).

<small>Of marble. Found in the village of Hagios Johannes, in the vicinity of Sparta. There are no restorations. PUBLISHED: *Archäologische Zeitung*, 1880, pl. 14; Dressel and Milchhöfer in the *Mittheilungen des Instituts in Athen*, II, p. 401, No. 228.</small>

Nine small genii are engaged in a Bacchic scene, all in various stages of intoxication. In the middle, one pours wine from a long, slender amphora into a krater. On either side of him is a musician, one playing a full blast upon the double pipes, the other striking the cymbals. At the right is a jolly group of three, two staggering in affectionate embrace, the third with his right hand pressed against his head, as though the after-effects of his merriment were beginning to be felt, his empty cup hanging from his left hand. At the left is a group whose faces wear a more serious expression, and whose legs move more heavily. Evidently they have passed the joyful stage, and he with the torch is vainly trying to escort the other two. The conception and grouping of these figures is charming, and the execution, though not of the best, is such as to warrant our dating the sarcophagus in a period earlier than that of the Roman dominion in Greece.

173. **The Death of the Niobids.** Roman Sarcophagus in the Vatican.

<small>Of marble. Found during the second half of the 18th century, outside the Porta S. Sebastiano, Rome, in a vineyard belonging to the Casali family. Presented by Cardinal Casali to Pius VI., and by him placed in the Vatican. RESTORATIONS: The left arm of Apollo with the bow, and the right arm of Artemis with the arrow. PUBLISHED: Visconti, *Museo Pio Clem.*, IV, pl. xvii; Stark, *Niobe*, p. 179 ff.; etc.</small>

The relief on the sarcophagus represents Apollo and Artemis slaying the children of Niobe. Both divinities are introduced in the composition rather awkwardly, being brought into too close proximity with their victims, whose faces are turned upwards, as though the arrows came from above, not as we see them, from the same plane. At the left is Artemis, next to whom Niobe endeavors to protect a daughter fallen over her knee, while the smallest daughter runs to her mother from the other side. Following this group, the old nurse supports another daughter who has sunk to the ground; and still another, probably the eldest, rushes forward in an attitude of despair. The faithful pedagogue or tutor clasps the smallest boy in one arm and looks as though for aid toward the largest of the sons, who, armed with two spears like a huntsman, his cloak wound about his left arm, rushes into the scene from the background. Between them another son has fallen to his knees and with one arm screens his face. Finally, next to Apollo, one of the daughters is writhing in mortal pain, and a son lies dead upon the ground. The subject is continued on the sides of the sarcophagus, — on that adjoining Artemis, by two daughters with upraised arms and flying garments; and on the other, a son supporting his falling brother, from whose side a horse rushes away.

This sarcophagus belongs to a very numerous class (see Nos. 176 and 198), dating from the second and third centuries after Christ, characterized by their decorations in high relief of scenes mostly from Greek and Roman mythology. It is rather on account of the representations than from intrinsic value as works of art that these sarcophagi possess interest, the execution being as a rule mediocre, although the figures are often conceived with such spirit as to suggest that they have been copied from more important works. Several well-known statues have been identified with figures on these reliefs, which has led to the belief that the makers of the sarcophagi reproduced upon them famous groups, the treatment of which they modified and adapted to their own abilities and requirements. The story of Niobe was evidently a favorite theme with them, as it appears on several extant sarcophagi, and calls to mind the famous group described under No. 154, which doubtless served as a model for some of these designs. The figure of Niobe on this and other similar sarcophagi bears quite a striking resemblance to the large statue, and probably was studied from the same original.

174. Marble Vase, in the British Museum.

Formerly in the Towneley collection. RESTORATIONS: The greater part of this vase is modern, the original parts being the Mænad and two of the Satyrs, the legs and part of the left arm of the Satyr playing on the cymbals, the head of one of the swans, and the greater portion of the neck of the vase. PUBLISHED: *Ancient Marbles of the Brit. Mus.*, I, pl. 9; Ellis, *Towneley Gallery*, II, pp. 215–16; *Guide to Græco-Roman Sculptures of Brit. Mus.*, part II, No. 2.

A Bacchic scene, in which most of the figures are in attitudes familiar in representations of Satyrs and Mænads. The style of the vase shows it to be an imitation of a bronze type.

175. The Vase of Sosibios, in the Louvre.

Of Parian marble. Formerly in the Villa Borghese. RESTORATIONS: The base of the vase. PUBLISHED: Clarac, *Musée de Sculpture*, pl. 126, No 332, and pl. 130; Fröhner, *Sculpture Antique du Louvre*, No. 19, p. 50 ff.; etc.

This amphora derives its name from the inscription, scarcely legible on the cast, on the base of the altar which forms the centre of the relief, "Sosibios the Athenian made this."

Towards the altar, on which is a sacrificial fire, comes from the left, Artemis, followed by a figure in long drapery playing the lyre, and a Satyr playing the double pipe. From the right Hermes, with pointed beard and holding the caduceus, is followed by a dancing Bacchante, behind whom comes a warrior in the movement of the Pyrrhic dance. On the back are two dancing Bacchantes, one with a thyrsos, the other playing a tambourine. The date of the vase is probably not earlier than the first century B. C.

176. The Murder of Aigisthos and Klytaimnestra, Roman sarcophagus in the Vatican.

Of marble. Formerly in the Palazzo Barberini. RESTORATIONS: The head of Orestes at the right end. PUBLISHED: Visconti, *Museo Pio Clem.*, V, pl. 22, p. 141 ff.; Gerhard, in the *Beschreibung der Stadt Rom*, II 2, p. 254, Nos. 33, **34**; Wolters' Friederichs, Nos. 1825, 1826; etc.

This sarcophagus belongs to the class described under No. 173. As often happens on these sarcophagi, the subject is divided into **several scenes, without** any indication of the division. In the centre, Orestes, with drawn sword, stands above the prostrate form of his murdered mother, Klytaimnestra; and Pylades, also with drawn sword, moves towards him from behind. Aigisthos, who was murdered on his throne, has dragged it over with him in falling. To **his left** the old nurse of Orestes turns **in horror from the scene.** To the right **of** Orestes, **a** youth, probably **a slave**, cowers behind a household altar, which he has lifted **from** the ground and holds before his face as though **to screen** himself from **the** impiety that **is** being committed. **Behind** him **two Furies,** bearing a curtain, approach Orestes. **The** serpen**t and** torch of one **are** visible.

The **above-named** figures **form** one group and scene, while **at the two** ends of **the front** of the sarcophagus Delphi is represented, and **the end of** Orestes' wanderings. At the left he clings with **one hand to** the tripod of Apollo, holding his sword in a **defiant** attitude with **the** other; at his feet sleeps a Fury, **about whom** is coiled a serpent. At the other end is a group **of three** sleeping Furies, signifying that Apollo's promise **has been** fulfilled, and their pursuit of Orestes has ceased. **On either side of** the sarcophagus **is a sphinx.**

177. **Large Female Head,** in the Custodians' House at the entrance **to** the Akropolis, Athens.

> Of Pentelic marble. Found 1876 during the excavations on the southern slope of the Akropolis. There are no restorations.
> PUBLISHED: Julius, in the *Mittheilungen des Instituts in Athen*, I, p. 269 ff., pl. xiii; Mitchell, *History of Ancient Sculpture*, p. 484, and Selections, pl. X.

This is probably the head of some female divinity, although its identification is difficult, owing to the absence of distinctive attributes, and **because no** fragment of the statue to which it belonged was found. The execution shows that it dates from a good period, and it is probably the original work of an Athenian sculptor of the fourth century B. C.

GRAVE MONUMENTS OF THE FOURTH CENTURY B. C.

The reliefs which decorated the graves of private individuals at Athens and elsewhere in Greece form one of the most interesting groups of the surviving monuments of Greek art, because they enable us to appreciate the skill and taste of common artisans during the epochs of the great masters, and to form some conception of the extent to which the artistic impulse pervaded all classes in those times. During the last twenty-five years these reliefs have been found in great numbers, chiefly in and about Athens, but also in other parts of Greece. Most of them are inscribed with the names of the persons they commemorate, and of those hitherto found not one bears a name of historical celebrity, — a fact which, taken in conjunction with the circumstance that they are never signed by the artist, shows that they were the common form of grave monument of their time, and were not regarded as important works of art. As might be expected in works of this kind, the quality of the execution varies greatly in the different reliefs, yet even the rudest of them shows great delicacy of feeling; and the simple treatment of the drapery, as well as the idealized type of the faces, illustrates the influence of the great sculptors upon the minor works of their age.

Beyond this, these monuments possess an especial interest as illustrations of the manner in which death was regarded by the Greeks. Naturally such works would be executed in accordance with the taste of the people by whom they were ordered, and would therefore reflect the common sentiment concerning death and the separation caused by it. The last parting between the deceased and his or her family is a favorite subject, and one cannot fail to be impressed by the peacefulness of these scenes. Applied to sepulchral subjects, the tranquillity which characterizes the great sculptures of the fifth and fourth centuries becomes extremely **pathetic**. While grief is apparent in every figure, it is never represented in a vehement or extravagant manner, but subdued and restrained, so that resignation is the feeling most forcibly expressed. Of the horrors of death or the grave there is never a suggestion.

A comparison of these reliefs with the primitive grave monuments in the First Greek Room (Nos. 1, 7-15) shows what an enormous development even the minor forms of sculpture underwent in the century following the Persian wars. The stele of Aristokles (No. 13), for example, shows the type of grave monument prevalent in Attika up to the period of the Persian invasion; and although the simple shaft or stele continued to be popular in subsequent epochs, a variety of other forms grew up around it. The type illustrated in Nos. 178-188 probably originated about the middle of the fifth century B. C., but did not attain its full development before the beginning of the fourth century, to which our specimens belong.

> NOTE. — No. 162, described on p. 105, belongs to this group. See also Nos. 196, 199, below.

178. Head of a **Woman**, in Lansdowne House, London.

> Of Pentelic marble. PUBLISHED by Michaelis in the *Archäolog. Zeitung*, 1880, p. 81, pl. 9; and *Ancient Marbles in Great Britain*, p. 437, No. 1.

This remarkably beautiful fragment is from an Athenian grave monument of the first quarter of the fourth century, and is one of the finest examples of its class. The woman's mantle was drawn over her head like a veil, and her wavy hair bound by three fillets. The manner in which grief is expressed in the countenance is especially worthy of note.

179. Monument of **Dexileos**, in the cemetery outside the Dipylon Gate, Athens.

> Of Pentelic marble. Found 1863, lying by its original site, on which it has been re-erected. There are no restorations. PUBLISHED: Wescher in the *Revue Archéologique*, N. S., VIII, pl. 15, pp. 82 ff. and 351 ff.; Wolters' Friederichs, No. 1005; Sybel, *Katalog*, 3312; etc.

This is one of the few Attic grave monuments which give us their exact date. On the pedestal of the relief, not shown in the cast, is an inscription which shows that Dexileos died in the battle of Corinth, B. C. 394, in the twentieth year of his age. The relief, which shows the influence of Pheidian art, represents the youth in a moment of triumph over an enemy, who, fallen on one knee, and leaning upon his shield, is trying to ward off the thrust of Dexileos' lance with his sword. The marble shows that color was applied, and that bronze was used for the reins and bridle, also for a wreath on the head of Dexileos, for his lance, and for the sword of his opponent.

180. Fragment of a Stele, with Akroterion. In the Theseion, Athens.

Of Pentelic marble. Found in Salamis. PUBLISHED: *Expéd. Scientif. de Morée*, III, pl. 23, 1, 2; Wolters' Friederichs, No. 1110; Sybel, *Katalog*, No. 3370; etc.

The inscription states that this is the monument of one Epikrates. This simple form of stele, surmounted by an akroterion, was a common grave decoration during all periods of Greek art, and especially during the fifth century B. C.

181. Grave Monument, in the National Museum, Athens.

Of white marble. Date and place of discovery uncertain. (In 1829 it was in Ægina, in the possession of an Englishman named Dawkins, and said to have been found there. Cf. *Annali*, 1829, p. 135; but Sybel, *Katalog*, No. 76, gives Lamia as the probable place of discovery.) There are no restorations. PUBLISHED: *Expéd. Scientif. de Morée*, III, pl. 41, 1-3; Wolters' Friederichs, No. 1012; etc.

The significance of this representation is not clear. A youth wearing an himation, the right half of his body bare, holds in the left hand a small bird; the right hand is raised to what appears to be a bird-cage, at which he is looking. Below this is a square pillar, on which is an animal somewhat resembling a cat. Leaning against the pillar is a small boy, who from the analogy of similar representations we know to be the slave of the youth. Along the cornice above the relief runs a honeysuckle ornament.

182. **Monument of Damasistrate**, daughter of Polykleides. In the National Museum, Athens.

> Of white marble. Formerly in the Piræus. Date and place of discovery not known. There are no restorations. PUBLISHED: Mitchell, *History of Ancient Sculpture*, fig. 208, p. 497; Sybel, *Katalog*, No. 71; etc.

Damasistrate, whose name appears in the inscription above the relief, is seated in an arm-chair, her feet resting upon a stool. With her left hand she holds her veil, and with the right clasps the hand of a man who stands opposite her, probably her father or husband. Between the two stands a woman, her left hand to her face, which is turned towards the man with an expression of sorrow. Behind the chair of Damasistrate is a smaller woman, whose head-dress and costume indicate that she is a handmaid.

183. **Monument of Phainippe**, in the National Museum, Athens.

> Of Pentelic marble. From Salamis. There are no restorations. PUBLISHED: *Expéd. Scientif. de Morée*, III, pl. 42, 2; Wolters' Friederichs, No. 1047; Sybel, *Katalog*, No. 75; etc.

Seven figures are crowded into this representation, the subject of which, like that above, is the parting between the deceased and her family. As is usual in these groups the principal figure is seated, and wears a veil over her head. She gives her hand to a woman standing in front of her. Against her knee leans a small boy. Between the two women, in the background, stands a bearded man leaning upon a staff. At the extreme left, in flat relief, is the head of a young woman; another stands above the chair of Phainippe, and the head and shoulders of a young girl appear at the back of her chair.

This relief is obviously the production of an ordinary workman, and betrays the common origin of these gravestones better than any other of our series. The figures are awkwardly jammed into the given space, and are rudely chiselled; but in spite of these facts, the composition has caught some of the spirit of the art of its time, which gives it a charm and renders it both interesting and instructive.

On the cornice above the relief are the names, Phainippe, Smikythion, Kleo.

184. Gravestone, with low relief, in the National Museum, Athens.

Of white marble. Date and place of discovery unknown. There are no restorations. PUBLISHED: Sybel, *Katalog*, No. 85; etc.

A woman seated on an armless chair, with footstool, holds her veil in her left hand, the right resting on her lap. Before her stands another woman, who with the left hand draws her mantle forward from her shoulder. On the cornice above is a honeysuckle pattern of a simple type. Below, the stone is left rough for insertion in a base.

185. Monument of Hegeso, daughter of Proxenos. On its original site outside the Dipylon Gate, Athens.

Of Pentelic marble. Found, 1870, on the spot where it now stands. There are no restorations. PUBLISHED: Mitchell, *History of Ancient Sculpture*, fig. 212, p. 502; C. Curtius in the *Archäolog. Zeitung*, 1871, pl. 42, pp. 19, 34; Sybel, *Katalog*, No. 3332; etc.

This is the most beautiful of these grave monuments that has yet been discovered. It dates from the beginning of the fourth century B. C., and might well be the work of a man who had been employed on the Parthenon frieze, to which it bears a great resemblance, both in the character of the relief, and the excellence of the execution. Hegeso, her head partially covered by a light, thin veil, sits on a chair of very graceful design, looking at an object she has taken from the casket held by her handmaid, who stands before her. The object, held in the raised right hand, was indicated wholly by color, as there is no trace of it in the relief. The subject is one of absolute simplicity, and is treated in that spirit. Delicacy and elegance characterize the execution of every detail; the management of the drapery and the contrast between that of the two figures, the one broken into small graceful folds, the other severely simple, are especially admirable.

Farther along on the same wall, —

186. Monument of Mynnion, in the National Museum, Athens.

Of white marble. **Found in Athens**, 1858. There are no restorations. PUBLISHED: Wolters' Friederichs, No. 1027; Sybel, *Katalog*, No. 99; etc.

Two women standing, the one on the left larger and apparently older than the other, whom she touches affectionately under the chin. Possibly mother and daughter. Date, the first part of the fourth century B. C.

187. Large Grave Monument, with figures in high relief. In the yard in front of the National Museum, Athens.

Of Pentelic marble. Found, 1861, outside the Dipylon Gate, Athens. There are no restorations. COLORS were noted at time of discovery as follows: Red on the background, blue on the garment of the seated figure. PUBLISHED: Wolters' Friederichs, No. 1050; Sybel, *Katalog*, No. 2614; etc.

On the left sits the principal figure of the group, a bearded old man. His garment falls from his right shoulder, leaving the breast bare. With his right hand, now missing, he grasped the hand of a younger man who stands before him. The latter is clad in a coat of mail, and holds in his left hand a scabbard. Between them, in the background, stands a matronly woman whose face expresses deep sorrow. The figures are all life-size.

In the conception of the group there is much dignity, but the execution is careless, many details being treated in a very sketchy manner.

On the adjoining wall, —

188. Grave Stele, in the Piræus Museum.

Of marble. PUBLISHED: Martinelli's *Catalogue*, No. 282.

On the stele is represented in low relief an amphora, only the upper half of which is preserved. The neck is very long and slender. On either side of it are the handles, in the form of long volutes, and into each handle is introduced the figure of a man dancing, with one hand raised. The shoulder of the vase is covered with scales, below which are other forms of decoration.

189-195.

SCULPTURES FROM THE MAUSOLEUM.

The Mausoleum was a tomb at Halikarnassos, on the southwest coast of Asia Minor, built by Artemisia, Queen of Karia, in memory of her husband and brother Mausolos, who died about 353 B. C. What little is known about the splendid edifice is described at length in Mrs. Mitchell's *History of Ancient Sculpture*, p. 453 ff., and need not be repeated here. Four of the leading sculptors of Athens were engaged upon its decorations, Skopas, Bryaxis, Leochares, and Timotheos, and though Artemisia died while it was yet incomplete, the sculptors finished the building for their own satisfaction. It was soon regarded as one of the seven wonders of the world, which position it maintained for ages. It was preserved in substantially its original condition until the twelfth century of our era, about which time it was destroyed, probably by earthquake. In 1402, the Knights of St. John took possession of the place, and used the fragments of the tomb for the construction of a castle. A great part of the beautiful frieze was used as building material, and remained walled into the fortress until 1846, when it was removed, through Viscount Stratford de Redcliffe, then British ambassador to Constantinople, and transferred to the British Museum. In excavations conducted by Mr. C. T. Newton, in 1857, the base of the structure and many architectural and sculptural fragments, including all those exhibited here, were discovered by him. The results of his discoveries were published in his *History of Discoveries at Halicarnassus, Cnidus and Branchidæ*, London, 1862; and the smaller *Travels and Discoveries in the Levant*, London, 1865. All the sculptures are now in the BRITISH MUSEUM.

189. **Statue of Mausolos.**

Of white marble. Put together from sixty-five fragments. RESTORATIONS: the left foot. PUBLISHED: Newton, *Travels and Discoveries*, II, p. 114 ff., pls. 6, 9, 10.

From Pliny's description of the Mausoleum we know it to have been **forty** cubits (about one hundred **and forty** feet) high, **its roof** pyramidal **and** surmounted by a colossal chariot drawn **by** four horses. As fragments **of** that chariot were found with those of this statue and **its** companion (No. 190), Newton supposed that the two **figures** stood in the chariot, an opinion still maintained, but **not** without opposition.

Mausolos, whose portrait this is generally admitted to be, is represented in middle life, and with a resemblance to Lucian's description of him, — "tall, handsome, and formidable in **war**." The hair rises from the forehead, and originally **fell** nearly to the shoulders. The face is short and broad, and indicative **of** both intelligence and firmness. The drapery is skilfully handled, but **not** in the broad, simple masses of earlier sculpture.

190. **Statue of Artemisia (?).**

Of white marble. RESTORATIONS: The face, forearms, the veil on both sides of **the** head, and the left foot. These restorations are not on the original, but on a cast of it restored by Mr. William W. Story, and placed at the side of the original in **the** British Museum. Mr. Story presented this copy of the restored figure to our Museum. PUBLISHED: Newton, *Travels and Discoveries*, II, p. 115 ff., and pl. 10; etc.

This statue is the companion of No. 189, with which it was found. Its identification is not so easily established as that of Mausolos, as it may represent Artemisia, or with equal probability, a tutelary goddess. The figure is matronly, the drapery carefully arranged to offer contrast to that of Mausolos, the mantle being longer and in simpler folds; and the hair is represented in stiff, symmetrical curls across the forehead, **an inartistic** method of treatment which may possibly be **explained** by the height at which it was to be seen, though **it compares** most unfavorably with the head of Mausolos.

In spite of their **colossal size** these two statues are less **impressive** and less **interesting** than those of Sophokles (132), Demosthenes **(138), and** others of that class, whose vitality and originality **they lack.** The attitude of both **figures** is constrained, **and in** their conception the artist **has** displayed neither **the vigor** nor the **grace** that characterize the best works **of the fourth century.**

191–195. **Selection from** the Frieze.

> Of a coarse white Asiatic marble. The blocks **in** this selection are those discovered by Newton, in 1857. There are no restorations. COLORS **were** noted at the time of discovery as follows: "the ground of the relief was a blue equal in intensity to ultramarine, the flesh a dun red, and the drapery and armour picked out with vermilion, and perhaps other colors." — Newton, *Travels*, II, p. 131. PUBLISHED: Newton, *Discoveries at Halicarnassus, etc.*, I, pls. 9, 10; *Travels and Discoveries*, II. p. 128 ff., pls. 13, 14, and No. 194, pl. 5.

With the exception of **No. 194, the blocks in this** selection form **a** continuous **subject, and should be** arranged in the following order, beginning from **the left: 193–192–195– 191.** At the **right** end of No. 193 may **be** seen the heel **of the first man of** 192, and at the end **of** this block the heel of **the horse, No.** 195, showing the connection between the blocks.

The subject **is** the **favorite one of the battle of** the Greeks and Amazons, **which is treated with** great spirit. As was stated above, **page 118, the** decorations of the Mausoleum were by four **of the leading** Athenian sculptors **of the** fourth century B. C., **and in the** treatment of this **frieze we** recognize the distinctively **Attic** style of that **period.** The proportions of **the** figures **are more** slender than in works of the fifth century (cf. **the** Phigaleian frieze, above these blocks), **and the execution** more delicate; but the composition **is not less easy or** graceful, and shows that the inventive **power of the** sculptors was still fresh.

196. Large Relief in the Villa Albani.

> Of Pentelic marble. Found about 1764 in Rome, in a vineyard belonging to the Duca di Caserta, near the Arch of Gallienus. RESTORATIONS: The nose of the standing figure, a piece in his left forearm, also a piece in the face and the right ear of the horse. PUBLISHED: Winckelmann, *Monumenti Inediti*, No. 62; etc.

Although this relief was found in Rome, it is unquestionably an original Greek work of the finest period of Attic sculpture, its date being probably not far from the year 400 B. C. In the type of the faces, which do not have the pathetic expression of the later sculptures, in the proportions of the figures, and in the character of the execution, the style of the Pheidian age and the influence of his school are evident. In shape and action the horse resembles closely the beautiful animals of the Parthenon frieze.

The character and object of this slab are difficult to determine, as its large size makes it unique among extant reliefs of its period. That it formed part of a frieze is unlikely, because the representation appears to end at the two sides of the block, and the subject is complete in itself. Its resemblance to the monument of Dexileos (No. 179) has led to the theory that it is, like that, a funeral monument, which is quite probable. It represents a warrior, who has leaped from his horse to deal a last blow at his enemy, who lies at his feet with one arm raised in supplication.

An unusual feature in relief-work of the period to which this belongs is the introduction of landscape effect in the background, such as the rocks at the left side of the slab.

197. Portion of the Amazon Sarcophagus, in the Cabinet of Antiquities, Vienna.

> Of white marble. Said to have been found in Greece. Formerly in the possession of the Fugger family. There are no restorations. PUBLISHED: Sacken, *Die antiken Skulpturen des k. k. Münz und Antiken-Cabinets*, pl. 2, 3. Wolters' Friederichs, No. 1822; etc.

This fragment is of importance because it belongs to one of the few genuine Greek sarcophagi that are known. The contrast which it offers to the Roman sarcophagi (of which Nos. 173, 176, and 198 are typical examples) is very striking, as regards both the quality of the execution and the character of the relief. The subject is the favorite battle of the Greeks and Amazons, which is continued in the same style of workmanship on all four sides of the sarcophagus. The sculptor may have copied his figures from some more important work, dating not earlier than the second half of the fourth century B. C. The slender proportions and the expression in the faces give the relief a general resemblance to the frieze of the Mausoleum (see Nos. 191–195), which is, however, of much better execution. As in all Greek battle scenes, the interest of the spectator is held by the indecisive nature of the contest. The number of disabled is the same on both sides, and the mastery of one Amazon over her opponent is balanced by the seizure of another by a Greek. The action of the figures is well distributed, and is spirited throughout.

198. Rape of the Daughters of Leukippos. Front of a Roman sarcophagus. In the Uffizi Gallery, Florence.

<small>Of Greek marble. Date of discovery unknown. Came into the possession of the Medici family 1584, and formerly in the Villa Medici, Rome. Nearly every figure in the relief has been extensively restored. PUBLISHED: Winckelmann, *Monumenti Inediti*, fig. 61; Dütschke, **Antike Bildwerke in** *Oberitalien*, Vol. III, p. 36, No. 74.</small>

The story illustrated in this relief is that of the rape of the daughters of Leukippos, a king of Messenia, by the Dioskouroi, Kastor and Polydeukes. Leukippos had two beautiful daughters, Phœbe and Hilæira, whom the Dioskouroi met in their wanderings, and, fascinated by their beauty, seized and carried them forcibly from their home and parents, slaying the two youths to whom they were betrothed, and afterwards married them. The details of the story are not sufficiently known to enable us to identify the different figures in the scene, except those in the two principal groups, by which the subject is identified.

This monument is of Roman origin, and belongs to the

class described under No. 173, p. 109. The reliefs have been so extensively restored that a judgment of the merit which the sculpture originally possessed is hardly possible. The figures are distributed with a symmetry suggestive of Greek design, and it is not unlikely that the relief may have been copied from some earlier and better work.

199. **Orpheus, Eurydike and Hermes.** Bas-relief in the Villa Albani, Rome.

<small>Of Pentelic marble. RESTORATIONS: Both feet of Orpheus, the right foot of Eurydike, right hand and half the forearm of Hermes. PUBLISHED: Zoega, *Bassirilievi della Villa Albani*, I, pl. xlii, p. 193 ff.; Wolters' Friederichs, No. 1198; etc.</small>

This relief represents the tragic moment in the story of Orpheus when he turns to look at Eurydike as she is led out of Hades. At the left is Hermes, the conductor of souls, who has accompanied Eurydike, and now takes her hand to lead her back. Affectionately and regretfully she places her hand upon the shoulder of Orpheus, who raises one hand to hers, while in the other he holds his lyre.

This is a most instructive example of the quietness of Greek art in its greatest epoch, to which allusion has been made in the introduction to the grave monuments, p. 112. Although the moment depicted is the most terrible in the lives of the two principal characters, there is a total absence of sensationalism in their attitude and expression. A calm resignation to fate characterizes all three figures, yet it will be noticed that this "frozen sorrow" appeals more directly and forcibly to the mind than the wildest manifestations of grief, because its truth and depth are undisturbed by emotional extravagance, which appeals to the senses rather than the intellect.

The purpose which this slab originally served is not known. Possibly it may have been part of a grave monument, as its subject has a sepulchral significance. There are two other copies of the same relief, one in the Museum of Naples, the other in the Louvre. All three are probably Roman replicas of a work of the Attic school, and their style indicates that the original dated not far from the year 400 B. C.

200. The Apoxyomenos. Statue in the **Vatican.**

Of bluish-white marble. Found by Canina in September, 1849, in Trastevere, Rome. RESTORATIONS: The fingers of the left hand. (This restoration, by Tenerani, was made in accordance with a misinterpretation of Pliny, N. H., xxxiv. 62. The die should be omitted.) PUBLISHED: Collignon, in Rayet's *Monuments de l'Art Antique*, II, pl. 55; E. Braun in the *Annali dell' Instituto*, 1850, p. **223** ff., etc. On the occupation in which he is engaged, see especially Kuppers, *Der Apoxyomenos des Lysippos*, Berlin, 1874.

This statue represents a Greek youth cleaning himself after the exercises of the palæstra. To keep the skin and muscles in fine condition it was the custom of Greek athletes to rub themselves thoroughly with olive-oil before they began to exercise, and also after bathing. As this would have prevented wrestlers from grasping and holding each other, they sprinkled fine sand over the oil. After the exercises, the athlete scraped from his body the oil, sand, and dust with an instrument called the strigil, which is represented in the left hand of the statue.

This is a fine copy of a famous statue by Lysippos, the greatest sculptor of the period following that of Skopas and Praxiteles. He was not of the Attic school, but a native of Sikyon, where he inherited the traditions of the art of Polykleitos (see Nos. 114 and 127). He was the contemporary and favorite sculptor of Alexander the Great.

The original of this statue was of bronze, and in the time of Pliny stood in the Baths of Agrippa at Rome, where it was such a favorite with the people that when the Emperor Tiberius carried it to his palace, leaving a copy in its place, they forced him by their clamor in the theatre to return it. So far as we are able to judge, this replica reproduces the original much better than is usual among Roman copies. It is an excellent illustration of the descriptions of Lysippos' style, which was marked by a most careful elaboration of details, and by the peculiar proportions of his figures, the heads of which were smaller, and the legs longer, than those of the works of his predecessors.

201. Head of Herakles, in the town of Dimitzana, Greece (midway between Tripolitza and Olympia).

Of grayish marble. Formerly in the village of Magula, near Sparta. There are no restorations. PUBLISHED: *Mittheilungen des Inst. in Athen*, 1878, p. 80, and 1879, p. 127, No. 3.

This is evidently an architectural decoration, of a late epoch, and served possibly as the key-stone of an arch. Herakles is represented as beardless, and wearing the lion-skin cap.

202. The Rondanini Medusa. Head in high relief, in the Glyptothek, Munich.

Of Parian marble. Formerly in the Palazzo Rondanini, Rome. In Munich since 1808. RESTORATIONS: The block to which the head is affixed, the end of the nose, the heads of the serpents above the forehead, and pieces in the hair and serpents. PUBLISHED: Brunn, *Beschreibung der Glyptothek*, p. 161, No. 128; Wolters' Friederichs, No. 1597; etc.

In contrast to the early type of the Gorgon, of which there is an example in one of the metopes from Selinus (First Room, No. 26), and which lasted at least until the second half of the fourth century B. C., this mask shows the ideal of later Greek art, in which Medusa was conceived not as a monster who created terror by her ugliness, but a being possessed of beauty, whose dread power came from her coldness and want of all feeling or compassion. She is therefore represented as beautiful, but with an element of cruelty in her beauty that shows itself most of all in the coarse, sensual mouth, which is partly open, and displays the upper teeth.

The date at which this type originated cannot be determined with exactness, though it was probably not earlier than the end of the fourth century B. C. The relief itself is of Roman workmanship.

203. Marble Vase, in the Villa Albani.

PUBLISHED: Zoega, *Bassirilievi della Villa Albani*, II, pl. lxxxiv, p. 177 ff.; Wolters' Friederichs, No. 2116.

Around the body of the vase are represented six Mænads in long flowing drapery, in various attitudes of the Bacchic dance. They carry thyrsi, or Bacchic staves, wreaths, sacrificial animals and knives.

204. Square Pedestal, or Altar. In the Augusteum at Dresden.

<small>Of Parian marble. Formerly in the Chigi collection, in the Palazzo Odelscalchi, Rome. Purchased by Augustus II. of Saxony, and carried to Dresden, 1728. PUBLISHED: Becker's *Augusteum*, pls. 33, 34; Hettner, *Bildwerke der kgl. Antikensammlung zu Dresden*, 1881, No. 194, p. 105.</small>

This was probably the pedestal of a candelabrum, intended to be placed against a wall, as one side is not sculptured. On each of the other three sides are niches for images; and at the base, a griffon projects at each corner, serving as a support for some small figure or object, all four of which have disappeared. The decoration is in the over-wrought style of the Roman Empire.

205. Sleeping Satyr, called the **Barberini Faun.** Statue in the Glyptothek, Munich.

<small>Of Parian marble. Found in the time of Urban VIII. (Barberini, 1623–1644), buried in the moat of the Castle of S. Angelo (the Mausoleum of Hadrian). Until 1813 in the possession of the Barberini family. Then acquired by Ludwig I. of Bavaria, at that time Crown Prince, and placed in Munich, 1820. RESTORATIONS: The end of the nose, the left forearm, the right elbow and fingers of the right hand, the entire right leg, part of the left from the middle of the thigh; also part of the animal's skin and of the back of the seat. PUBLISHED: Clarac, *Musée de Sculpture*, pl. 710 A, No. 1723; Brunn, *Beschreibung der Glyptothek*, No. 95, p. 120; etc.</small>

A Satyr is represented sleeping off the effects of a revel, sprawled over a rock on which he has laid his pantherskin. The cause of his heavy slumber is suggested by the Bacchic wreath on his head, and more forcibly by the ungraceful but characteristic attitude in which he reposes.

The contrast between this Satyr and those of the Praxitelean type (see in Second Greek Room, No. 82) is very striking. The aim of Praxiteles and his school was to idealize the satyric nature, representing only its most attractive, poetic side, and reducing its animal qualities to the least possible suggestion, by carefully concealing the tail and pointed ears. Here, on the contrary, the art is thoroughly realistic. The Greek artist could not be brutal, and that phase of realism is therefore avoided; but in the conception of this Satyr, naturalism is the chief feature. This appears first of all in the posture of the figure, and is worked out even more carefully in the sensual, half-savage face. The expression of the open mouth is strongly suggestive of sonorous breathing.

As an example of naturalistic Greek sculpture, this work ranks very high. The apparent ease with which the sculptor has carried out his conception, and the rugged freedom of the execution, indicate that it is an original Greek statue, not a copy, its probable date being the early part of the Hellenistic epoch (B. C. 332–150).

206. Head of Hypnos, of bronze, in the British Museum.

Found near Perugia, 1855. PUBLISHED: Brunn, in the *Monumenti dell' Instituto*, VIII, pl. 59, and *Annali*, 1868, p. 351 ff.; Murray's *History of Greek Sculpture*, II, pl. xxi, p. 259; etc.

This exquisite head of the god of sleep, wearing the wings of the night-hawk, is the only surviving fragment of a statue of which several copies, in bronze and marble, exist. The best of these, a marble statue in Madrid, shows that he was bending far forward, with one arm outstretched as though pouring slumber over some person upon whom he is looking down. The relief on a sarcophagus in Pisa (published in the *Archäol. Zeitung*, 1862, pl. 159, fig. 1), groups a similar figure of Hypnos with the sleeping Endymion, and possibly the statue to which this head belonged may have been a member of such a group.

This is probably a work of the fourth century B. C., of the school of Praxiteles.

207. Round Altar, of marble, in the Louvre.

Discovered on the site of the ancient Gabii about 1792. Formerly in the Borghese collection, Rome. RESTORATIONS (beginning with the Bacchante carrying the vase and plate of fruit as No. 1): "No. 1, the whole figure with the exception of the left foot; No. 2, almost the whole figure, except the two legs, the upper part and paws of the panther-skin, and the end of one of the flutes; No. 3, a piece in the middle of the drapery; No. 4, a few insignificant bits; No. 5, almost the whole dancer, except the left leg and arm, and part of the drapery;

No. 6, the legs" (Fröhner). PUBLISHED : Clarac, *Musée de Sculpture*, pl. 140, No. 140, and pl. 258, No. 18 ; Fröhner, *Sculpture Antique du Louvre*, No. 3.

This is evidently an altar consecrated to Dionysos, and its decoration is the familiar dance of Satyrs and Bacchantes. The composition is graceful and pretty, and like all Greek Bacchic reliefs, gives full expression to the merriment of its subject. The figures have been largely restored, but what remains of the original parts enables us to see that the restorations are carefully and intelligently done.

208. The Borghese Warrior. Marble statue in the Louvre.

Found during the pontificate of Paul V., Borghese (1605–1621), at Capo d' Anzo, the ancient Antium. Formerly in the Villa Borghese, Rome, whence it was carried to Paris, 1808. RESTORATIONS : The right arm from just below the shoulder, and the right ear. PUBLISHED : Rayet, *Monuments de l' Art Antique*, II, pls. 64, 65 ; Bouillon, *Musée des Antiques*, II, pl. 16 ; Wolters' Friederichs, No. 1425 ; etc.

The action of this figure has been variously interpreted, but most probably the statue represents a warrior in a position of combined defence and attack, in close combat with an opponent above him, perhaps a horseman or Amazon. The tension of the muscles shows the posture to be that of an instant only. With his body bent forward to the utmost extent, and firmly supported on the right leg, he stretches out his left arm to receive on his shield the blow of a sword or axe directed from above ; while with his own weapon clutched in his right hand; and the left leg just about to recover its spent force, he is ready to swing about and thrust the moment his shield is struck. The contracted brow and eager, weary face indicate that the combat has been long and fatiguing, and has now reached its most desperate point.

This explanation of the motive is the most generally accepted, and by far the most satisfactory of the many that have been offered.

At the time of its discovery the statue was thought to represent a gladiator, and thus the name of the "Borghese

Gladiator" became attached to it, nothwithstanding its origin in a Greek school of art, in which gladiators were unknown. Recently M. Rayet (cited above) has attempted to revive an old theory that the subject represented is a runner in the armed race (Hoplitodromos) just reaching the goal. In spite of the ingenious arguments by which this theory is supported, the figure cannot be said to have either the character or the action of a racer.

Like the "Barberini Faun" (No. 205), this statue belongs to the epoch when naturalism had taken the place of ideality in the tendency of Greek art, and is therefore a characteristic example of the Hellenistic period (see p. 131.) Not only is the greatest attention given to the expression of the face, about which the earlier sculptors were indifferent, but the broad simplicity which characterizes the modelling of athlete statues of the fifth and fourth centuries is here replaced by a most elaborate display of anatomical knowledge. As an illustration of the muscular action of the human figure the work is masterly, yet this technical skill and knowledge do not compensate for the greater intellectual power which the earlier sculptures exhibit.

The inscription on the tree records the name of Agasias, son of Dositheos, of Ephesos, as the sculptor. He belonged to a family of Ephesian sculptors, and lived probably during the last half of the second century B. C.

209. Marble Vase, in the Museum of Naples (?).

The body of the vase is decorated with curved flutings, on which are two Bacchic groups in relief, each of three figures. That on the front represents Dionysos walking towards the right, followed by two nymphs. He is bearded, and clothed in a long mantle. In his right hand he holds a wine-cup (*kantharos*), and in the left a thyrsos. The nymphs join hands, and the foremost holds in one hand a corner of the god's mantle.

On the back Dionysos is also represented, followed by two nymphs. The god is clothed in a Thracian costume, with a large hat, tight-fitting chiton, and high boots. One of the nymphs following carries flowers in her mantle; the other is tightly wrapped in her garments.

Of the casts in this room the following numbers were purchased from the bequest of Charles Sumner: Nos. **150, 151, 154, 158, 160, 161, 165–171,** 174, 175, **198, 199, 202–204, 209.**

Nos. **156, 200,** 205, are the property of the Boston Athenæum.

Nos. 153, **197,** are the property of the Institute of Technology.

No. 190 **was presented to the** Museum **by Mr.** William W. Story.

FIFTH GREEK, OR HELLENISTIC, ROOM.

HELLENISTIC ART.

The casts in the first four rooms illustrate the progress of Greek sculpture from its rude beginnings through its efforts first to represent the human figure, then to use that figure as the embodiment of an idea. We have followed the art through the age of perfection, the age in which the noblest ideals were created, and then through the period in which refinement more than sublimity was the sculptor's aim. Now we come to the last epoch of Greek sculpture, — an epoch created under the influence of Alexander the Great, and lasting from his death, B. C. 332, to the rise of the Roman dominion in Greece, 146 B. C. This, known as the Hellenistic epoch (in distinction to the pure Hellenic) presents a series of characteristics unknown in earlier art, which are to be accounted for by the political and social conditions of the age.

With the triumph of Philip of Macedon the political greatness of Athens fell. At the same time, and probably for the same reasons, her intellectual, and especially her artistic, activity declined. The schools of Skopas and Praxiteles carried out the ideas of these masters, but there was no great Athenian sculptor to succeed them. Yet the seed which Athens had sown spread over the whole ancient world. Alexander, in his eastern conquests, carried the language and the influence of Athenian civilization through the East, and both in his time and after his death schools of art sprang up in Asia Minor and in Egypt, which looked to Athens and her works for their inspiration.

Sculpture, together with the other arts, having become

the servant of the sovereign rather than the state, was put to service she had never known before. Alexander called **upon** every form of art for the display **of his** own magnificence. His example **was** followed **in a** constantly increasing degree by his successors, who erected magnificent temples, altars and monuments, in all of which the personal element was more conspicuous than that of adaptability to the purpose for which the works were intended; and the desire for display more apparent than the sentiments of religion and patriotism, which had been the inspiration of earlier art. Under such conditions sculpture naturally lost its old ideals. The creative power of sculptors, though **not** actually crushed, sank almost to insignificance. In **the** numerous statues and reliefs of this period which are now **known,** one of the most striking features is the absence **of** new types. In representations of divinities the types of the fifth and fourth centuries were adapted to the needs of the time (for instance the Otricoli Zeus, No. 134), but so far as we know no new ideal was created to replace **them.** This lack of originality was recompensed to a certain extent by extraordinary skill in technique. The Hellenistic was pre-eminently a scientific age. Aristotle as well as Pheidias had left his heritage, and the Hellenistic sculptors show more of the academic element in their works than any who preceded them. There can be little doubt that anatomy, of which the sculptors of the Hellenic age knew no more than may be studied from **a** well-developed athlete in action, was thoroughly familiar **to** the sculptors of **the** Borghese Warrior (No. 208) **and** the Laokoön (No. 250).

The chief characteristics, then, of the sculpture **of** the Hellenistic age, illustrated in this room, and in Nos. **205 and** 208 of the Fourth Room, may be summed up as a love of display and sensationalism, an absence of creative power, and marvellous technical perfection. The principal schools of the epoch were those of Pergamon, Alexandria, and Rhodes.

215. The Apollo Belvedere. **Statue in the** Vatican.

Of white (Carrara?) marble. Found near **the** end of the 15th cen**tury** at Capo d' Anzo (Antium). Bought by Julius II., then

Cardinal, and placed in his apartment in the Palazzo Colonna. When he became Pope (1503), removed it to the Belvedere of the Vatican. RESTORATIONS: By Montorsoli, the left hand and wrist, and the fingers of the right hand. PUBLISHED: Visconti, *Museo Pio Clem.*, I, pl. 14; Müller-Wieseler, *Denkmäler d. alten Kunst*, II, pl. xi, No 124; Mitchell, *History of Ancient Sculpture*, p. 621 ff ; etc.

As restored by Montorsoli, this statue represents Apollo watching the effect of an arrow just discharged, the stump in the left hand suggesting his bow. This restoration suits the attitude and character of the figure so well that probably it would never have been questioned but for the existence of a small ancient bronze copy of the same figure in the Stroganoff collection, St. Petersburg, of which the left hand is original. This, instead of holding a bow, grasps the folds of some soft material, only a fragment of which remains. The object thus held is believed by many to have been an ægis, and according to their theory, both statuette and statue represented Apollo repelling his enemies by holding before them the terrible shield of his father Zeus, on which was the Medusa head that turned beholders into stone. Many eminent authorities have adopted this theory, which nevertheless remains a matter of conjecture. The object in the hand of the statuette has never been proved an ægis, and may have been nothing more than the end of the cloak, as has been suggested. Moreover, for technical reasons it is difficult to believe that the outstretched arm of the statue could have sustained the weight of such a mass. That Apollo was represented in his character of archer is indicated by the quiver strap across the breast; and until some more incontestable restoration than that of the ægis is proposed, it is wiser to retain the present.

This statue is probably a replica of a bronze original of the Hellenistic epoch. The studied elegance of the form, the theatrical pose, the unnaturally slender proportions, all of which show a striving for effect, are characteristic of the third and second centuries B. C., and the head shows the remodelling, according to the taste of that time, of an older type of considerable power and beauty. The face expresses the same haughty scorn that is indicated in the

Apollo of the Zeus Temple at Olympia (Second Room, No. 59). Comparison between these two statues of the same divinity is extremely instructive, as illustrating the wide difference between early and late sculptors in their aims and aspirations. The former struggled to give expression to great thoughts **in a material** over which they had not gained complete **mastery, while the** latter endeavored to make **up** in elegance **of execution** what they lacked in power **or** originality **of** conception.

216. Bacchic Relief, in the British Museum.

Of marble. Found by Gavin Hamilton, 1776, on the site of the ancient Gabii. Formerly in the Towneley collection. PUBLISHED: *Ancient Marbles in the Brit. Mus*, pt. II, pl. 12; Ellis, *Towneley Gallery*, II, p. 109.

This relief forms part of a Bacchic procession, such as are frequently represented in later Greek sculpture. A Bacchante in the wild frenzy of the Bacchic dance, playing upon **a** *tympanum*, leads two Satyrs, one of whom plays the double flute, the other **dances,** swinging in **his** right hand a thyrsos and on his left arm **his** nebris, or panther-skin. At his side walks a panther.

The work itself is of Roman execution, probably of the early years of the Empire, but is copied from an earlier relief, which undoubtedly originated in the Hellenistic epoch, probably soon after its beginning.

217. Head from Pergamon, in the Berlin Museum.

Of Parian marble. **Found** among the ruins of the great altar, during the German excavations, in the spring of 1880. There **are no** restorations. PUBLISHED: *Zeitschrift für bildende Kunst*, 1880, XV, p. 161 ff.; Murray, *History of Greek Sculpture*, II, pl. xxxii, No. 2; etc.

This **is** one of the most beautiful fragments of sculpture discovered **at** Pergamon. It is supposed to have belonged to **a** statue of Aphrodite, but of the figure nothing has been found. A resemblance has been traced between this head and that of the Venus of Melos as regards the style of treatment. This may be observed especially in the two faces, though the hair of the Pergamon head is treated in larger, heavier masses than that of the Venus of Melos,—an indication of a later origin.

If this head is a work of the Pergamenian school, it is distinguished from the other works of that school with which we are familiar by the extreme softness with which the flesh is modelled. The figures in the relief from the great altar (No. 247), and the statue of the Dying Gaul (No. **261**), which are characteristic examples of the Pergamenian style, exhibit a realism in treatment entirely lacking in this head, which, in both its refinement and its ideality, resembles the Athenian works of the fourth century B. C.

218. The Artemis of Versailles (called "Diane à la Biche"), in the Louvre.

Statue of Parian **marble**. Date of discovery not known. Was carried from **Rome** to the chateau of Meudon, France, in the first half of the 16th century. Then moved to Fontainebleau, afterwards to Paris, and from Paris carried to Versailles by Louis XIV., where it remained until the French Revolution, and was finally placed in the Louvre, February 16, 798 (18 pluviôse, an VI). RESTORATIONS: The nose, both ears, a piece of the neck, the right hand and half the forearm, the left hand and arm as far as the deltoid, the end of the large toe of left foot, the right foot and upper part of the leg, the two ends of the quiver, and small pieces in hair, drapery, etc. Of the hind, the nostrils, ears, horns (except the base), and the greater part of the legs. (Fröhner.) PUBLISHED: Clarac, *Musée de Sculpture*, pl. 284, No. 1202; Bouillon, *Musée des Antiques*, I, pl. **20**; Fröhner, *Sculpture Antique du Louvre*, No. 98; etc.

Artemis is represented as a huntress, wearing a short chiton like those of the Amazons, around which is wound her chlamys, or cloak, as a sort of sash. The animation of both face and figure shows that she is in the full movement of the chase, and just about to draw an arrow from her quiver. At her side leaps a stag or horned hind, which some writers have supposed to be the animal pursued by Herakles on Mt. Keryneia, though more probably it is introduced simply as an attribute of Artemis, without reference to any especial myth.

This statue bears a striking resemblance to the Apollo Belvedere (No. 215), not only in the elegance of the execution and the unusually long and slender proportions, but even in details, such as the pattern of the sandals, and the family likeness in the faces, which is so strong as to render it most probable that the originals of the two statues were works of the same sculptor. The attempt has been made (see Overbeck, *Plastik*, II, 317 ff.) to identify those originals with a group erected at Delphi to commemorate the repulse of the barbarian invaders at that place, 279 B. C. This attempt is unwarrantable, however, because beyond the fact that the date of that group corresponds with the period in which these statues may possibly have originated, there is no ground for establishing the identity.

The type of Artemis which represents her as a huntress, in the Amazon costume, dates as far back as the middle of the fifth century B. C., but was modified with the successive changes of style of that and the following centuries, and is shown here in one of its latest forms. This variety of the type does not date earlier than the third or second century B. C.

219 and 220. Two Figures from the Group of Attalos.

Of marble. No. **219**, in the Museum of Naples. Formerly in Rome, in the Farnese collection. RESTORATIONS: Both arms, the right leg from knee down, and part of the scimitar. PUBLISHED: *Monumenti dell' Inst.*, IX, pl. xxi, No. **7**; Clarac, *Musée de Sculpture*, pl. 871, No. 2217; etc.

No. **220**, in the Museum of the Marciana, Venice. Formerly in Rome, in the possession of a Cardinal Grimani, who bequeathed it to the Republic of Venice, 1523. RESTORATIONS: The right arm and some of the toes of the right foot. PUBLISHED: *Monumenti*, IX, pl. xix, No. 2; Clarac, *Musée*, pl. 868, No. 2211.

Both figures and the rest of the group are discussed by BRUNN in the *Annali dell' Inst.*, 1870, pp. 292-323.

Attalos I., King of Pergamon (B. C. 241-197), dedicated on the Akropolis of Athens four groups of statues, in commemoration of his victories over the Gauls of Mysia. These groups were erected on the southern wall of the Akropolis, and represented the battles respectively of the Gods and Giants, the Greeks and Amazons, the Greeks and Persians at Marathon, and Attalos and the Gauls.

To Professor Brunn belongs the credit of identifying with these groups a number of small statues now scattered among various museums of Europe, but all traceable to Rome. Although the evidence in favor of this identification is circumstantial, it is so strong as to amount almost to demonstration. Of those figures, Nos. 219 and 220 are characteristic specimens. The former is evidently from the group representing the battle of Marathon, as the costume, especially the long trousers (*anaxirides*) and the scimitar, are distinctively Persian. No. 220 is probably from the group of the Gauls, the face being of barbaric type.

The execution of these figures is thoroughly characteristic of the Hellenistic style of sculpture, and particularly of the Pergamenian school, as may be seen by comparison with the relief from the great altar of Pergamon, No. 247. The action of the bodies is emphasized by the expression of the faces, in which the pathetic element is developed to its greatest extent. The prominence given to representation of the muscles is another point of resemblance to the figures of the altar and the sculptures of that epoch generally.

Whether these are the original statues erected by Attalos, or copies of them, must, of course, remain a question. The modelling shows a free and vigorous handling, which gives considerable ground for the former opinion, which is held by Brunn and others. If this be correct, the year 200 B. C. may be assumed as the date of these figures, as the dedication of the groups on the Akropolis took place about that time.

221. **Small Herma of Herakles**, in private possession in Sparta.

> Of red (*rosso antico*) marble. There are no restorations. Published in the *Mittheilungen d. Inst. in Athen*, II, p. 343, No. 83.

A small, decorative piece of sculpture of a late epoch, representing Herakles, bearded, his shoulders wrapped in a lion's skin.

222. The Torso of the Belvedere, in the Belvedere of the Vatican.

> Of marble. Found probably in the Campo del Fiore, a Roman street on the site of the Theatre of Pompey, during the pontificate of Julius II. (1503-1513). There are no restorations.
> PUBLISHED: Visconti, *Museo Pio Clem.*, II, pl. x, p. 66 ff.; Collignon in Rayet's *Monuments de l'Art Antique*, II, pl. 63.

This magnificent fragment represents Herakles, distinguished by his powerful frame and the lion's skin on which he sits, resting upon a rocky seat. The right leg was bent so that the foot rested against the rock, on which a trace of it is still observable. The left leg was extended. In what manner the arms were occupied, there is almost nothing to show. Evidently the action of the figure was directed towards the left, and the right arm was extended in that direction, more than which is not determinable. Lysippos is said to have made, for Alexander the Great, a small bronze statuette of Herakles in a similar position. According to the descriptions of that statuette, the hero was seated upon a rock that was almost hidden by the lion's skin. In his right hand he held a wine-cup, while the left grasped his club, the head being turned somewhat upwards. It is often supposed that the Torso may be an enlarged copy of that bronze.

This figure was one of the chief promoters of sculpture during the Renaissance. Michelangiolo regarded it with enthusiastic admiration, and declared himself its pupil. Its influence has not declined with the development of modern knowledge of Greek art, as it still retains its place among the grandest statues of Rome. The inscription on the pedestal states it to be the work of Apollonios son of Nestor, of Athens, an otherwise unknown sculptor, whom the character of the inscription shows to have lived during the first century B. C., about the time of Sulla. Although the execution possesses much of the quality of original work, it is scarcely credible that such a sublime conception should have been created at so late an epoch. More probably the work of Apollonios is a very skilful copy of an Athenian statue of a much earlier period. It will be noticed that the modelling of the muscles is much less elaborate than in the Pergamenian and other Hellenistic sculptures, and has more resemblance to the treatment of the Parthenon statues, though possibly more refined. In both the treatment and the majestic spirit of the conception, the influence of the Pheidian school is strongly felt. It is, therefore, very probable that the original of the figure was made even before the epoch of Lysippos, to which it is usually assigned, and its date may have been as early as the end of the fifth, or beginning of the fourth, century B. C.

223. Fragment of a Statuette, in the Museum at Sparta.

Of marble. There are no restorations. PUBLISHED: *Mittheilungen d. Inst. in Athen*, II, p. 341, No. 79.

The powerful muscles of this little figure indicate that it represents Herakles, although there are no other attributes by which to identify it. The execution has the average character of works of a late Greek period.

224. Small Torso of Herakles, in the Museum at Sparta.

Of marble resembling Pentelic. There are no restorations. PUBLISHED: *Mittheilungen d. Inst. in Athen*, II, p. 341, No. 80; *Bulletino dell' Inst.*, 1873, p. 184 (Hirschfeld).

The attitude and proportions of this fragment are similar to those of the Belvedere Torso, though the arms and shoulders are turned in the opposite direction. The modelling is careful and delicate, and displays considerable skill.

225. Torso of Marsyas, in the possession of Mrs. Hiland, at Concord, N. H.

Of red marble (*pavonazetto*). Found at Alexandria, 1879, by Lt. Com. Gorringe in clearing the foundation of the obelisk known as "Cleopatra's Needle," preparatory to its removal to New York. Brought to America with the obelisk, 1880, and bequeathed to its present owner by Lt. Com. Gorringe at his death, in 1885. There are no restorations, and the figure is unpublished. (The site of the discovery is shown in Gorringe's *Egyptian Obelisks*, N. Y., 1882, pl. viii, and the figure is one of the "several fragments of statuary" referred to on p. 12.) Ht. of the fragment, M. 0.548.

The subject of this little torso, which is just half life-size, has been made familiar by a considerable number of larger and more complete copies of the same original, existing in various European collections. It is the Satyr Marsyas bound and hung by his hands to a tree, about to be flayed by Apollo, — the penalty of his having ventured to engage in musical competition with the god.

Enough of this fragment remains to show the beginning of the left arm, the thighs, and the lower end of the beard, which rested against the breast. Although the outlines of the loins and breasts are indicated in a somewhat hard and mechanical manner, the modelling is generally good, and shows the realistic characteristics of the Hellenistic age. The realism of the figure is heightened by the dull red color of the marble.

This cast was presented to the Museum by the late Lt. Com. Gorringe.

226. Zeus or Asklepios, Head of Parian marble, in the British Museum.

Found, 1828, in the island of Melos. Afterwards in the collection of the Duc de Blacas. There are no restorations. PUBLISHED: Collignon, in Rayet's *Monuments de l'Art Antique*, I, pl. 42; Mitchell, *Hist. of Anc. Sculpture, Selections*, pl. XIII; Overbeck, *Kunstmythologie*, vol. II (Zeus), p. 88, Atlas, pl. II, Nos. 11 and 12; etc.

The fact that this head was discovered among the ruins of a sanctuary of Asklepios, gave rise to the opinion that it represented that divinity, although it has more affinity with the types of Zeus. The differences between the types of these two gods have been pointed out in connection with a head in the British Museum (Third Room, No. 137), from which it will be seen that this is more probably a head of Zeus. Less stern than the Otricoli Zeus (Third Room, No. 134), the face is equally majestic, and suggests the tremendous power that belongs to the father of gods and men. The projecting brow, the deep, sharp angle at which the eyes are set, the dignity of the mouth, and the thick heavy masses of hair are all peculiarly characteristic of Zeus.

This is probably a work of the Hellenistic epoch; it is certainly not older than the fourth century B. C.

227 and 228. Terra-cotta Reliefs, formerly in the Campana collection.

> PUBLISHED in the *Museo Campana*, No. 227, pl. LX; No. 228, pl. LXI.

These two reliefs are from an architectural decoration, probably a frieze, the subject of which is the marriage of Peleus and Thetis. In No. 227 Peleus receives his bride, who comes to him heavily veiled and draped, according to Greek custom, attended by a companion. No. 228 represents Herakles and one of the Hours or Seasons, bringing gifts. Herakles bears a bullock on his shoulders, and his companion carries in her left hand a staff from which are suspended a hare and a brace of birds. In the right hand she carries a pig. These reliefs belong to a very large class of terra-cottas found principally in Rome, and probably the products of the early Empire, during which they served as decorations in the houses of the wealthy. As in this case, the reliefs of this class usually show great skill in treatment, and bear the unmistakable stamp of Greek workmanship. They may therefore be presumed to be the work of Greek artisans in Rome.

229. Votive Relief, in the British Museum.

> Of marble. Formerly in the possession of Cavaceppi (about 1768), later in that of the Duke of Bedford, and presented by him to Mr. Towneley in 1805, with whose collection it passed to the British Museum. RESTORATIONS: Slight and unimportant. PUBLISHED: *Ancient Marbles in Brit. Mus.*, pt. II, pl. 5; *Guide to Græco-Rom. Sculptures in Brit. Mus.*, pt. I, No. 200; etc.

The slight remains of an inscription on the base of this relief show that it was dedicated to Apollo, who is represented at the right sitting upon the *omphalos*, a stone which marked Delphi as the centre of the world, his right hand raised and holding some object. In the centre stand two females, whose size indicates that they are goddesses, and therefore probably Leto and Artemis, the mother and sister of Apollo. At the left are three mortals, probably father and two sons, who approach the divinities, and doubtless represent the family of the dedicator. Each wears a coat of mail under his cloak.

230 and 231. Dionysos received by Ikarios. Two marble reliefs.

> No. 230 in the Museum at Naples. From Capri. RESTORATIONS: The head of the last figure on the right. PUBLISHED: *Guida del Museo Nazionale di Napoli*, 1884, No. 6713.
> No. 231 in the British Museum. First published by Lafreri, 1549. Placed by Sixtus V. in the Villa Montalto, now Grazioli; later in the Towneley collection, with which it passed to the British Museum. RESTORATIONS: The left arm and top of head, including the wreath, of Silenos; the head and right arm of the Satyr following him, the head, upper part of body and part of the drapery of the last figure at the right, and part of the column under the herma at the left. Besides these restorations, there has **been** much retouching of the whole. On the couch was a female figure which has disappeared, and her drapery has been worked over to form part of that of Ikarios. The last Satyr to the right supported a Bacchante in his arms, traces of whom are visible. PUBLISHED: *Ancient Marbles in the Brit. Mus.*, II, **pl.** 4; *Guide to Græco-Roman Sculptures*, pt. I, No. 176; etc.

The name here given to these reliefs is that by which they are generally known, although their interpretation is a matter of dispute. Ikarios was a mythical Athenian, who, according to tradition, received Dionysos with hospitality on the god's **first** visit to **Attika.** In return for this reception Dionysos initiated him into the secrets of wine making. Whether the reliefs, of which these two are but examples of a numerous class, illustrate this event, or are merely a form of votive tablet to Dionysos, is difficult to determine. At all events, the scene represents the reception of Dionysos by a mortal. In the background is a house, separated by a high wall from a court in which the action takes place. On a couch covered with cushions and rugs recline **a** man and a woman (in No. 231 the latter **has** been erased, as noted above). Before them is a table, on which are a kantharos, or wine-cup, and sundry articles of food. The man, his right arm extended, turns his head as though **in** surprise towards the gate, where stands Dionysos, bearded, clothed in **a long** mantle, and leaning, as though heavy with wine, upon **a small** Satyr who supports him from behind, while another removes his sandal. Following Dionysos through the gateway comes a jolly Bacchic group: first a Satyr, dancing, with a long thyrsos in his arm, **next a** drunken Silenos playing the double flute, then a second Satyr with right arm upraised, and finally a Bacchante supported by a Satyr (in No. 231 the Bacchante has disappeared, though traces of her drapery worked over into that of the Satyr are apparent). In their main features these two reliefs correspond perfectly, but there are some slight differences in detail; as for example, in No. 231 the Satyr decorating the house with flowers, the trees and pillar in the background, and the masks on the footstool at the left, none of which appear in No. 230.

Whether the originals of this class of reliefs had a votive significance or were merely *genre* representations, it is probable that the considerable number now extant, in marble and terra-cotta, served a decorative purpose only. Their style is that of the Hellenistic epoch, but it is doubtful whether the works themselves are earlier than the Roman Empire.

232. Bacchic Scene. Relief in the Museum at Naples.

> Of marble. Formerly in the Palazzo Farnese, Rome. There are no restorations. PUBLISHED: *Museo Borbonico*, III, pl. xl; Winckelmann, *Monumenti Inediti*, part I, head-piece of the *Indicazione*.

Dionysos is escorted by his companions through a grove, to the music of pipes and cymbals. In the centre is the god, represented as youthful, heavy with wine, his arm about the shoulder of a supporting Satyr. Both of them carry thyrsi. Before them go a Satyr carrying a large krater of wine, and a Bacchante playing the cymbals high above her head. Behind follows another playing the double pipe. Between Dionysos and his supporter is a panther, and on either side of them a small Satyr. This is a decorative work of a common type, the origin of which is not earlier than the Hellenistic epoch.

233. Menander, seated statue in the Vatican.

> Of Pentelic (?) marble. Found during the pontificate of Sixtus V. (1585–1590), near the church of S. Lorenzo in Panisperna, on the Viminal, Rome, and placed in the Villa Montalto, now Grazioli. Purchased by Pius VI., and removed to the Vatican. RESTORATIONS: The left hand, with the scroll. PUBLISHED: Visconti, *Museo Pio Clem.*, III, pl. xv, p. 65 ff.; Gerhard in the *Beschreibung der Stadt Rom*, II 2, p. 169; etc.

This statue was established as a portrait of Menander by Visconti, who pointed out its resemblance to a small head inscribed with the poet's name, and thereby disposed of the popular tradition that it represented the Roman general Marius. Pausanias, in his description of the Dionysiac Theatre in Athens (I, 21, 1), mentions a statue of Menander which he saw there, and it has often been supposed that the statue in the Vatican might be the very one referred to; but this is impossible, because the pedestal of the statue seen by Pausanias was discovered some years ago in its original position, with the name Menander upon it, and is too small for the base of this figure.

While it cannot, therefore, be the original statue erected to the poet's honor in the place where his plays were produced, this is one of the finest examples of Greek portrait-sculpture that survive, especially on account of the marvellous ease and naturalness of the pose. The manner in which energy and force of character are made to manifest themselves even in this attitude of repose, is remarkable. The head is modelled with great power, and an especial regard for individuality of expression, while the figure is treated rather carelessly as to details.

Menander died in 291 B. C., at the age of fifty-two, and this portrait evidently represents him in the last years of his life. It is therefore a work of the Hellenistic epoch, in which portraiture was a favorite theme among sculptors, doubtless because of the opportunity it afforded for the display of virtuosity in the representation of individual traits and distinctions. The contrast between this style of portraiture and the more ideal style of the preceding epoch may be studied by comparing this statue with that of **Sophokles** (Third Room, No. 132).

234. Crouching Aphrodite, statue in the Vatican.

Of Carrara marble. Found, 1775, on the Salone estate, at Prato Bagnato, on the Via Prænestina, about six miles from Tivoli. Bought by Pius VI., who placed it in the Vatican. RESTORATIONS: The hair, right hand, fingers of left hand, fore half of right foot, and first two toes of left. Also the greater part of base. PUBLISHED: Visconti, *Museo Pio Clem.*, I, pl. x, p. 58 ff.; Clarac, *Musée de Sculpture*, pl. 629, No. 1414; etc.

Aphrodite is here represented in the style of late Greek art, which used the name of the goddess merely as an excuse for displaying the nude female form in a variety of graceful poses. Of religious significance, or of the nobler ideal of Aphrodite, as embodied in the "Venus of Melos" (Third Room, No. 140), there is no suggestion. The figure is simply that of a pretty woman bathing, her occupation being indicated by the waves on the base, and the hydria (water-jar) on which she rests.

There are many extant replicas of this statue, all of which date from the Roman Empire. They probably served no higher purpose than decoration, being especially appropriate as fountain-figures. That they reproduce some famous statue is quite probable, though the attempt to identify the original with the statue mentioned by Pliny (N. H., XXXVI. 35) as the work of a sculptor named Daidalos, has not been successful.

235. **Boy and Goose**, marble group, in the Louvre.

> Found at Roma Vecchia, the ancient Pagus Lemonius. RESTORATIONS: The head of the boy and that of the goose. PUBLISHED: Clarac, *Musée de Sculpture*, pl. 293, No. 2226; etc. See, especially, a paper by E. A. Gardner, in the *Journal of Hellenic Studies*, VI (1885), p. 1 ff., on the different types of this subject.

This group, which formerly served as decoration for a fountain, is a characteristic example of the *genre* style of the Hellenistic period. A sturdy little boy, scarcely more than an infant, is trying to hold a goose nearly as tall as himself, and in his struggle almost chokes the poor bird, whose neck is clutched in both hands. Both boy and goose are cleverly and charmingly executed, particularly the chubby figure of the former, which is modelled with great skill and feeling. The spirit of the action would be better appreciated were it not for the support under the body of the goose. The presence of this, and the character of the technique, indicate that the original of which this is a copy was of bronze. In that material no such support would be required, and the effect would be increased accordingly.

On the statement of Pliny (N. H., XXXIV. 84), that a sculptor named Boethos made a child strangling a goose, this group has for many years been regarded as a copy of that work, in spite of the fact that we know nothing more about it than this mention. Since there are not less than fifty-two extant representations of boys with geese, which cannot be reduced to less than six distinct types, of nearly the same period, it is certainly not advisable to attempt to identify any one of these with a work of which we know so little. Whoever may have been its sculptor, the original of this group was probably a work of the early part of the Hellenistic period, and of bronze, as stated above.

236. Nike, Apollo, Artemis, and Leto. Marble relief in the Villa Albani.

PUBLISHED: Zoega, *Bassirilievi*, II, pl. xcix, p. 239 ff.; Morcelli, etc., *Descr. de la Villa Albani* (1869), No. 1014, and Appendix II, p. 174.

In the background is a Corinthian temple decorated with a frieze of racing chariots, and separated from the foreground by a high wall. In front of this, at the right, stands Nike at the side of a round altar, pouring from a wine-jug into a patera held by Apollo, who approaches from the left followed by his sister and mother, Artemis and Leto. Apollo carries a large lyre, upon which he plays with his left hand. Artemis catches the garment of Apollo in her right hand, holding in the left a large torch. On her shoulder is her bow. Leto carries a long sceptre in her left hand, and with the right holds an end of her himation or shawl.

While the temple and other accessories are of a late style, all four figures are executed in imitation of archaic types, with the drapery arranged in stiff zigzag folds. The manner of clasping objects with the thumb and forefinger is also characteristic both of genuine archaic art and its late imitations. The relief belongs to the class of works described above, p. 13.

237. **The Ludovisi Ares,** statue in the Villa Ludovisi, Rome.

> Of fine Greek marble. Found near the Palazzo Santa Croce, Rome. Date of discovery unknown, but earlier than 1633, as the statue is entered in the inventory of the works of art of the Villa Ludovisi, dated Jan. 28 of that year. RESTORATIONS: On the Ares, the greater portion of the nose, the right hand, except the piece against the knee, end of thumb and forefinger of left hand, with the handle of the sword and a piece of the sheath, and the right foot except the heel. On the Eros, head, neck, left arm with the quiver, right forearm, right foot and part of the lower leg. PUBLISHED: Raoul-Rochette, *Monuments Inédits*, pl. XI, p. 49; Schreiber, *Antike Bildwerke der Villa Ludovisi*, p. 82, No. 63; etc.

Ares, the god of war, sits meditatively upon a rock, his left knee clasped in both hands, one of which holds his sword. Upon the ground at his side are his helmet and shield, and just in front of the seat, under his right leg, sits a small Eros. The mantle of the god has fallen about his waist, leaving the figure nearly nude. A mark on the left shoulder and the remains of a support on the same side show that originally another statue was grouped with this, of which unfortunately nothing remains. A theory that has received very general acceptance is that the second figure may have been Aphrodite, standing by Ares, and endeavoring to divert his thoughts from war to love. While such a restoration would suit the statue well, and explain the introduction of Eros, it is based upon nothing but conjecture, as we possess neither the example nor the description of an analogous work from which to learn how the statue was grouped.

The long slender limbs of this figure, its athletic body and fine head bear such resemblance to the Apoxyomenos of Lysippos (Fourth Room, No. 200) as to warrant the belief that its original was a work of either that artist or his school, dating therefore from the second half of the fourth century B. C.

238. **Large Double Herma,** in the National Museum, Athens.

> Of the pillar only a section is given in the cast. Found in the Stadion, Athens, 1869. There are no restorations. PUBLISHED: Sybel, *Katalog*, No. 36; etc.

A Herma is a quadrangular pillar surmounted by a head, which in early Greek art was usually that of Hermes, whence the name. Originally they had a religious significance, and throughout historical times were especially venerated at Athens, as is shown by the alarm and indignation felt at the mutilation of them on the night before the Sicilian expedition was to sail, described by Thucydides. These hermæ were erected in all kinds of public places, before temples, tombs, gymnasia, etc., and were placed along roads, with distances marked upon them. They were also used to mark the boundaries of lands, and in Athens there was one at the door of every house. In later times they were used for decorative as well as religious purposes, and while the former class underwent great variety of form and type, especially in the treatment of the bust, the religious hermæ retained their simple archaic character. It is to this class that our example belongs. The heads preserve a type much older than the period of their execution, which may have been as late as the Roman dominion in Greece. The bearded face is probably Hermes, the other Dionysos, or possibly Apollo. This Herma formerly stood in the Stadion at Athens, among the ruins of which it was found.

239, 240. Two Bacchic Reliefs.

No. 239 represents a Bacchic dance of a type familiar through a number of examples in the preceding room. The group consists of two Satyrs and a Mænad, all in dancing attitudes. The original is the Villa Albani, Rome.

No. 240 is in the gallery of the Uffizi, Florence. It represents a Bacchic orgy, and shows the followers of the god of wine in various stages of frenzy. The tripod on the column locates the scene at Delphi, where Dionysos was worshipped in the winter months, and Apollo in the summer. Dionysos himself leans against the tree, a long thyrsos in his hand.

PUBLISHED: Welcker, *Alte Denkmä'er*, II, pl. v, 9 ; Dütschke *Antike Bildwerke in Oberitalien*, III, No. 516.

241, 242. Busts of Comedy and Tragedy, in the Vatican.

> Found at Hadrian's Villa during the pontificate of Pius VI., and placed by him in the Vatican. PUBLISHED: Visconti, *Museo Pio Clem.*, VI, pl. xx, 1, 2; Gerhard in the *Beschreibung der Stadt Rom*, II 2, p. 224, Nos. 1 and 2.

These two busts, which personify Comedy and Tragedy, were found at the entrance to the theatre of Hadrian's Villa, which they formerly decorated. They are works of the Roman Empire, and date probably from the time of Hadrian.

243. Apollo playing on the Lyre, statue in the Vatican.

> Of Carrara marble. Found, 1774, in the so-called Villa of Cassius near Tivoli, and placed by Pius VI. in the Vatican. RESTORATIONS: The end of the nose, the chin, right hand and arm from above the elbow, left hand and part of the arm which projects from the drapery, the visible portions of both feet, and pieces in the drapery. Also the upper half of the lyre, including the upper part of the Marsyas on it. PUBLISHED: Visconti, *Museo Pio Clem.*, I, pl. xv, p. 101 ff.; Clarac, *Musée de Sculpture*, pl. 496, No. 967; Stephani, in the *Compte Rendu de St. Petersbourg*, 1875, pp. 122–153; etc.

Apollo, crowned with a laurel wreath, is represented as the god of music, moving with stately step to the accompaniment of his lyre, his head raised as though in the act of singing. His musical victory over Marsyas is brought to mind by the figure of the latter on the lyre. The costume, which gives the figure rather a feminine appearance, is that of a Kitharoidos or lyre-player, consisting of a long, flowing chiton which reaches to the feet, and is girded considerably above the waist by a broad band. Over this is a chlamys, or cloak, much longer than that usually worn by men. (Cf. for example, that of the Apollo Belvedere in the same room.)

Augustus, after his victory at Actium, which he believed due to the intervention of Apollo, dedicated to him a temple on the Palatine, in which was placed a statue of the god playing upon the lyre, the work of Skopas. It is possible that the figure before us is a replica of that statue, which the poet **Propertius** describes as "Apollo in a long garment playing songs" (*Pythius longa carmina veste sonat*), and which is represented on coins of Augustus and the following emperors with a general resemblance to this figure. The coin-types, however, differ so much from one another in regard to the action of the arms as to teach little more of the original than that it was erect, in **the** long costume described, and carried the lyre on the left side.

Apart from the question of the connection **of this** statue with the Palatine Apollo of Skopas, the type **of** head, the character of the drapery, and the style of the execution point to the **fourth** century B. C. **as** the **date of** its original.

244. Thalia, statue in the Vatican.

Of Carrara marble. Found with Nos. 243 and 245 in 1774 at Tivoli, on the site of the so-called Villa of Cassius. Placed by Pius VI. in the Vatican. RESTORATIONS: The Satyr's staff, except a fragment on the upper arm, both forearms, and nearly the entire tympanum, of the original presence and position of which there were traces on the figure. PUBLISHED: Visconti, *Museo Pio Clem.*, I, pl. xviii; Gerhard, in the *Beschreibung der Stadt Rom*, II 2, p. 214, No. 10; etc.

Thalia, the Muse of Comedy, **clothed in** long, **full** drapery, is seated upon a rock. On her head she wears an ivy wreath, an emblem of Dionysos, the patron divinity **of the** theatre. At her side is a comic mask, by which she is distinguished from Melpomene, the Muse of Tragedy. In her right hand she holds a staff such as are carried by Satyrs in Bacchanalian representations, and on her knee rests a tympanum, a favorite instrument of the Bacchantes. These symbols are probably introduced because of the importance of the dance of Satyrs and Bacchantes as a feature of the comic drama.

This statue is undoubtedly the product of a Roman chisel, as it possesses all the characteristics of a Roman copy, notably the hard, mechanical manner in which the drapery is treated. That it reproduces a Greek original is most probable, but of that work or its sculptor we have no knowledge. Mention is made in ancient writers of groups of **Muses by** several eminent sculptors of different epochs.

245. **Clio,** statue in the Vatican.

> Of Carrara marble. Found with Nos. 243 and 244 in 1774 at Tivoli, on the site of the so-called Villa of Cassius. Placed by Pius VI. in the Vatican. RESTORATIONS: The nose, neck, right breast, right forearm, the left **arm from above** elbow, with part of the scroll, the right knee, and **extremity of** the left foot. PUBLISHED: Visconti, *Museo Pio Clem.*, **I,** pl. xvi; Clarac, *Musée de Sculpture*, pl. 500, No. 985; etc.

As noted above, this statue was found with the Apollo, No. 243, Thalia, **No.** 244, and statues of several **other** Muses. It is perhaps the best of the group, displaying in its conception remarkable charm and beauty. The pose is graceful and easy, and expresses perfectly the reflective nature **of** the Muse of History. The execution, however, like **that of the** Thalia, **is** hard and dry, indicating that **the** statue **is a Roman copy of a** better work.

246. **Statue** restored as Euterpe, in the **Louvre.**

> Of Pentelic marble. Formerly in the Villa Borghese, Rome. RESTORATIONS: The head is ancient, but does not belong to the statue. The nose, mouth, and chin are modern. Also the neck, the right hand and portion of the arm which projects from the drapery, **the** left hand and arm, including the sleeve and the part of the pilaster covered by it, both flutes, **and the** left foot. PUBLISHED: Clarac, *Musée de Sculpture*, pl. 295, No. 1016; Fröhner, *Sculpture Antique du Louvre*, No. 379; **etc.**

A female figure in full drapery stands with feet **crossed** leaning upon **a tall square** column. On the front **of this,** near the base, **is a bird** standing upon a palm branch, **and** on the side **an olive-tree,** both sculptured in low, flat relief. Upon **what ground** the statue is restored as Euterpe **it** would be **difficult to** say, there being nothing upon the original figure to justify the flutes and the two hands, which are the distinctive attributes of that Muse. The drapery is treated easily **and with a** considerable degree of merit.

247. **Combat between Zeus and the Giants.** Selection from the reliefs of the **Great Altar at Pergamon,** in Asia **Minor.** Now in the Berlin Museum.

> Of bluish white marble, probably of an Asiatic variety. Found July 21, 1879, during the excavations undertaken by the German government, under the management of Karl Humann. It had

been built into a rude wall east of the altar. There are no restorations. PUBLISHED: Rayet, *Monuments de l'Art Antique*, II, pl. 61; Humann, etc., *Ergebnisse der Ausgrabungen zu Pergamon*, I, 1880, p. 27, pl. iii; Brunn, *Pergamenische Gigantomachie*, Berlin, 1884; etc.

The monument to which this relief belonged was one of the most magnificent and most characteristic works of the Hellenistic age. Eumenes II., king of Pergamon, B. C. 197-159, to whom the city owed its famous library and many other public institutions, was probably the one who dedicated to Zeus Soter (the Saviour) this altar, of such magnitude and splendor that it is unique among the Greek edifices known to us. As with other works of the age, its purpose was evidently one of display rather than the mere fulfilment of religious needs, the object being to place the altar proper, which was used for sacrifices, in as magnificent a setting as possible. To this end it was raised upon a platform or substructure about 16 ft. high and nearly square in plan, measuring about 123 ft. 7 in. by 113 ft. 6 in. This was erected in a most imposing situation, a terrace near the top of the lofty Akropolis, seven hundred feet above the surrounding plain, the site being that of the agora, or market-place, of the city. One side of the platform was pierced by a broad staircase leading up to the altar, which stood in the centre, surrounded, except at the head of the staircase, by an Ionic colonnade.

The most important feature of this structure, artistically, was the broad band of sculpture which encircled the walls of the platform, taking its start at either side of the staircase. This was a single composition, about seven feet six inches in width, and probably not far from four hundred feet long, representing the battle of the Gods and Giants. Although the altar has long since been destroyed, and its decorations scattered, the German excavations have brought to light the fragments of over 350 feet of the relief, which now adorn the Museum of Berlin. Of this No. **247** is a characteristic specimen. Zeus is engaged in combat with three giants, one of whom, at the left, is struck down by a thunderbolt which pierces his left leg; another, fallen to his knees, grasps his left shoulder as though in agony, and his left arm is swollen and somewhat contracted. **There** being no trace of any weapon which has caused this, it has been supposed that the artist intended to represent him as paralyzed by the sight of the ægis, which Zeus brandishes above his head. The third giant prepares to defend himself against the thunderbolt Zeus is about to hurl. He is older than the other two, bearded, and with legs that end in serpents, one of which springs at the eagle of Zeus above his left arm.

The qualities of this work which first impress the spectator are its spirit and power. Through the entire composition runs the same animation, the same feeling of rush and noise, displayed in this group. In the figures with which the relief is crowded from beginning to end, there is neither repetition of motive nor any sense of effort in the grouping. The whole subject is composed with the utmost facility. The merit of the modelling varies in different sections, showing that many hands were employed upon it, yet it is always vigorous. No extant work of Greek art exhibits greater technical perfection. The dignified torso of Zeus, the forms of the giants, the deep cutting of the folds of the drapery, all show marvellous skill. The types are not new or original; but those of the best periods have been chosen, and worked over with a love of detail, especially in the anatomy, which has already been mentioned as a characteristic of Hellenistic sculpture. Its perfection in these qualities, however, makes this relief an excellent example of one of the chief lessons of Greek art — that cleverness alone will not suffice to make a work really great. Behind the technical power there must be ethical qualities which this work lacks. However spirited the composition may be, it lacks the true religious feeling which the earlier sculptors would have given it. Their great mythological representations were inspired by piety; this by the love of display. It is evidently an attempt to make as gorgeous a composition as possible; and while it has succeeded in this, the endeavor for startling effect is constantly apparent, resulting in a restlessness and confusion which present a strong contrast to the quiet simplicity of the sculptures of the best period. It embodies in their full development the virtues and the faults of what may be called the Barocco period of Greek art.

248. **Pseudo-Archaic Relief, in the** Villa Albani.

Of marble. RESTORATIONS: According to Zoega, the only part of this relief which is original is the lower left-hand corner, including only a portion of the seated figure, — the top and back of head, both hands with the objects they hold, the legs from the middle of the thigh, and the front leg of the seat being restored, — and the remainder of the relief is modern. PUBLISHED: Raffei, *Saggio di Osservazione*, Rome, 1773, frontispiece; Zoega, *Bassirilievi*, II, pl. cxii, No. 1; Müller-Wieseler, *Denkmäler der alten Kunst*, II, No. 257; etc.

This relief is so extensively made up of pieces which, whether ancient or modern, do not belong together, that it does not merit detailed description. The right and left halves do not belong together, and of the latter, the altar, the upper part of the temple, and the attributes held by the sitting figure, are of extremely doubtful authenticity. This figure is identified as Aphrodite by the rabbit or hare under her seat, both animals being sacred to that goddess. The figure at the right is Athena. The style of the relief is that of the Roman imitation of archaic Greek sculpture.

249. **Mask of a Satyr, in** the collection of **antiquities, Dresden.**

Of marble. Found at Pompeii, and bought of Prof. Zahn, in 1841. COLORS, in traces, are still preserved: on the eyes reddish brown and blue, and in the hair yellow and reddish brown. PUBLISHED: Hettner, *Bildwerke der kgl. Antikensammlung zu Dresden*, 1881, p. 90, No. 124. See also Treu, *Sollen wir unsere Statuen bemalen?* Berlin, 1884, p. 33.

A decorative piece of sculpture, the chief interest of which lies in the preservation of some of the colors in the original. These are noted above.

250. **The Laokoön Group, in the Vatican.**

Of Greek marble. Found during the pontificate of Julius II., in 1506, among the ruins of the palace of Titus, on the Esquiline, Rome, and purchased by the Pope. RESTORATIONS: The right arm of the father, with the portion of the serpent extended along it, the right arm of the son on the left, with the coil of the serpent at the top, the right hand and part of the forearm of the son on the right. There are also a number of minor restorations. PUBLISHED: Visconti, *Museo Pio Clem.*, II, pl.

39; Mitchell, *History of Ancient Sculpture*, p. 601 ff., fig. 243, etc. Of the controversial literature regarding the date, etc., of the group, the list is very long; much of it is given in Blümner's **second** edition of Lessing's *Laokoon*. See also Kekulé, *Laokoon*, **Berlin,** 1883, **and** Trendelenburg, *Laokoongruppe*, Berlin, 1884.

Laokoön, a **Trojan priest, is a character that** figured prominently in **the post-Homeric legends of Troy.** To us he is best known **by the story of his death in the second** book of the Æneid, **but this was also described by many** earlier **writers,** among **them** Sophokles, **in works now lost.** As we **are able to** judge from fragments, the story **varied in different authors.** According to that illustrated by **this** group, and **also** followed by Virgil, Laokoön warned and urged the Trojans **to** have nothing **to** do with the wooden horse **left by** the **Greeks** outside the city when they pretended to **sail away; but the people, rej**oicing **at** what they thought **their final** delivery from war, determined to carry the horse **into the** city amid sacrifices and feasting. Laokoön **as priest, aided** by his **two sons, was** about to sacrifice **a bull at the altar of** Poseidon, **when** two enormous **serpents rushed from the sea, and entwined** themselves **first about the sons, then about** Laokoön himself, who came **to** the rescue, **and all three were** killed. The legends agree that the **monsters** were the **instrument of some divinity, but** differ **as to which one, and as to the** reason of the punishment.

It is easy to understand how such **a** subject, **the representation of which required the greatest technical skill, should** have attracted the sculptors of the Hellenistic age, **which,** as mentioned above, p. 132, **was** distinguished for its virtuosity. **Pliny (N.** H., XXXVI. 37) describes as one **of the most wonderful** works known to him (*opus omnibus et picturæ et statuariæ artis præferendum*) a marble group of **Laokoön** and **his** sons, that stood in the palace of Titus on the Esquiline, the **work** of the Rhodian sculptors, Agesander, Polydoros, and Athenodoros. **As the** Vatican **group, of** which **the cast is before** us, was found on the **site of** the palace mentioned, and is the only known **group representing** the subject, there can be little doubt **that it is the** identical work to which Pliny alluded. It was evidently the **cleverness of the** execution that excited his admiration, as he mentions that the father, sons, and serpents were all cut from a single block of marble, — though modern examinations have shown that the group was composed of **several** closely fitted pieces.

The modern restorations of **the** figures **are** incorrect in several particulars, especially **the** right arm **of** the father. **A mark on** the back of **his** head **shows** that this **arm was** not outstretched, but bent sharply **at the elbow so that the** hand, or the serpent grasped by it, **came in contact with** the head. Thus the pyramidal character **of the** composition was preserved, and the harmony between the main and subordinate lines maintained. **The** right arm of **the son** on the left is also an incorrect restoration.

In the conception **of** this group there **is no** attempt **to** go below the surface. The sculptors have not given **expression** to **an** idea. It is simply the representation **of** physical agony of the most wearying kind, which fatigues **the spectator** as well as the sufferer. The contrast in conception between the Laokoön and the Dying Gaul is pointed **out** below (p. 157). The former does not stop with suggestion; every circumstance of the torture is elaborately represented in faces and limbs. It appeals to the senses only, because the suffering is that of the senses only. Of mental or moral distress there is not a suggestion.

Technically the group displays a studied perfection. The composition, evidently the result of thought rather than inspiration, is carefully managed so as to avoid awkwardness, and the action of the human figure in pain is represented with academic exactness. The modelling is refined to the point of over-elaboration, details being wrought with such minuteness that the effect of the whole is weakened, in contrast to **the free,** bold treatment of the Pergamon relief (No. 247). **In** technique it bears the relation to that relief of a later, imitative style, but whether this is due to direct study **of** the relief itself or **to** the powerful influence **of** the Pergamenian school over those of subsequent epochs, **is** a matter of dispute.

The date of the Laokoön **has** long been the subject of controversy, for the determination of which there is not sufficient material. Opinions range between the year 300 B. C. and the reign of Titus, in the first century of our era. Judged by its style alone, the most probable date of its origin is midway between these two, between 150 and 100 B. C.

251. The Dying Gaul, statue in the Capitoline Museum, Rome.

Of Asiatic (?) marble. Found in Rome in the 16th century. Formerly in the Villa Ludovisi, from which it was carried to the Capitol by Clement XII. (1730–1740). RESTORATIONS: The end of the nose, the right hand and arm, part of the left knee, the toes, and part of the plinth, including the sword and a portion of the horn. PUBLISHED: Bouillon, *Musée des Antiques*, vol. II, pl. xx; *Nuova Descrizione del Museo Capitolino*, 1882, p. 231 ff.; Wolters' Friederichs, No. 1412; etc.

The opinion, formerly prevalent, that this statue represented a dying gladiator, has long since been proved fallacious, partly by the fact that it is undoubtedly a product of Greek art, which knew nothing of gladiators, — a peculiarly Roman institution, — and partly by the strong resemblance of face and figure to the descriptions of the ancient Gauls, or Galatians, the barbarous people who invaded Greece and Asia in the third century B. C., and were finally restrained by Attalos I., king of Pergamon. The ring or torque about the neck was a distinctive decoration of these men, and the thick, mane-like hair, and habit of wearing no beard except the moustache, which the Greeks regarded as barbarous, were also peculiar to them. Beyond doubt, therefore, we have here a Gaul who, defeated in battle, is dying from a wound either received from an enemy, or, as some think, inflicted by himself in order to escape slavery.

There are few statues in which pathos is expressed in so high a form as in this, an effect produced chiefly by the quiet, restrained manner in which the artist has suggested rather than expressed the emotions of pain and despair, thus stimulating the spectator's imagination and appealing to his sympathy. This quality will be better appreciated by comparison with the Laokoön (No. 250), in which physical suffering is expressed in the wildest and most vehement form, both in faces and figures, with an amount of detail which leaves no room for the imagination. In the Gaul pain is indicated by the wound, which is clearly mortal, yet this is subordinated to the mental anguish produced by defeat. The face is not distorted, the limbs are not violently contracted, and even in his humiliation the warrior maintains a dignity which renders this statue one of the noblest expressions of pathos in Greek art. The characteristic virtuosity of the Hellenistic epoch is displayed in the treatment of the flesh, which is represented as hard and tough, in contrast to the soft, supple skin of athlete statues, the object being to distinguish the barbarian from the Greek in this as well as in other particulars.

The general resemblance in style between this and the figures of the Attalos group (see Nos. 219 and 220), and the fact that it represents a Gaul, point to Pergamon as the place where the statue originated. It probably belongs among the earlier works of the Pergamenian school, dating about the end of the third century B. C.

252. Round Altar, in the Villa Albani, Rome.

Of Pentelic marble. There are no restorations. PUBLISHED: Zoega, *Bassirilievi della Villa Albani*, II, pl. xcvi; Overbeck, *Kunstmythologie*, II, *Demeter*, pp. 487 ff.; Wolters' Friedrichs, No. 2144; etc.

Against a tree, which may be taken as the centre of the representation, leans a male figure, whose cloak falls in such a way as to leave the body exposed. At the other side of the tree are two female figures, one of large, matronly proportions, and clothed in heavy drapery; the other, smaller and more lightly draped. Around the other side of the altar are three females thickly draped and veiled, who walk in procession, catching hold of one another's garments.

From its resemblance to a common type of that divinity, the male figure may be assumed to be Dionysos, in whose service the altar was probably used, but of the subject represented or the names of the other figures no satisfactory explanation has ever been given.

The altar is probably a work of the early Empire, the relief reproducing types of the Hellenistic epoch.

Of the casts in this room Nos. 229–232, 234, 236, 243–246, **248**, **252**, were purchased from the bequest of Charles Sumner.

Nos. **215, 218, 233, 237, 250, 251**, are the property of the Boston Athenæum.

No. **225** was presented by Lt. Com. Gorringe.

ROMAN ROOM.

265. Young Satyr, marble statue in the British Museum.

> From the Maccarani Palace, Rome. Formerly in the Towneley collection. RESTORATIONS: The arms from the elbows, the legs from knees down, and the trunk supporting the left side. The staff in the left hand is correctly restored, as a portion of the original is attached to the upper part of the arm. PUBLISHED: *Ancient Marbles in Brit. Mus.*, II, pl. 24; *Guide to Græco-Roman Sculptures*, I, No. 183, p. 96; etc.

A Satyr of the late Hellenistic type, with elfish face, pointed ears, and horns protruding from the brow. He wears the *nebris* or fawn's skin, characteristic of Satyrs, and carries their favorite staff or crook. The great number of figures of this type, in various attitudes, discovered in and about **Rome,** attest their popularity among the Romans, by whom they were used to decorate houses and villas.

266. Heads and Figures from the Column of Trajan. On this and other walls.

The column of Trajan stands in the Forum designed by that Emperor, in Rome. Its purpose was to commemorate his victories over the Dacians, a barbarous people of the Danube country, and also to serve as the sepulchre of his ashes. It is composed of a square base from which rises a tall round shaft, surmounted by a capital. Above this is a pedestal on which stood originally the statue of the Emperor, now supplanted by one of St. **Peter.** The height from the ground to the upper surface of the capital is 117 **ft.** 7 in., and the pedestal rises about 17 ft. above this. The diameter of the shaft at the bottom is a trifle less than 12 ft., at the top about 10 ft. The whole is of Parian marble.

The most characteristic feature of the column is a spiral relief, which, beginning from the bottom, illustrates Trajan's two wars against the Dacians. This relief, about 2 ft. wide at the bottom, gradually increases in width, until at the top it measures 4 ft. The increase, however, is not regular, some places being wider than those above them. Its length is about 660 ft., and into this space are crowded over 2,500 human figures, divided, according to Pollen (see below), into 109 subjects, illustrating all the incidents of the wars. Examination has shown that the entire surface of the marble was covered with colors and gilding, by which the details were made much clearer than they are at present.

Our selections show the general character of the sculpture. Artistically it does not rank high, being in conception nothing more than a faithful record of facts, without an element of ideality; and the execution is, as a rule, mediocre. But as an historical document it is of the highest value, because of its fund of information regarding not merely the events of the campaigns, but the types, costumes, weapons, methods of warfare, etc., of the people represented upon it. In the history of art it is important, because it is the last great monument of classic sculpture.

> The column and its reliefs are fully illustrated in the great work of Fröhner, *La Colonne Trajane*. They are also described by J. H. Pollen, *The Trajan Column*, London, 1874 (So. Kensington Handbooks); S. Reinach, *La Colonne Trajane;* etc.

267. Bust of Cicero (?), in the Museo Chiaramonti, in the Vatican.

This bust belongs to the rather numerous class of doubtful portraits of Cicero.

268. Satyr. Statue in the Capitoline Museum.

> Of red marble (*rosso antico*). Found in Hadrian's Villa, near Tivoli, and placed in the Capitoline Museum by Benedict XIV., 1746. RESTORATIONS: The end of the nose and chin, the right arm

with the bunch of grapes, the left hand with the staff, the legs, except the front half of the right foot and nearly all the left, the tree-trunk and syrinx, the head of the goat, with part of the neck and the fore feet. PUBLISHED: Bottari and Foggini, *Museo Capitolino*, I, pl. 34; *Nuova Descrizione del Museo Capitolino*, 1882, p. 292, No. 1; etc.

This, like its neighbor (No. 265), is a piece of decorative sculpture, of the class of subjects popular in the time of the Roman Empire. A Satyr, of the late Hellenistic type, smiles at the emblem of Dionysos, which he holds in his right hand. In the fawn's skin which he wears as a garment are other fruits, and the basket at his side is filled with grapes. The goat standing by him typifies the favorite animals of the Satyrs, which are also sacred to Dionysos.

The material of this statue, rosso antico, shows that it was executed during the Roman Empire, and probably in the time of Hadrian, — in whose villa it was found, — as the adoption of this material for statues is believed to have begun during his reign.

269. Apotheosis of **Homer,** marble relief in the British Museum.

Found at Bovillæ, on the Via Appia, about twelve miles from Rome, as early as the middle of the 17th century. Formerly in the Palazzo Colonna, Rome, and purchased for the British Museum, 1819. RESTORATIONS: Part of Homer's right foot, the left hand of Mythos, with the patera, the heads of Sophia, Apollo, the Delphic priestess, the poet on the base, Terpsichore, Urania, Calliope, Erato and Euterpe. Also both upper corners, with the left arm and end of the peplos of Thalia. PUBLISHED: Mitchell, *History of Ancient Sculpture*, p. 668, fig. 276; *Guide to Græco-Roman Sculptures in Brit. Mus.*, 1879. I, pp. 73–80; etc.

Although artistically this **work is** of small value, being a rather clumsy attempt to **make** sculpture in relief trespass upon the province of landscape painting, it is interesting because of its subject, and because it is one of the few allegorical representations which classic art has left us. Beginning with the lowest row, at the left is Homer throned, receiving the adoration of those who approach from the right. Inscriptions, nearly obscured in the cast, give us the names of all the figures in this row. Behind Homer are *Chronos* (Time), the winged figure, and *Oikoumené*, (the World, — humanity?) crowning him. The throne is supported by two small kneeling figures, personifying the Iliad and the Odyssey. Before Homer is an altar, by which stands a Karian bull, about to be sacrificed. The bull is led by a boy, *Mythos* (the genius of Myth). The altar-flame is kindled by *Historia* (History), behind whom come *Poiesis* (Poetry), with two torches; *Tragodia* (Tragedy); *Komodia* (Comedy), and a child, *Physis* (Nature). In the corner is a group of four, personifying Virtue, Memory, Faith, and Wisdom. The principal figure in the second row is Apollo, standing in a cave with his lyre. The cone-shaped object at his right, on which is his quiver, fixes the locality of the scene, being the *omphalos* or symbol of Delphi. The mountain represented is therefore Parnassos, and Apollo is standing in the Korkyrian cave. The other figure in the cave may be a priestess or a nymph. The other female figures on the mountain are the nine Muses, — to the left of Apollo, Polyhymnia, next her Urania, with her globe, and Terpsichore, seated, playing upon a lyre. Beginning at the left of the row above, we have Clio, Calliope, Erato, Euterpe, Thalia, and on the ledge above, Melpomene. Some of these names are conjectural, but most probably belong to the respective figures. At the top is seated Zeus, holding a sceptre, and accompanied by an eagle. On the right of the relief, between the second and third row, is an isolated figure difficult to name. Goethe, who wrote a memoir on the subject, suggested that this might represent the statue of the poet by whom the relief was dedicated.

Directly below Zeus is an inscription recording the name of ARCHELAOS, son of Apollonios, of Priene, as the sculptor. His date is unknown, but the character of the inscriptions indicates the first century B. C. as the probable date of the relief.

270. Statuette of an Amazon, in the Augusteum at Dresden.

Of Pentelic marble. Found in the island of Salamis, 1813. Formerly in the collection of Baron Stackelberg, from which it passed to the Dresden Museum in 1845. RESTORATIONS, by Thorwaldsen: The head, neck, a small piece on right breast, the left forearm, the right hand, with greater part of the axe, both legs from knees down, and the lower part of the mantle, with the base. PUBLISHED: Clarac, *Musée de Sculpture*, pl. 810 A, **No.** 2031 B; Hettner, *Bildwerke der Antikensammlung zu Dresden*, 1881, p. 62, No. 40; Wolters' Friederichs, No. 518; etc.

This little figure, found in Greece, is undoubtedly the work of a Greek artist, and most probably a reduced copy of a large statue. It represents an Amazon in repose, and is especially interesting because it presents a decided contrast to the common type of Amazon, which is that of No. 90 in the Second Greek Room. That type represents them as wearing simply a short chiton, while this figure wears, in addition to that garment, a cloak and high boots. The head, as noted above, is modern, and the addition of a helmet is conjectural, as well as the shield on the left arm; but for the attitude of the head and of both arms, traces of the original furnished the indications, so that these are correct.

The treatment of the figure shows that it was intended to be seen only from the front. Its original probably dated not far from 400 B. C.

271. Bust of Cicero (?), in the Capitoline Museum, Rome.

This head, like No. 267, is one of the doubtful portraits of Cicero. Visconti thought it a portrait of Caius Asinius Pollio.

Of the bust only the head is ancient, both the drapery and the pedestal being modern.

272. Portrait Bust, formerly thought to be **Seneca**.

The individual whose features are here reproduced is represented in more extant busts than any other man of antiquity, with the single exception of Sokrates; yet his identity still remains a mystery. It was formerly thought that these heads, the finest of which is a bronze bust from Herculaneum in the Museum at Naples, were portraits of the Roman philosopher Seneca; but a head in the Berlin

Museum, which is established as a portrait of him by the name inscribed upon it, shows a very different type of face, and proves that the name which has been ascribed to this and others like it rests upon no foundation.

273. The Venus of the Capitol.   Statue in the Capitoline Museum, Rome.

> Of Greek marble. Found in Rome, between the Viminal and Quirinal hills, and placed in the Capitoline Museum by Benedict XIV., 1752. RESTORATIONS: The nose, the forefinger and a small piece of thumb of the left hand, the fingers of the right hand. PUBLISHED: Bouillon, *Musée*, I, pl. 10; Clarac, *Musée de Sculpture*, pl. 621, No. 1384; *Nuova Descrizione del Museo Capitolino*, 1882, p. 148 ff. ; etc.

Like the crouching Aphrodite in the Fifth Greek Room (No. 234), this statue represents the goddess without any religious significance whatever, and with no attempt to express the higher qualities of her nature, such as are shown in the Venus of Melos (Third Room, No. 140). Both face and form are those of an extremely pretty woman, but with no suggestion of divinity in either expression or proportions.

The sentiment of shame, indicated by the action, while appropriate to a woman, is unworthy of a goddess, and shows that the sculptor used the name of Aphrodite, or Venus, merely as a pretext for the representation of a beautiful female figure, a characteristic of the degenerate epoch in which the statue originated.

That its motive was very popular with the later Greek and Roman sculptors is attested by the many similar statues of those epochs in the various European museums. Of these the Venus of the Capitol and the Venus de' Medici (of which there is a marble copy in the entrance hall) are the most famous examples. The attitude of both is the same, but the Capitoline displays an older, maturer form than the other, and in point of execution is the finer of the two. The original exhibits a remarkable elasticity and suppleness of texture which the cast fails to reproduce.

The date of this statue is a matter of conjecture. It is certainly not older than the Hellenistic epoch; and the elegance which is aimed at in the treatment offers reason for believing that it is a work of the Roman Empire.

274. Lucius Junius Brutus (?). Bronze bust in the Palazzo dei Conservatori, on the Capitol, Rome.

Presented to the city of Rome by Cardinal Rodolfo Pio da Carpi in the 16th century. RESTORATIONS: Only the head is ancient. The nude bust on which this rests was made for the cast, the original being on a much larger bust, modern, draped as a toga. PUBLISHED: Visconti, *Iconographie Grecque*, I, pl. ii, figs. 1 and 2; etc.

From a general resemblance which this head bears to that of Lucius Junius Brutus on certain Roman coins, Visconti and others have taken it to be a portrait of him, and it is generally so considered, although the resemblance is not so exact as to make the identity unquestionable. It is a fine example of Roman portrait sculpture, showing a face of strong individuality, expressive of a serious and determined character.

275. Diogenes. Statuette in the Villa Albani, Rome.

Of Carrara marble. RESTORATIONS: Both arms from above the elbows, almost the entire left leg, and the right from knee down. Also the dog and the tree trunk. PUBLISHED: Clarac, *Musée de Sculpture*, pl. 842, No. 2111; Wolters' Friederichs, No. 1323; etc.

Of Diogenes there is no authenticated portrait, but the name has been given to this figure because it so well illustrates the characteristics of the chief of cynics, as tradition has preserved them. There are a number of instances of ancient sculptors having represented famous men according to their mental or moral traits, without regard for — or more probably without a knowledge of — their actual appearance in life, and this statuette is probably of that class.

276. Klytie, so called. Marble bust, in the British Museum.

Purchased by Towneley of Prince Laurenzano, at Naples, 1772, and formerly in the Towneley collection. RESTORATIONS: Two leaves of the flower. PUBLISHED: Ellis, *Towneley Gallery*, II, p. 20; *Guide to Græco-Roman Sculptures in Brit. Mus.*, 1879, I, p. 68, No. 149; Wolters' Friederichs, No. 1648; etc.

The name by which this bust is popularly known was given to it by its former owner, Mr. Towneley, because he thought the flower which forms its base represented the sunflower into which Klytie was changed. It is more probably a portrait, as the face is of an individual type; and the character of the sculpture, as well as the manner in which the hair is arranged, suggests the reign of Augustus as its most probable date.

The attribute of the flower has no especial significance, being used merely as an ornamental termination of the bust. The motive of a head rising from a flower is common in late Greek art. Examples of it occur on the frieze, No. C 19, in the Architectural Room, and on a vase in the large case (E) of the Room of the Greek Vases.

277. **Statue of an Orator**, called the **Arringatore**, in the Museo Archeologico, Florence.

Of bronze. Found, 1566, at a place called Pila, near Lake Thrasymene. PUBLISHED: Müller-Wieseler, *Denkmäler der alten Kunst*, I, pl. lviii, No. 289; Dennis, *Etruria*, II, p. 95; etc.

Although the Etruscans were famous in antiquity for their works in bronze, excavations in Etruria have thus far yielded very few statues in that material which are undoubtedly of Etruscan origin. This statue of an orator is therefore an important monument, as the inscription on the edge of the garment is in the Etruscan language, and shows the statue to be the portrait of one Aulus Metellus, of an Etruscan family. He is represented in the act of speaking, his right arm raised, and the left covered by the *pallium* which he wears over his tunic.

Owing to the small number of works with which to institute a comparison, the date of this statue is not easily determined. It shows a strong affinity to Roman sculpture in style, and probably belongs to the period of Roman domination in Etruria, when Etruscan art was gradually being merged in that of Rome; that is, about the beginning of our era.

278. **Head of a Youth** (Alexander the **Great**?), in the British Museum.

> Of Parian marble. Found in Alexandria. Since 1872 in the British Museum. PUBLISHED: Murray, *History of Greek Sculpture,* II, pl. xxxii, p. 345; Wolters' Friederichs, **No.** 1602; etc.

This head is regarded by the authorities of the British Museum as a portrait of Alexander, but its resemblance to other extant portraits of him is so slight as to render this identification questionable. With the Hellenistic manner of representing Oriental youths, such as Mithras and Paris, it has much more affinity, and may well have belonged to a statue of one of them.

279. **Aktaion attacked by his Dogs.** Marble group, in the British Museum.

> Found by Gavin Hamilton, 1774, among the ruins of the Villa of Antoninus Pius near Civita Lavinia. Formerly in the Towneley collection. RESTORATIONS: The head (which is ancient, but does not belong to the figure), the right arm and left hand, fore part of the head and both ears of the leaping dog, and a portion of each ear of the other. PUBLISHED: *Ancient Marbles in Brit. Mus.*, II, pl. 45; Wolters' Friederichs, No. **457**; etc.

Aktaion **was a famous** mythical **huntsman who** was transformed by **Artemis to a** stag and **devoured by** his own dogs, the cause **of the** punishment being, **according** to one legend, that **he** boasted himself **a** better **hunter than** the goddess; according to another, **that** he had **seen her** bathing. This group represents him at the moment when **the** transformation is beginning, and already his hounds are attacking him. A similar group is represented on a sarcophagus in the Louvre (Clarac, *Musée*, pl. 113-115), which makes it probable that both are copied from a larger work.

280. **Bust of Antinous, from** the colossal statue **in** the Vatican.

> **Of** marble. The statue was found by Gavin Hamilton, at Palestrina, towards the end of the last century, and was placed first in the Palazzo Braschi, Rome, having been presented to the Duke Braschi by Pius VI. It was later removed to the Lateran and thence to the Vatican. PUBLISHED: Levezow, *Antinous*, pls. 7, 8, p. 85; Wolters' Friederichs, **No.** 1660; etc.

Hadrian's extravagant attachment for the beautiful Antinous is attested by the many portraits of him, statues, busts, and reliefs, which have been discovered in all parts of the Roman Empire. Of these, this head is one of the finest, and represents the Emperor's favorite in the character of Dionysos, crowned with a chaplet of ivy. When discovered, the statue to which the head belongs was nude, but marks upon the marble showed that originally it had worn some kind of a garment of bronze, and in restoring the figure this was substituted by a long mantle of marble.

Antinous died A. D. 122, and the statue dates from about that time. The extraordinary combination of a marble statue with metallic drapery is characteristic of the taste of Hadrian's epoch.

281. Augustus. Marble statue, in the Vatican.

Found, 1863, in the ruins of the Villa of Livia at Porta Pia, a town on the Via Flaminia, about nine miles from Rome. RESTORATIONS: Part of one ear, the forefinger of the left hand, and the sceptre. PUBLISHED: Martha, in Rayet's Monuments de l'Art Antique, II, pl. 71; Monumenti dell' Instituto, vol. VI–VII, pl. lxxxiv, and Annali, 1863, p. 432 ff.: etc.

This statue is a noble witness to the technical excellence of sculpture in the Augustan age. It represents Augustus as commander-in-chief of the Roman armies, wearing his armor and military cloak, and probably holding the sceptre, as restored. The pose of the figure is not only easy and natural, but thoroughly majestic, harmonizing finely with the dignity of the face; and the execution is masterly, displaying in its best aspect the elegance peculiar to Augustan sculpture. In the modelling of the head, power is combined with an extreme delicacy, especially in the sensitive lines about the mouth. The draping of the mantle, though somewhat too elaborate, is skilfully managed. The reliefs on the cuirass show a painstaking method of treating details which detracts from the effect of the work as a whole, a characteristic fault of the best Roman sculpture as well as that of the Hellenistic epoch.

In the conception of the statue there is a mixture of realism and idealization; for while the face has the individual traits of a fine portrait, and the armor is represented with minute fidelity to nature, the feet are unshod, as in statues of gods and heroes, and **the** Cupid and dolphin **are** accessories of an ideal character. Doubtless these **are** introduced as an allusion to Venus, the ancestress of the Julian family.

The reliefs on **the** breastplate enable **us to** date the statue almost exactly, since **the** group in **the** centre represents a Parthian giving up **to** a warrior **in** Roman uniform one of the standards captured from Crassus. This subjugation of the Parthians took place B. C. 20, when Augustus was forty-three years of age. The statue represents him **as** about that age, and was probably made soon after **the** conquest. The other figures **on** the relief are, **at** the top Cœlus, **a** personification of heaven; below him **the** Sun in his chariot, preceded by the goddesses of morning. **At** either side of the central group is **a** captive barbarian; below, Apollo on a griffon and Diana on a stag, and **at** the bottom Tellus, the earth.

This statue gives valuable testimony **as** to the polychromy of ancient sculpture, as COLORS were noted **on** it when discovered, and are still distinguishable in parts, as follows: "The tunic of Augustus is *crimson*, the mantle *purple*, the fringe of the armor *yellow;* on the nude portions of the body no traces of color are noticeable, except the indication of the pupils with a *yellowish* tint; and the hair **no** longer shows color. But the relief decorations of the cuirass are painted with especial care, although the flat surfaces are left without **color.** The god of heaven, rising from *blue* waves or clouds, **holds** a *purplish* garment in both hands; the chariot of the sun-god is *crimson;* before him soars a female with outspread *blue* wings; the goddess of **the** earth wears a wreath of wheat in her *blond* hair. Apollo in a *crimson* mantle rides upon **a** griffon with *blue* wings; the *light-haired* Diana, **in a** *crimson* garment, is borne by a *reddish brown* stag. In the middle stands **a** Roman commander in *blue and red* armor, *crimson* tunic and *purple* mantle, **with a** *blue* helmet. A bearded warrior in *crimson* tunic and *blue* **trousers** holds up a Roman standard with insignia painted *blue*. The **barbarian on** the right, with *auburn* hair, **in** a *purple* mantle, holds a war-trumpet; the figure on the left is likewise *light-haired*, and clothed in a *blue* mantle." — Translated from Jahn, *Aus der Alterthumswissenschaft*, p. 260. (It must be remembered that the colors here described are those which always last longest, and it is by no means to be supposed that they were the **only ones** originally applied.)

282. A Roman in the act of Sacrificing. Statue in the Vatican.

> Of Pentelic marble. Said to have been brought from Greece to Venice, where it stood in the Palazzo Giustiniani; and was bought for the Vatican by Pius VI. RESTORATIONS: The head, which is ancient, but does not belong to the statue, and both hands, with the patera. PUBLISHED: Visconti, *Museo Pio Clem.*, III, pl. 19; Wolters' Friederichs, No. 1677; etc.

A Roman citizen in his character of priest is represented as pouring a libation from the patera in his right hand, presumably upon the sacrificial fire. Although both hand and patera are modern, the restoration is undoubtedly correct. The sacred nature of the act is indicated by the veiling of the head in the toga, as required in sacrifices by the Roman ritual. The head, it is true, does not belong to the figure, but the lines of the toga about the neck and shoulders show that the original head was similarly covered.

This statue is an excellent model for the study of the Roman citizen's costume, especially the arrangement of the toga, the abundant folds of which present a striking contrast to the simplicity of Greek garments. The drapery is, in general, well managed, but in the plaster has an unpleasant effect of heaviness and solidity.

283-310. Busts of the Roman Emperors.

Twenty-seven busts of emperors and one of Agrippa, from originals in various museums. The name and date of each are given on the labels. It will be seen that the faces of these men well illustrate their characters as described by Suetonius and the other historians and satirists of Rome. Excepting those of Vitellius and Nerva, each bust may be considered as contemporaneous with the person represented, and thus the course of portraiture through the decline of Roman art may be followed.

Only the heads from which these casts are taken are ancient. The busts themselves, as shown in this collection, are either from the modern ones upon which the heads are now set (Nos. 304, 306, 308), or made expressly for the casts, without regard to the originals.

311. Statue of a young Roman lady, in the Louvre.

Of Pentelic marble. Found in Rome towards the end of the last century. RESTORATIONS: The right arm and hand, with the corner of the garment which it holds, and the left hand. PUBLISHED: Clarac, *Musée de Sculpture*, pl. 300, No. 2265; Wolters' Friederichs, No. 1686; etc.

This statue is evidently a portrait, and its style indicates it to be that of a young patrician of the early Empire. The pose of the figure is pretty and graceful, except about the feet. The arrangement of the drapery here, which neither shows nor suggests the right foot, produces a stiff effect. As a whole, the statue is rather above the average of Roman portrait figures.

312. Relief from the Arch of Titus, Rome.

Still in its original position. There are no restorations. PUBLISHED: Mitchell, *History of Ancient Sculpture*, fig. 283, p. 677 f.; W. Knight, *The Arch of Titus and the Spoils of the Temple*, London, 1867; etc.

The arch to which this relief belongs was erected in the year of Titus' death, A. D. 81, to commemorate his victories over Judæa, and especially the capture of Jerusalem, A. D. 70. That event forms the subject of the relief, the position of which on the arch is shown in the photograph that hangs on the wall.

Through a richly decorated archway, apparently the gate of a city, march the Romans, their brows crowned with victorious wreaths, leading their captives, and bearing the sacred symbols of the Jewish religion — the table of the shew-bread, and the golden seven-branched candlestick. The representation of objects so often mentioned in the Old Testament, and the fact of the commemoration on a Roman monument, of an event of such importance in the history of our religion, give this relief an interest considerably in excess of its artistic value. It is a characteristic example of the realistic, matter-of-fact manner in which Roman sculptors treated historical subjects.

313. Satyr playing the Scabellum. Statue in the Gallery of the Uffizi, Florence.

Of Greek marble. RESTORATIONS: The greater part of the head, both arms, and toes of the right foot. PUBLISHED: Maffei, *Raccolta di Statue Antiche,* pl. 34, p. 38; Clarac, *Musée de Sculpture,* pl. 715, No. 1709; etc.

The scabellum (Gr. *kroupesia*, lit. a wooden shoe) was an instrument played by the feet, producing the same clattering sound as castanets. It was used by flute-players, and in theatres by the leader of the orchestra, to beat time. Probably this Satyr is represented as performing that office for some Bacchic dance.

The figure is spirited and well modelled. The thick, bushy hair, the horns projecting from the brow, and the type of the face indicate the Hellenistic age as the earliest date at which the statue could have originated. It is probably an original work of that epoch, dating between the year 300 B. C. and the foundation of the Roman Empire. An exact date for works of this class it is impossible to fix.

This cast was presented to the Museum by M. Denman Ross, Esq.

314. Pudicitia, so called. Marble statue in the Vatican.

Formerly in the Villa Mattei. Placed in the Vatican by Pius VI. RESTORATIONS: Most of the face and coronet, the right hand, with the part of the veil held by it, and part of the forearm. Also part of the left hand, several of the toes of both feet, and pieces of the drapery. PUBLISHED: Venuti and Amadutio, *Monumenta Mathæiana,* I, pl. lxii; Clarac, *Musée de Sculpture,* pl. 764, No. 1879; etc.

This statue derived its name from the long, full drapery and the veiled head and shoulders, which were considered appropriate attributes of the goddess of modesty. The name has been questioned, however, the statue being considered by some authorities as a portrait of Livia, wife of Augustus. Most probably neither appellation is correct. A possible key to the proper interpretation of the figure is the unmistakably sepulchral character of both attitude and drapery. As a considerable number of replicas of this type have been discovered, the majority evidently products of artisans rather than artists, it is not impossible that they were all erected as ideal figures over the graves of matrons.

The execution of the statue shows it to be of Roman origin, not earlier than the Empire.

315. Agrippina the Younger. Marble statue, in the Museum at Naples.

Formerly in the Farnese collection, Rome. RESTORATIONS: The nose, both hands, the front half of the feet, the legs of the chair, and the footstool. PUBLISHED: *Museo Borbonico*, III, pl. 22; Clarac, *Musée de Sculpture*, pl. 929, No. 2363; etc. Cf. an article by von Duhn in the *Annali dell' Instituto*, 1879, p. 176 ff.

The younger Agrippina, it will be remembered, was one of the most notorious women in the history of imperial Rome, a typical character of that heartless and licentious age. She was the daughter of Germanicus and Agrippina, the wife of Claudius, and the mother of Nero. This statue was recognized as her portrait by Visconti, who identified it by the resemblance of the features and the mode of wearing the hair to a head of the empress on a coin of Claudius. The identity is not absolutely certain, but has found general acceptance.

The attempt has been made to show that in the expression of the face and the clasped hands the sculptor had a moral object, as of wishing to represent her reflecting with repentance upon her past life, but it is extremely questionable whether any such thoughts are expressed in the figure.

The striking contrast between the wrinkled face and the youthful freshness of the form is explained by the fact that the motive of the statue is not original, being borrowed from a much older type which is reproduced with slight variations in several extant statues, examples of which are given in the two pictures on the pedestal. One is a photograph of the well-known "Agrippina the elder," in the Capitol, a Roman portrait statue of the same class; the other a drawing by Mr. C. H. Walker of a statue in the Torlonia Museum, Rome. The latter is undoubtedly a Greek work, several centuries older than the other two, and brings us nearer the original of the type, which was probably a product of the last part of the fourth century B. C.

This statue is therefore an interesting example of the Romans' practice of adapting Greek ideal statues to their own portraits. Another instance has already been noted in the Third Room, No. 129, but the Agrippina is the more instructive of the two, showing how, for the sake of flattering, the sculptor did not hesitate to combine an old and ugly face with a young and beautiful figure.

316. The Wolf of the Capitol, in the Palazzo dei Conservatori, on the Capitol, Rome.

Of bronze. Has stood on the Capitol since 1473; before then was in the Lateran. (A monk of the 10th century writes of a part of the Lateran palace as being called the "place of the wolf, which is the mother of the Romans," etc., — a probable reference to this statue. — *Annali*, 1877, p. 379.) RESTORATIONS: Both children, the work of Guglielmo della Porta (?), a sculptor of the 16th century. PUBLISHED: Rayet, *Monuments de l'Art Antique*, I, pl. 27; Stevenson, in the *Annali dell' Instituto*, 1877, pp. 375–381; Burckhardt, *Cicerone*, 5th ed., vol. I.

Livy (X, 23) and Dionysios of Halikarnassos (I, 79) describe a bronze group of a she-wolf suckling Romulus and Remus, that stood in the Lupercal, the traditional spot where the founders of Rome were nurtured; and Cicero in several passages refers to a similar group that stood on the Capitol, where it was struck by lightning. Whether the original of this cast is identical with one of these wolves, is a much-disputed question, which there is unfortunately no means of deciding. The fact that the right hind leg has been broken open from within, as though by the effect of lightning, offers a dangerous temptation to accept it as the one mentioned by Cicero, and the notes above show that it was regarded as an ancient image as far back as the tenth century. On the other hand, Burckhardt (*ubi supra*) and a few other German writers claim that it is not older than the early part of the Middle Ages, because of its stylistic affinity to the wolves of Siena, the lion of Brunswick, the animals of the Pisan sculptors, and other mediæval works. But this resemblance does not necessarily preclude the antiquity of the statue, which may be an example of an equally primitive school of sculpture, of a much earlier age. There is good reason to regard it as a genuine specimen of early Etruscan art, and therefore to admit the possibility of its being one of the famous "Mothers of Rome."

On the landing of the main staircase : —

317. **Sleeping Ariadne.** Marble statue, in the **Vatican.**

> Date and place of discovery unknown. Bought by Julius II. (1503–13), and placed by him in the Belvedere of the Vatican, whence it was subsequently removed to the Gallery of Statues. RESTORATIONS: The nose, upper lip, some fingers of the left hand, the right hand, and some parts of the drapery. PUBLISHED: Visconti, *Museo Pio Clem.*, II. pl. 44, p. 280 ff ; Clarac, *Musée de Sculpture*, pl. 689, No. 1622; Wolters' Friederichs, No. 1572; etc.

The fact that the band upon the **left arm has the form of a** serpent was formerly considered an indication that this was a statue of Kleopatra, but **a twisted** serpent was a favorite design for jewelry among **Greek** and Roman women, and has no attributive significance. A number of reliefs on Roman sarcophagi and elsewhere, in which the figure of Ariadne occurs in precisely this attitude, show that she is the subject of the statue, and that she is represented in the troublous sleep during which she was deserted by Theseus at Naxos, and in which she was found by her **future husband,** Dionysos. The attitude suggests the **uncomfortable** nature of her repose, the head, very much **inclined,** resting heavily upon the right hand, while the left **arm is** supported in a manner anything but restful.

That this statue is not **an original** work is attested partly **by** the number of similar figures, mostly in reliefs (there **is** one statue like it in Madrid), and partly **by its** technical characteristics, the execution displaying the **lifeless, mechanical** qualities of an ordinary Roman reproduction. Its original may have been a work of the last epoch **of Greek** art, but more probably was executed, like this **copy,** during the Empire. The conception shows a want of the freedom which distinguishes the spirit of Greek sculpture; both figure and drapery are evidently "posed" with a studied effort for grace and elegance. The careful manner in which the drapery is arranged so as to expose a portion of the body below the girdle, is characteristic of Roman taste.

Nos. 269, 270, 273, 277, 279, 280, 311, 315, 317, were purchased from the bequest of Charles Sumner.

Nos. 283–289, 291–303, 307, 310, were given to the Museum by Dr. Jacob Bigelow.

Nos. 290, 309, were given to the Museum by the heirs of Dr. Jacob Bigelow.

No. 313 was the gift of Mr. M. D. Ross.

No. 266 is the property of the Institute of Technology.

SUPPLEMENT.

CASTS FROM GREEK AND ROMAN WORKS
IN THE
ARCHITECTURAL ROOM.

THE casts in this section of the architectural collection are marked C, — classic. Owing to the crowded condition of the room, it has not been possible to place them together, or in chronological order.

On the eastern wall and on screen No. 1 :—

C 1-16. Details from the Erechtheion, Athens.

As the Parthenon illustrates the dignity and grandeur of Greek architecture at the highest point of its development, so the Erechtheion demonstrates its capacity for grace and elegance of design. Less than a third the size of the Parthenon, almost under whose shadow it stands, the aim of its builders seems to have been to avoid all possibility of comparison with its imposing neighbor, by giving it an entirely different shape, by adopting another style of architecture, and by contrasting the simple masses of the larger building with a profusion of exquisite detail upon the smaller. The relative position and size of the two are shown on the model of the Akropolis in the Third Greek Room, where it will be seen that the axis of the Erechtheion varies just enough from that of the Parthenon to emphasize the absence of relation between the two.

The unique plan of the Erechtheion is partially due to its peculiar position. It was built against the wall of a terrace, in a location **dictated** by the traditions of Athens, according to which this was **the** site of the house of Erechtheus, the first hero **of** Attika, and also the scene of the contest between Athena and Poseidon for dominion over the city. (See **p.** 70) Here, moreover, had **stood from** the earliest times the shrine of Athena Polias, the guardian deity of Athens, which, with the other buildings on **the** Akropolis, was destroyed by the Persians B. C. 480. **That the** Athenians could have neglected their principal **shrine more than** fifty years is incredible, yet up to the present **no record or** remains have been found of a building **erected on this site between the** date of the Persian invasion and **that of the Erechtheion,** which **we** may presume to have been begun after **the** completion of the Parthenon (B. C. 438), since the famous inscription **recording** the report of the commissioners appointed to **examine its** condition in the year 409 shows that it was **then incomplete.**

The terrace on **which it stands is** of a **form** that brings the eastern and **southern sides of** the building upon **a** higher level than the northern and western. The main portion of the edifice is oblong in plan, measuring about 66 **ft. 7** in. × 36 **ft. 9** in. (M. 20.30 × 11.21). The architecture **is** Ionic, treated with **a** variety and luxuriance unequalled **in** any other example of that style. At the EAST END is a portico of six columns, rising from a base (*krēpidoma*) of three steps. Of this portico **we** possess casts **of** but two details:—

        C **1,** section **of the base of a** column, and
        C **2,**   "   "   "   an anta.

Both of these **are** at the base of the Porch of the Maidens.

At the western extremity **of the** NORTH WALL is another portico, also of six columns, four on the front and **two on** the sides. In refinement of design and elegance of execution the decoration of this portico surpasses that **of all** other ancient buildings, and **it may** be considered **the** most beautiful structure **of** its kind in the world. Perhaps **no work** of Greek art loses so **much** of its effect by reproduction as the details of this decoration, because the vigor and crispness of the carving, which are very striking **in** the marble, cannot be reproduced in **plaster.**

The casts from this portico are: —

C 3 and 4, on the wall. Two casts of one of the corner capitals, C 4 showing the manner in which the corner volute curves outward so as to present a face on each side.

C 5. Base of the same column (at the base of the Porch of the Maidens).

C 6, 7, 8 (C 8 on screen No. 1, the others at the base of the Porch of Maidens). Details from the door opening from the portico to the interior of the building.

C 9. Decoration from the capital of an anta.

C 10, 11, 12, 13. Same decoration, from the walls of the building. This decoration, the famous "honeysuckle ornament" of the Erechtheion, was carried along all four walls just below the frieze, which was doubtless one of the most charming members of the building, being of a polished black limestone, to which figures of white marble were attached. This is, unfortunately, in such fragmentary condition, the greater part being lost, that neither subject nor composition is any longer recognizable.

So little is known of the arrangement of the interior that it will not be discussed here, and we come finally to

C 14. The Porch of the Maidens, or Karyatides, as they are more commonly called. The latter name was used in the time of Vitruvius to designate figures of this kind, and he ascribes its origin to the capture and destruction, by the Athenians, of the town of Karya, in the Peloponnesos, the women being sold into slavery. That any such event is commemorated in this porch is extremely improbable. The inscription referred to above (p. 179) speaks of these figures simply as "maidens," and their resemblance to figures on the Parthenon frieze makes it most probable that the type is that of the Athenian maidens of the time.

This portico is on the south side of the Erechtheion, looking towards the Parthenon. In the original there are six figures, two at the sides as well as the four on the front.

So much has been said and written about the marvellous manner in which architecture and sculpture are blended in these figures that it will suffice here to call attention to the skill with which each is treated as freely as a statue, yet without sacrificing any of its character as a supporting member. The burden is borne firmly, yet with perfect ease; the feeling of support is carried through the straight lines of the drapery; that of repose is suggested by the curved lines and by the bent knee.

The reproduction of this **portico was presented to the** Museum by the late George B. Dorr, Esq.

C 15. Section of the entablature above the figures. This entablature, it will be noticed, is made as light as possible by the **suppression of the frieze which runs along** the other walls of the building.

C 16 (on screen No. 1). Detail from the decoration of the antæ behind the maidens.

> THE ERECHTHEION is described in all handbooks of Greek art. It has been made the subject of especial studies and illustrations by Inwood, *The Erechtheion of Athens*, folio, London, 1827; von Quast, a translation of the same into German, with corrections, Potsdam, 1843; Beulé, *L'Acropole d'Athènes*, 1st edition, Paris, 1853-4, vol. II, chaps. VII-IX; etc. For the latest investigations concerning the building see the *Mittheilungen des deutschen Instituts in Athen*, passim.

C 17. Throne of the **Priest of Dionysos,** in the Dionysiac Theatre, Athens.

This chair, of Pentelic marble, was discovered during the excavation of the theatre in 1862. It still stands in its original position, in the centre of the front row of the auditorium. On either side of it, occupying the entire row, are ranged the seats of the other religious dignitaries of the city, each inscribed with the title of the official to whom it belonged. As dramatic representations formed part of the worship of Dionysos, in whose honor they were always given, his priest occupied the post of honor at the performances, and had a seat of more elaborate construction than the others. On the back is a decorative design, in low relief, representing two Satyrs, back to back, separated by a grape-vine. Below the seat is a smaller relief, Assyrian in style, the significance of which is not clear. Two men, kneeling, attack two griffons. Under this relief is the inscription, "Of the Priest of the Eleutherean Dionysos." On the outside of each arm is a winged youth pitting one cock against another, probably an allusion to the cockfights that took place in the theatre annually. The form of the letters in the inscription shows that the date of the throne is not earlier than the first century after Christ.

> **The** throne is published in the *Revue Archéologique* 1862, pl. 20, p. 350. An excellent description of the theatre and the thrones in it is given in Dyer's *Ancient Athens*, pp. 307-344. The situation of the theatre is shown on the Model of the Akropolis, in the Third Greek Room.

C 18. Marble Seat.

> Found at the eastern end of the Parthenon, 1836, between the outer and inner row of columns. Now in the Akropolis Museum, Athens. PUBLISHED: Sybel, *Katalog*, No. 6153; Wolters' Friederichs, No. 1332.

The ornamentation of this seat has probably nothing more than a decorative significance. Its style is that of the late Greek or Roman period, the figure on the back being an imitation of the archaic style.

C 19. Terra-Cotta Relief. Italo-Greek.

> Found at Capua, 1869, and now in the Museo Gregoriano of the Vatican. See Wolters' Friederichs, Nos. 2249-50.

Both the **site** of its discovery and the style of the decoration show this to be a product of the schools of Magna Græcia. This peculiar form of scroll-work, and the introduction of the heads, is a design often met with on the vases of Southern Italy, specimens of which may be seen in case E, in the Room of Greek Vases.

The date of the relief is not earlier than the year 300 B. C.

C 20. Candelabrum. Roman. Formerly in the Farnese collection, Rome; now in the Museum at Naples.

> PUBLISHED: *Museo Borbonico*, vol. I, pl. xliii.

C 21. Upper half of the body of an Amphora, used as decoration of a grave. Found outside the Dipylon Gate, Athens, and now in the National Museum there. Athenian work of a good period.

> Martinelli's *Catalogue*, No. 188.

On the wall adjoining the Porch of the Maidens: —

C 22. Figure from a Roman pedestal, resembling a figure in the relief No. 216 in the Fifth Greek Room.

PUBLISHED: Righetti, *Il Campidoglio*, II, pl. 30.

C 23. Bas-relief, of terra-cotta, used as an architectural decoration. Roman.

PUBLISHED: *Museo Campana*, pl. lxxxvii.

C 24. Decoration of a pilaster. Roman. In the Villa Medici, Rome.

PUBLISHED: Piranesi, *Raccolta di Vasi*, pl. 40.

C 25 (on the steps of the Porch of the Maidens, at the side). Scroll from the Monument of Lysikrates, Athens. Cf. No. C 60.

C 26. Ionic capital and base, with a portion of the shaft. From a temple at Daphne, near Athens. Roman epoch.

The following numbers are on screen No. 1: —

C 27. Section of a cyma, with lion's head as water-spout. From Metapontum. Italo-Greek.

C 28, 29. Sections of Greek stelai, showing handle of an amphora in relief. Cf. No. 188, Fourth Greek Room. Athens.

C 30. Scroll decoration, from a temple at Rhamnos. Greek.

PUBLISHED: Von Quast, *Das Erechtheion*, pt. III, pl. xxiii.

C 31. Head of an animal. In the Vatican. Roman.

C 32. Small triglyph frieze. Roman.

C 33. Fleuron, from the temple of Vesta at Tivoli. Roman.

C 34. Akroterion, from a Greek grave stele, in Athens.

C 35. Akroterion, from a Greek grave stele, in the Louvre.

C 36. Akroterion, from a Greek grave stele, in Athens.

C 37. Akroterion, from the Parthenon, Athens.

C 38. Leg of a seat or bench, Roman style, from the École des Beaux Arts, Paris.

C 39-41. Three pilaster capitals, style of the Roman Empire, from the École des Beaux Arts, Paris.

C 42. Ionic volute, from the Temple of Apollo at Phigaleia. Greek. Second half of the fifth century B. C.

C 43-49. Akroteria, Roman style. No. C 44 in Rome.

C 50. Roman moulding, from Athens, in the British Museum.

C 51. Roman Ionic volute, from Athens, in the British Museum.

C 52. Akroterion, Roman, from Athens, in the British Museum.

C 53. Palmetto decoration. Greek style, from the École des Beaux Arts, Paris.

C 54. Detail from the pedestal of Trajan's Column, Rome.

C 55. Corner fragment, with decoration. Athens.

C 56. Table leg. Roman style.

C 57. Table leg. Roman style.

C 58. Leg of a chair or bench. Roman. In the Vatican.

C 59. Sphinx, which served as the central support of a table. From Pompeii, in the Museum at Naples.

PUBLISHED: *Museo Borbonico*, vol. IX, pl. xliii.

The following numbers are on the round pedestal in the middle of the room : —

C 60, encircling the pedestal. **Frieze from the Monument of Lysikrates,** Athens. Erected B. C. 335-4.

This monument, a photograph of which hangs upon the pedestal, is the sole survivor of many that stood along the famous " Street of Tripods," commemorating musical and dramatic victories. It was erected by Lysikrates, a citizen of Athens, to celebrate his victory as *choregos* — that is, provider and supporter of a chorus — in a musical contest. The inscription recording these facts says further that the chorus was of boys, and that the year was that of the archonship of Euainetos (B. C. 335-4).

The primary object of the graceful little edifice, the total height of which is not quite thirty-four feet, was to serve as an appropriate support for the tripod received as a prize. Its architecture is Corinthian — the earliest extant example of that style in Athens. The photograph shows the position of the frieze, which is still *in situ*. Its subject is taken from a popular legend concerning Dionysos, according to which he once sailed, in the form of a beautiful youth, with a band of Tyrrhenian pirates, who, attracted by his beauty, attempted to capture him and sell him as a slave. Suddenly the cords with which they bound him loosened themselves, the sea turned the color of wine, the masts were transformed to serpents, and Dionysos assumed the shape of a lion. The pirates, terrified, jumped into the sea, only to be changed into dolphins.

In the relief Dionysos is not alone, but surrounded by Satyrs, young and old, who assist in the punishment. The scene is the sea-shore. The god himself is seated upon a rock, caressing his favorite animal, the panther. On either side are young Satyrs and large kraters of wine. Beyond these the action begins, and is carried easily and gracefully around the monument, suggesting the story, rather than representing it with literal fidelity. Both in the selection of the theme, which is more comic than tragic, and in the charm of the composition, the frieze shows the characteristics of the younger Attic school of sculpture. The figures have the slender proportions of the larger sculptures of the period, and the influence of the masters of the school is felt especially in the delicacy with which the details are modelled.

> This monument is fully illustrated in a series of twenty-six plates in Stuart and Revett's *Antiquities of Athens*, vol. I, chap. IV. It is also described and illustrated in Mitchell's *History of Ancient Sculpture*, p. 485 ff., figs. 203, 204; etc.

At the top of the pedestal: —

C 61. **Greek Vase**, in the Campo Santo, at Pisa, with relief representing a Bacchic scene. The vase is probably of Roman workmanship, the types of the figures being borrowed from earlier works.

> "Apart from its artistic beauty, this vase is interesting on account of its connection with the revival of sculpture in the 13th century. That it was one of the antique objects studied by Nicholas of Pisa, which led to the regeneration of what was then well-nigh a lost art, is certain, as he repeated one of the groups upon it — namely, that of the Indian Bacchus supported by Ampelos — in his bas-relief of the Presentation in the Temple, which forms one of the series of reliefs around his celebrated pulpit in the baptistery at Pisa. Trained by the Byzantine workmen who were employed about the Cathedral at Pisa, and surrounded by men of his own profession, who were nothing more than stone-cutters, and whose highest idea of sculpture was the carving of bas-reliefs and ornaments for the portals of churches, he had the genius to recognize, in the antique vases and sarcophagi which had lain neglected and despised about the streets of Pisa since the days when she was a Roman colony, and had been used as building material for the walls of her cathedral, the true objects of study for one who, like himself, knew nothing of the treatment of draperies, the grouping of figures, or the principles of composition. He accordingly took them as his masters, and in due time produced those bas-reliefs of the pulpits of Pisa and Siena, which are as superior to the works of his contemporaries as the bas-reliefs of the Parthenon are superior to his own."
>
> *From the former catalogue.*

The other casts on this pedestal are from small friezes and other architectural decorations, mostly of terra-cotta, all except No. C 77 dating from the early Roman Empire. Most of them have much of the feeling of fine Greek work, and are doubtless the products of Greek artisans employed at Rome.

C 62 and 63. Dancing Satyrs. 62 is from an altar in the Villa Albani, Rome.

C 64. Figure resembling those in the relief No. 153, in the Fourth Greek Room. It is from a vase in the Vatican.

PUBLISHED: Pistolesi, *Il Vaticano*, VI, pl. 47, 3.

C 65. Section of a frieze, of terra-cotta, — Paris and Helen (?). In the Museo Kircheriano, Rome.

C 66. Section of a frieze, of terra-cotta. In the Museo Kircheriano, Rome.

C 67. Ditto. Dionysos and a Satyr. In the British Museum.

Cf. *Museo Campana*, pl. xxxiii.

C 68. Section of a frieze, terra-cotta. In the centre a Victory. In the Villa Poniatowski.

C 69. Bas-relief. A griffon. In the Vatican.

C 70. Ditto. A pastoral group. From a sepulchral altar in the Vatican.

C 71. Ditto. Section of a frieze. A Nike sacrificing a bull. Terra-cotta, in the British Museum.

C 72. Ditto. Dionysos and Satyrs.

C 73. Ditto. Satyr and Mænad dancing, holding the infant Dionysos in a basket. Terra-cotta, in the British Museum.

PUBLISHED: *Museo Campana*, pl. l.

C 74. Bas-relief. Two "Seasons." In the Villa Albani.
PUBLISHED: Zoega, *Bassirilievi*, II, pl. xcv.

C 75. Ditto. Hermes and Aphrodite (?).

C 76. **Ditto.** "Achilles and Penthesilea."
PUBLISHED: *Museo Campana*, II, pl. lxii.

C 77. Akroterion, of terra-cotta. **Archaic** Etruscan.

C 78. Stem of Lilies. Modern.

C 79. Akroterion.

C 80. Fragment of a Greek inscription, of the **Roman** period.

C 81. Moulding.

C 82. Prow of a vessel. From the relief of the "Embarcation of Helen," in the Palazzo Spada, Rome.

C 83. Bas-relief, architectural decoration. Two Satyrs drinking.
PUBLISHED: *Museo Campana*, pl. xlii.

C 84. Front of a Roman cippus. In the Capitoline **Museum**, Rome.

The following numbers are on screen No. 2 : —

C 85. Roman moulding. **From the** Temple of Jupiter Tonans.

C 86. Roman moulding. **In the Vatican.**

C 87. Roman moulding. Time **of Nero.**

C 88. Roman moulding.

C 89. Roman **moulding.** From the **Pantheon, Rome.**

C 90. Roman moulding.

C 91. Roman moulding.

C 92. Roman moulding. Temple of Jupiter Tonans.

C 93. Section of a Roman frieze.

C 94. Large rosette, Roman style, from the École des Beaux Arts, Paris.

C 95. Patera, architectural, from the Temple of Jupiter Tonans.

C 96. Rosette.

C 97. Guilloche moulding. From the École des Beaux Arts, Paris.

C 98. Fleuron. From the Basilica of Antoninus.

C 99. Lion's head.

C 100. Rosette. Roman.

C 101. Rosette.

C 102. Fragment, Acanthus leaf. From the École des Beaux Arts, Paris.

C 103. Detail from a frieze, Roman, in the Villa Medici, Rome.

C 104. Acanthus leaf.

C 105. Boss, Roman.

C 106. Stucco decorations of the ceiling of a Roman house of the time of Augustus; discovered, 1879, in digging the banks of the Tiber for the new embankment, in the grounds of the Villa Farnesina.

C 107. Acanthus capital.

C 108. Rosette.

C 109. Rosette, from the tomb of the Scipios, B. C. 298.

C 110. Scroll, from the tomb of the Scipios.

C 111. Rosette, from the tomb of the Scipios.

C 112. Rosette, from the tomb of the Scipios.

C 113. Rosette.

C 114. Detail, Roman. From the Villa Doria-Pamfili.

C 115. Ornamental Roman base. From the Villa Giustiniani.

C 116. Roman Eagle. In the Vatican.

C 3, 8, 11, 12, 13, 16, 19, 22, 25, 27–49, 53–58, 60, 62–75, 80, 85–96, 98–105, 108–114, 116, are the property of the Massachusetts Institute of Technology.

C 14 was given to the Museum by Mr. George B. Dorr.

C 76, 77, 78, 79, 81, 83, were given to the Museum by Mr. C. C. Perkins.

INDEX.

NOTE. — Except where otherwise specified, the numbers in this index refer to the numbers of the casts, not to the pages.

Those numbers which have C prefixed to them are in the Architectural Room, described pp. 178–190.

Achilles, Borghese, so called, in the Louvre, 124.
Achilles and Penthesilea, so called, relief from the Campana collection, C 76.
Actæon, see Aktaion.
Ægina, statues from the Temple of, in Munich, 16 A–O.
Æsculapius, see Asklepios.
Agamemnon, archaic relief from Samothrake, in the Louvre, 32.
Agrippa? bust in the Capitoline Museum, 309.
Agrippina the Younger, statue in Naples, 315.
Aigisthos and Klytaimnestra, the murder of, sarcophagus in the Vatican, 176.
Aktaion attacked by his dogs, group in the British Museum, 279.
Akropolis of Athens, model of, 141.
Alexander the Great? head in the British Museum, 278.
Alkaios and Sappho? terra-cotta relief in the British Museum, 19.

Alpheios, figure from the east pediment of the Zeus Temple at Olympia, 57.
Altar, in the Louvre, 207.
—— round, in the Villa Albani, 252.
—— the Great, at Pergamon, 247.
Amazon, statue in the Capitoline Museum, 90.
—— statuette in Dresden, 270.
Amazon Relief, so called, in the Villa Albani, 196.
Amazon Sarcophagus, in Vienna, 197.
Amazons, on the frieze of the Temple of Apollo at Phigaleia, 151.
—— on the frieze of the Mausoleum, 191–195.
Amor see Eros.
Amphitrite and Poseidon, relief in Munich, 150.
Amphora, upper half of, marble, in Athens, C 21.
Antinous, bust from the colossal statue in the Vatican, 280.
Antoninus Pius, bust, 301.
Aphrodite, statuette in Argos, 121.

Aphrodite, of **Melos**, in the Louvre, **140**.
—— statue in the **Capitoline Museum**, 273.
—— crouching, in the **Vatican**, 234.
—— and Hermes (?), bas-relief, C 75.
Apollo? statue from **Thera**, in Athens, **20**.
——? statue from Orchomenos, in Athens, 21.
—— in the west pediment of the Zeus Temple at Olympia, 59.
—— Sauroktonos, statue in the Vatican, 83.
——? and the Omphalos, in Athens, 86.
—— the Pourtalès head, in the British Museum, 119.
—— head in the British Museum, 120.
—— slaying the Niobids, on a sarcophagus in the Vatican, 173.
—— Belvedere, in the **Vatican**, 215.
—— votive relief to, in the British Museum, 229.
—— on a relief in the Villa Albani, 236.
—— playing on the lyre, statue in the Vatican, 243.
—— in the Apotheosis of Homer, 269.
—— Temple of, **at** Phigaleia; selection **from** the frieze, 151.
Apotheosis **of** Homer, **relief** in the British Museum, 269.
Apoxyomenos, **statue** in the Vatican, 200.
Arch of Titus, relief from, 312.
Architectural details, Greek and Roman, pp 178-190.
Ares, in the Villa Ludovisi, 237.
—— or Achilles, Borghese, in the Louvre, 124.
Ariadne, statue in the Vatican, 317.

Aristokles, the stele of, in Athens, 13.
"Arringatore," the, bronze statue in Florence, 277.
Artemis, on a sarcophagus **in the** Vatican, 173.
—— **on** the vase of Sosibios, 175.
—— **of** Versailles, in the Louvre, 218.
—— **on a votive relief to Apollo, 229.**
—— on **a** relief in the Villa **Albani**, 236.
Artemisia, statue **from** Halikarnassos, in the British Museum, 190.
Asklepios? head in the **British Museum**, 137.
——? head from Melos, in the British Museum, 226.
Assos, archaic reliefs from, 28 A-E.
Assyrian reliefs, pp. 7-10.
Athena, seated; archaic statue **in** Athens, 34.
—— pseudo-archaic **statue** in Dresden, **35.**
—— statue from **the temple at Ægina, 16 E.**
—— Parthenos, **Lenormant statuette,** 112.
—— Parthenos, Varvakeion statuette, 113.
—— Giustiniani, in **the** Vatican, 125.
—— colossal bust in Munich, 126.
Athens, Model of the Akropolis, 141.
Atlas and Herakles, Metope in Olympia, 66.
Attalos group, figures from, in Naples, 219; in Venice, 220.
Augustus, statue **in the** Vatican, 281.
—— bust, 286.

Bacchic relief, in the British Museum, 216.
—— in the Museum at Naples, 232.

INDEX.

Bacchic relief, in **the Villa Albani**, 239.
—— in Florence, 240.
—— sarcophagus, in the Vatican, 159.
Bacchus, see Dionysos.
Barberini Faun, in Munich, **205**.
Bassæ, temple of Apollo at, **selection** from the frieze, 151.
Bellerophon and the Chimæra, terra-cotta relief in the British Museum, 17.
Belvedere Hermes, in the Vatican, 92.
Belvedere, Apollo of the, **in the** Vatican, 215.
—— Torso, in the Vatican, **222**.
Borghese Warrior, in the Louvre, 208.
Boy, praying, **in the** Berlin Museum, **133**.
—— drawing thorn from his foot, in the Palazzo dei Conservatori, Rome, 136.
—— and Goose, in the Louvre, 235.
Brutus, Lucius Junius (?), bust in the Capitoline Museum, 274.
Bull, figure carrying a, in **Athens, 22**.

Cæsar, Julius, **bust in Florence,** 283.
—— ? bust in the **Villa Ludovisi**, 284.
—— ? bust in the Capitoline Museum, 285.
Caligula, bust, 288.
Campana collection, terra-cotta reliefs from, 227, 228.
Candelabrum, Roman, in Naples, C 20.
Caracalla, bust, 307.
Caryatides, see Erechtheion.
Castor, see Kastor.
Centaurs, see Kentaurs.
Ceres, **see** Demeter.
Chariot, figure mounting a, **ar**chaic relief in Athens, **2**.

Cicero ? **bust in** the Vatican, 267.
—— ? bust **in the** Capitoline Museum, 271.
Claudius, busts, 289, 290.
Clio, statue in the Vatican, 245.
Clytie, so called, bust in the British Museum, 276.
Comedy, bust **in** the Vatican, 241.
Commodus, bust, **303.**
Cupid, see Eros.

Damasistrate, monument of, **in** Athens, 182.
Demeter, on the Eleusinian slab, 88.
—— head of, from Knidos, in the British Museum, 157.
Demosthenes, statue in the Vatican, 138.
—— head of, in Athens, **139.**
Dexileos, monument of, in Athens, **179.**
Diadumenos, **Farnese, in the** British **Museum, 127.**
Diana, see Artemis.
Diogenes, statuette **in the Villa** Albani, 275.
Dionysos, infant, and Silenos, **in** the Louvre, 84.
—— infant, and Hermes, in Olympia, 75.
—— infant, carried by a Satyr and a Mænad, in the British Museum, C 73.
—— received **by** Ikarios, relief in the **Museum** at Naples, 230; **in the** British Museum, 231.
—— on a relief in Naples, 232.
—— on a relief on an altar in the Villa Albani, 252.
—— in the frieze of the choragic monument of Lysikrates, C 60.
—— **on** a relief in the British Museum, C 67.
—— throne of the priest of, in the Dionysiac Theatre at Athens, C 17.

Dioskouroi archaic reliefs in Sparta, 29, 33.
—— on a sarcophagus in Florence, 198.
Diskobolos, standing, in the Vatican, 158.
—— after Myron, in the Vatican, 161.
Domitian, bust, 297.
Doryphoros, relief in the Museum at Argos, 114.
Dresden Pallas, **35**.

Eirene and Ploutos, group in Munich, 85.
Eleusis, large relief **from**, in Athens, 88.
Epikrates, stele of, 180.
Erechtheion, description of, pp. 178-181.
—— the Porch of the Maidens, C 14.
—— details of the architecture and decoration, C 1-16.
Eretria, female head from, in the Berlin Museum, 135.
Eros, torso in Sparta, 89.
Eurydike, on a relief in the Villa Albani, 199.
Euterpe? statue in the Louvre, 246.

Farnesina, stucco decorations from the, C 106.
Fates, so called, from the east pediment of the Parthenon, 102.
Faun, the Marble, 82.
—— the Barberini, in Munich, 205.
—— see Satyr.
Furies, on a sarcophagus in the Vatican, 176.

Galba, bust, 292.
Gaul, dying, statue in the Capitoline Museum, Rome, 251.
Gaul, from the Attalos group, in Venice, 220.

Germanicus, so called, in the Louvre, 129.
Gladiator, the Borghese, so called, in the Louvre, 208.
—— dying, formerly so called, in the Capitoline Museum, Rome, 251.
Grave monuments of the fourth century, introduction to, p. 112.
—— from Sparta, archaic, 7-12.
—— of Aristokles, archaic, in Athens, 13.
—— from Bœotia, archaic, in Athens, 14.
—— in Naples, archaic, 15.
—— from Karystos, in the Berlin Museum, 122.
—— large marble lekythos, in Athens, 162.
—— Head of a woman in Lansdowne House, London, 178.
—— of Dexileos, in Athens, 179.
—— of Epikrates in Athens, 180.
—— from Ægina, in Athens, 181.
—— of Damasistrate, in Athens, 182.
—— of Phainippe, 183.
—— with two women, in **Athens**, 184.
—— of Hegeso, **in** Athens, 185.
—— of Mynnion, in Athens, 186.
—— large, with figures in high relief, in Athens, 187.
—— in the Piræus Museum, 188.
—— amphora, marble, in Athens, C 21.
—— sections of, C 28, 29, 34, 35, 36.

Hadrian, bust, 300.
Halikarnassos, sculptures from, in the British Museum, 189-195.
Harpy Monument, reliefs from, in the British Museum, 6.

Head, of a youth (Alexander the Great?), in the British Museum, 278.
—— archaic, in the British Museum, 5.
—— female, from Eretria, in the Berlin Museum, 135.
—— large female, in Athens, 177.
—— of a woman, in Lansdowne House, London, 178.
—— from Pergamon, in the Berlin Museum, 217.
Hegeso, monument of, in Athens, 185.
Helios, metope from Ilion, in Berlin, 152.
Hellenistic Art, pp. 131 f.
Herakles and the Stag, relief in the British Museum, 3.
—— and the Kerkopes, metope from Selinus, in **Palermo,** 27.
—— on a relief in Dresden, 4.
—— and Atlas, metope in Olympia, 66.
—— head, in Dimitzana, **Greece,** 201.
—— small herma in Sparta, **221.**
—— torso of the Belvedere, **222.**
—— statuette in Sparta, 223.
Hercules, see Herakles.
Herma, double, in the National Museum, Athens, 238.
Hermes, head of, archaic relief in Athens, 31.
—— statue by Praxiteles, at Olympia, 75.
—— statue from **Andros,** in Athens, 91.
—— statue in the **Belvedere of the** Vatican, **Rome,** 92.
—— on the vase of Sosibios, 175.
—— on the Orpheus relief, in the Villa Albani, 199.
—— on a herma in Athens, 238.
—— and Aphrodite (?), bas-relief, C 75.
Hippodameia, torso from the east pediment of the Zeus Temple at Olympia, 51.

Homer, apotheosis of, relief in the British Museum, 269.
Horse's head, from the east pediment of the Parthenon, 104.
Hypnos, bronze head in the British Museum, 206.

Ikarios receiving Dionysos, relief in the Museum of Naples, 230; in the British Museum, 231.
Ilioneus, so called, statue in Munich, 93.
Inopos, so called, fragment in the Louvre, 131.
Inscription from Orchomenos, in the British Museum, 116.
—— Attic, in the British Museum, 117.
—— bronze, from Olympia, in the British Museum, 118.
—— from Oropos, in the British Museum, 123.
—— genuine? in the British Museum, 128.
Inscriptions found at Olympia, 77–81.

Jason, so called, in the Louvre, 115.
Jerusalem, capture of, relief from the Arch of Titus, Rome, 312.
Juno, see Hera.
—— Ludovisi, 130.
Jupiter, see Zeus.

Karyatides, so called, porch of the Erechtheion, C 14.
Kastor, colossal head of, in Rome, 156.
—— see Dioskouroi.
Kentaurs, in the western pediment of the Zeus Temple at Olympia; see 59 ff.
—— on the Parthenon metopes, 108–111.

Kentaurs, on the frieze of the Temple of Apollo at Phigaleia, 151.
Kephisos, so called, from the west pediment of the Parthenon, 105.
Kladeos, figure in the east pediment of the Zeus Temple at Olympia, 56.
Klytaimnestra, on a sarcophagus in the Vatican, 176.
Klytie, so called, bust in the British Museum, 276.

Lansdowne House, head in, 178.
Laokoön, group in the Vatican, 250.
Lapith head, from the Zeus Temple at Olympia, 64.
Latona, see Leto.
Lekythos, of marble, used as a grave monument, in Athens, 162.
Lenormant statuette of Athena Parthenos, 112.
Leto, on a votive relief to Apollo, 229.
Leukippos, rape of the daughters of, sarcophagus in Florence, 198.
Leukothea relief, so called, in the Villa Albani, 1.
Lions on the gate of Mykenæ, 24.
—— heads, in Olympia, 68-72.
Ludovisi Juno, 130.
—— Ares, 237.
Lysikrates, monument of, description of, p. 185.
—— **frieze** from, C 60.
—— **scroll** from, C 25.

Marcus Aurelius, bust, 302.
Mars, statue in the Villa Ludovisi, 237.
—— see Ares.
Marsyas, torso of, in the Gorringe collection, 225.
Mausoleum, sculptures from the, in the British Museum, 189-195.

Mausolos, statue in the **British Museum**, 189.
Medusa, head in relief, in **Argos**, 25.
—— **Rondanini, head in Munich, 202.**
"Melan" reliefs, of terra-cotta, in the **British Museum,** 17-19.
Melos, the Venus **of,** in the Louvre, 140.
Menander, statue in the Vatican, 233.
Mercury, see Hermes.
Metope, Helios, from Ilion, in Berlin, **152.**
—— from Selinus, 26, 27.
—— from Assos, 28 E.
—— from **the** Zeus Temple **at** Olympia, 66, 67.
—— from the Parthenon, **108-111.**
Milo, see Melos.
Minerva, Giustiniani, **in** the Vatican, **125.**
—— see Athena.
Mykenæ, the lions **of, 24.**
Myron, Diskobolos **of,** in the Vatican, 161.
Muses, in the Apotheosis **of Homer,** 269.

Neptune, see Poseidon.
Nero, bust, 291.
Nerva, bust in the Capitoline Museum, 298.
Nike, from **the** east pediment of the Parthenon, 103.
—— **of** Paionios, statue at Olympia, 73; inscription on the same, **74.**
—— on a relief in the Villa Albani, **236.**
—— sacrificing **a** bull, terra-cotta relief in the British Museum, C 71.
—— **Apteros,** temple of, in Athens, small fragments from the frieze, 163, 164; reliefs from the balustrade, 165-171.

Niobe, in the Uffizi Gallery, Florence, 154.
—— and her children, relief on a sarcophagus in the Vatican, 173.
Niobid, statue in the Vatican, 155.

Oinomaos, fragment from the east pediment of the Zeus Temple at Olympia, 52.
Olympia, sculptures from, 50–81.
—— introduction to, pp. 37–40.
Orator, the "Arringatore," bronze statue in Florence, 277.
Orchomenos, archaic grave relief from, in Athens, 14.
Orestes, on a sarcophagus in the Vatican, 176.
Orpheus? relief in Sparta, 30.
—— Eurydike and Hermes, relief in the Villa Albani, 199.
Otho, bust, 293.
Otricoli Zeus, 134.

Paionios, Nike by, at Olympia, 73.
Pan, on a marble vase in the British Museum, 160.
Paris and Helen (?), relief in the Museo Kircheriano, Rome, C 65.
Parthenon, introduction to, pp. 64 f.
—— sculptures from, 100–113.
—— frieze, 100.
—— metopes, 108–111.
—— statues from the pediments, 101–106.
Pedestal of a tripod, in Dresden, 4.
Pedestal, in Dresden, 204.
Peirithoös, head and fragments, from the Zeus Temple at Olympia, 62, 63.
Peleus and Thetis, marriage of, terra-cotta reliefs from the Campana collection, 227, 228.

Penelope? statue in the Vatican, 36.
Pergamon, the great Altar of, p. 151.
—— relief from the same, 247.
—— head from, in Berlin, 217.
Persephone, on the Eleusinian slab, 88.
Perseus and Medusa, terra-cotta relief in the British Museum, 18.
—— Metope from Selinus, in Palermo, 26.
Persian, from the Attalos group, in Naples, 219.
Pertinax, bust, 304.
—— ? bust, 305.
Phainippe, monument of, in Athens, 183.
Phigaleia, temple of Apollo at; selection from the frieze, 151.
—— Ionic volute from, C 42.
Pollux, see Dioskouroi.
Polykleitos, Diadumenos, Farnese, 127.
—— Doryphoros of, see 114.
Poseidon and Amphitrite, the wedding of; frieze in Munich, 150.
Praxiteles, the Hermes of, in Olympia, 75.
—— Satyr after, in the Capitoline Museum, 82.
—— Apollo Sauroktonos, after, in the Vatican, 83.
Praying Boy, so called, statue in Berlin, 19.
Proserpine, see Persephone.
Pudicitia, so called, statue in the Vatican, 314.
Pyrrhic Dance, relief in the Vatican, 153.

Relief, large, in the Villa Albani, 196.
Roman, statue of a, fragment at Olympia, 76.
—— lady, statue in the Louvre, 311.

Roman priest, sacrificing; statue in the Vatican, 282.
Rondanini, Medusa, in Munich, 202.

Samothrake, archaic relief from, in the Louvre, 32.
Sarcophagus, Amazon, in Vienna, 197.
—— death of the Niobids, in the Vatican, 173.
—— murder of Aigisthos and Klytaimnestra, in **the** Vatican, 176.
—— **rape** of the daughters of Leukippos, in Florence, 198.
—— Satyrs and Mænads, in the Vatican, 159.
—— in Sparta, 172.
Satyr, statue in the Capitoline Museum, Rome, 82.
—— **statue** in Dresden, 87.
—— statue, called the Barberini Faun, in Munich, 205.
—— statue, in the British Museum, 265.
—— statue, of rosso antico, **in** the Capitoline Museum, 268.
—— playing the Scabellum, statue in Florence, 313.
—— mask, in Dresden, 249.
Satyrs in reliefs, see Bacchic reliefs.
Scipios, Tomb of the, details **from,** C 109-112.
Seasons? relief **in** the Villa Albani, C 74.
Seat of the priest of Dionysos, in the Dionysiac Theatre, Athens, C 17.
—— marble, found in the **Par**thenon, C **18**.
Selinus, metopes from, in **Palermo**, 26, 27.
Seneca, formerly so called, bust, 272.
Severus, Alexander, bust, 308.
—— Septimius, bust, 306.

Silenos carrying the infant Dionysos, in the Louvre, 84.
Sirens on the Harpy Monument, p. 16.
Sophokles, statue in the **Lateran** Museum, Rome, **132**.
Sparta, archaic reliefs from, 7-12, 29, 33
—— archaic statue **in, 23**.
—— relief in, Orpheus ? **30**.
—— sarcophagus in, **172**.
—— torso of Eros in, **89**.
"Spinario," the, bronze statue in the Palazzo dei Conservatori, Rome, **136**.
Sphinx, Italo-Greek, in **the Mu**seum **of** Naples, C **59**.

Thalia, **statue in the Vatican,** 244.
Theseus, so called, **statue from the** east pediment **of the** Parthenon, 101
Throne of the priest of Dionysos, **in** the Dionysiac Theatre, Athens, C 17.
—— marble, found in the **Par**thenon, C 18.
Tiberius, bust, 287.
Titus, bust, 296.
—— the arch **of, relief from,** 312.
Torso of the **Belvedere, in the** Vatican, **222**.
Tragedy, bust, in the **Vatican,** 242.
Trajan, bust, 299.
Trajan's Column, heads and figures from, 266.
Tripod, pedestal of a, in Dresden, 4.

Varvakeion statuette **of Athena,** in Athens, 113.
Vase, marble, in the British Museum, **160**, 174.
—— of Sosibios, **in** the Louvre, 175.

Vase, in the Villa Albani, 203 ; in Naples ? 209.
—— in the Campo Santo at Pisa, C 61.
Venus of Melos, in the Louvre, 140.
—— of the Capitol, in Rome, 273.
Venus, see Aphrodite.
Vespasian, bust, **295**.
Victory, see Nike.
Vitellius ? **bust in the Capitol**, 294.
Votive relief to Apollo, 229.

Warrior, Borghese, in the Louvre, 208.

" Weber " head, so called, from the west pediment of the Parthenon, 106.
Wolf of the Capitol, 316.

Zeus, torso from the temple at Olympia, 50.
—— Otricoli, head, 134.
—— ? head from Melos, 226.
—— ? head in the British Museum, 137.
—— on a relief from the altar at Pergamon, 247.
—— in the Apotheosis of Homer, 269.
—— Temple at Olympia, p. 39 ff.
—— —— sculptures from, 50–71.

www.ingramcontent.com/pod-product-compliance
Lightning Source LLC
Chambersburg PA
CBHW020926230426
43666CB00008B/1588